Canadian Critical Race Theory

Canadian Critical Race Theory

Racism and the Law

Carol A. Aylward

Fernwood Publishing • Halifax

This book is dedicated to my now grown children,
April and Wade Aylward,
who during their childhood showed great patience and maturity
when their single mother went back to school,
and who taught me that the sacrifice was worth it.
It is also dedicated to my enslaved but indomitable ancestors,
without whom I would never have been born.

Editing: Douglas Beall
Design and production: Beverley Rach
Printed and bound in Canada by: Hignell Printing Limited

A publication of:
Fernwood Publishing
Box 9409, Station A
Halifax, Nova Scotia
B3K 5S3

Fernwood Publishing Company Limited gratefully acknowledges the financial support of the Ministry of Canadian Heritage and the Canada Council for the Arts for our publishing program.

Canadian Cataloguing in Publication Data

Aylward, Carol A.

Canadian critical race theory

Includes bibliographical references and index.
ISBN 1-55266-005-2

1. Equality before the law -- Canada.   2. Race discrimination -- Canada.
I. Title.

KE4410.A94 1999   342.71'0873   C99-950011-2

Contents

Foreword
by Derrick Bell

An old rhythm and blues lyric boasts: "I may not be the one you want, but I sure am the one you need." Reading Professor Carol Aylward's revelatory review of racism in Canada, a nation with a long democratic history and relatively few people of color, I was struck by how fitting that lyric is to beliefs about race and racism that are accepted as gospel on both sides of the border. Because these beliefs are, to a large extent, self-affirming or self-denying myths and thus dangerous, we need a work like *Canadian Critical Race Theory* to help us distinguish what role the law plays in enabling so many to ignore racial subordination so regularly severe that it appears normal.

Civil rights advocates in both countries will find great value in Aylward's work. She provides a succinct but quite readable review of Critical Race Theory, how it evolved and how it differs from Critical Legal Studies and the earlier Legal Realism jurisprudential theories. She then shows the applicability of the Critical Race Theory approach to several major cases involving race in both the United States and Canada. Most importantly, she illustrates how Critical Race Theory can be applied in litigating cases involving race. This involves viewing the situation from the perspective of a person of color and then identifying those aspects of racial oppression that are amenable to legal remedies. The crucial step is what she calls "reconstruction," a three-step process in which the litigator asks: What are the alternatives, if any, to the existing doctrine, legal rule, principle or practice that will not subordinate people of color or will lessen the subordination of people of color? What harm or benefit to the Black client and/ or the Black community might result from the adoption or nonadoption by the courts of the change sought? and What are the risks in pursuing a Critical Race Litigation strategy?

The balance of the book demonstrates how these principles can be applied in the various phases of litigation, particularly in jury selection and challenging racially discriminatory policies under Canadian human rights codes. There is a thoughtful and thought-provoking section on the ethical issues involved in utilizing Critical Race Theory in litigation. Issues of funding and whether the litigation is intended to serve the client or the community are reviewed with recommendations. Finally, under a heading "Community Activism and Coalition Building," the book discusses an essential and potentially risky subject for the lawyer: how

Critical Race Litigation strategies can be combined with strategies for political change.

Thirty years ago in the Preface of the first edition of my text, *Race, Racism, and American Law*, I wondered why the hard-won decisions protecting basic rights of Black citizens from racial discrimination become obsolete before they are effectively enforced. My question, pertinent then in the midst of the greatest surge of positive civil rights gains in American history, has become critically important in the wake of the rollback of legal precedents that even the pessimistic among us viewed as permanent. Clearly, we needed then what Professor Aylward has provided us with now: a perspective that connects legal issues with the realities of race, which we ignore at our peril.

Derrick Bell
Visiting Professor
New York University Law School

Foreword
by Leon Trakman

At a recent conference, I found myself in the company of several American critical race scholars. They were very laudatory about Canada. They believed that Canada was a truly multicultural society and that Canadians were racially tolerant. They particularly liked our equality rights jurisprudence. They were far less charitable towards American race relations and equality rights. American law was oppressive, dominated mostly by White males and duplicitous, they said. It marginalized racial minorities.

Professor Carol Aylward, in this enlightening book, confronts the stereotype of racial tolerance and harmonious race relations in Canada. She declares that "there exists in Canada a devastating anti-Black racism." Canada is not the egalitarian society it is sometimes held up to be. It is not a pristine "mecca for the oppressed of the world." Writing authoritatively and in her own voice, she presents an arsenal of arguments to bolster her thesis: slavery in Canada's past; segregation in education, employment, housing, transportation and social life, race riots and violence in Canada's recent past. Her book is replete with illustrations of racism in both Canada and the United States. She tells the story of racial unrest in Toronto following the verdict in the Rodney King case in California, and she narrates instances of excessive force being used by police against racial minorities in Canada. She describes efforts made to confront racism before both the Canadian and American courts. Her attacks upon racism in the law are relentless. Her forays are bolstered by detailed research and resonate with the voices of other critical race scholars.

Yet Professor Aylward's book is as farsighted and hopeful as it is devastating. Her ultimate story is not fixated on "trashing" or deconstructing the status quo. Her goal is to reconstruct. She argues for a new and informed critical race litigation that is strategic in focus. Her first strategy, or "step," is to enable critical race litigants to become aware of the history of racism in Canadian society. Her second step is to identify when race is an issue in a given circumstance. And her final step is to reconstruct an alternative mode of litigation in which "existing doctrine, legal rule, principle and practice ... will not subordinate people of colour."

Professor Aylward's book embodies many voices. Her own voice is personal. As a self-avowed, Black critical race theorist, she dedicates her book to her "enslaved but indomitable ancestors." But her book is also scholarly, succinctly describing critical legal studies and critical race theory in the United States and Canada. And her story is vivid in its details. She narrates the legendary saga of the Rodney King and O.J. Simpson cases in the United States, and she dissects the facts of the *R.D.S.* case in Canada, including the verdict of the Supreme Court.

I read Professor Aylward's book as a privileged White male. I came away believing its message is as important to mainstream scholars as it is to their debunkers.

Leon Trakman
Professor
Dalhousie Law School

Acknowledgements

I would like to thank all those who contributed to this book. I would particularly like to thank my law school colleagues Philip Girard and Leon Trakman for taking time out of their busy schedules to read and comment on earlier drafts of the manuscript and for providing valuable insights for its improvement. I would like to offer a special thank-you to my colleague Jennifer Bankier (a born editor) for her unselfish dedication to detail and for her friendship and support during this project. Her commitment to equity principles is unflinching and much appreciated. I would also like to thank Derek Edwards and Sam Moreau, former students, for impeccable research assistance during one summer of their law school careers, and Natalie Francis, student researcher in the Indigenous Blacks and Mi'kmaq Curriculum Review Project.

No manuscript is complete without professional editorial assistance, and I had the best in Fernwood's editor, Douglas Beall. Thank you. I wish to thank Beverley Rach for her excellent work in coordinating the production of this book and creating the cover. And thanks also to Marie Koehler, director of the film "Balancing the Scales," from which the still for the cover photo was taken.

I owe a debt of gratitude to the academics of colour in the United States and Canada who began the Critical Race Theory movement and inspired my own work in the field. Finally, a thank-you to Fernwood Publishing for boldly going where no Canadian publisher has dared to go before.

Preface

The prevailing myth in the United States is that Americans have overcome their racist past and are no longer racist; and the prevailing myth in Canada is that we are a country without a history of racism. Both myths have led to a failure by the courts to confront the issue of race and the role it plays in law. In one respect, however, Canada's history of racism presents more serious problems than that of the United States. In the United States, most observers would acknowledge that racism exists, and the controversy is over the role that law has played in its maintenance and perpetuation. In Canada, it is hard even to reach this issue because of a pervasive denial of the very existence of racism in Canadian society.

There is a dichotomy between Canada's public and international image as an egalitarian society free from the racism that plagues the United States and the racial reality that exists in this country. In Canada today, discrimination and racism exist in subtle and systemic forms and are concealed in systems, practices, policies and laws that may appear neutral on their face but have a serious detrimental effect on people of colour. Although race and racism are significant factors in Canadian society, these issues have not become a part of the litigation instinct of lawyers in Canada as they have in the United States.

American "Critical Race" scholars have begun a movement, however, that has had a significant impact on the birth of a "Critical Race Theory" movement in Canada. The growth of the Critical Race Theory (CRT) genre began in Canada during the 1980s and has followed along the same theoretical lines that American Critical Race theorists have travelled. Scholars of colour in Canada have also begun to articulate a dissatisfaction with existing Canadian legal discourse which, like its American counterpart, has failed to include an analysis of the roles that race and racism have played in the political and legal structures of Canadian society.

This book begins with an analysis of the birth of Critical Race Theory in the United States and Canada. American scholars of colour, the pioneers of the movement, have decried the failure of legal discourse to place racial questions on the legal agenda, and they argue for an analysis of law that will recognize the complex relationships among race, racism and law, as well as for new approaches to deal with these complexities.

The failure of both "Legal Liberalism" and the "Critical Legal Studies" (CLS) movement to place racial questions on the legal agenda left scholars of colour skeptical about the state of existing legal discourse.

Critical Race theorists were attracted to the CLS movement because it challenged liberal concepts about the "neutrality" and "objectivity" of law and because it recognized the fact that law legitimates existing "maldistributions" of wealth and power. However, in the end, Critical Race theorists rejected CLS because of its refusal or inability to recognize the central role that race and racism play in law, as well as the movement's failure to give credit to the experiences of people of colour. Critical Race theorists also rejected the CLS view of rights discourse and its disinclination to use law as a tool against oppression and subordination.

This book documents how Canadian Critical Race theorists are beginning to develop a body of thought designed to move us beyond theory to practical applications. Canadian Black lawyers and others are gradually beginning to seriously consider the role of race in litigation and to develop effective "Critical Race Litigation" (CRL) strategies to address the issue. As demonstrated by cases such as *R. v. R.D.S.* (1994), *R. v. Parks* (1993), *R. v. Williams* (1998) and *R. v. Cole (D)* (1996),[1] these strategies are increasingly placing issues of race before the Canadian courts.

Introduction

"Law and order exist for the purpose of establishing
Justice and ... when they fail in this purpose they
become the dangerously
structured dams that block the flow of social progress"
—Martin Luther King Jr. (1963)

In Canada, as well as in the United States, it can be said that law has failed in its purpose of establishing justice for Black members of society. This book is about the role law plays in the perpetuation of racism and the disenfranchisement of Black Canadians. It is about challenging through Critical Race theory and practice the subtle and not-so-subtle forms of discrimination perpetuated by law. This book is designed to be a theoretical and practical guide, not just for the legal practitioner and student who wishes to broaden her or his knowledge in the area of race advocacy, but also for the layperson who has a social interest in the topic. It is also designed for the social activist who, although already engaging in Critical Race Theory and advocacy, lacks a clear understanding of the role of law in her or his work and wants to develop a better understanding of that role and its practical implications on a daily basis in the fight against the perpetuation of racism through law.

Canada and the United States have similar colonial histories that gave rise to anti-Black racism and oppression, which have often been reinforced and perpetuated by law. The similarities between the two countries run deep and the concept of "race" is a powerful force in both societies. Although most Canadians would deny the existence of widespread racism and, in particular, anti-Black racism in their country and would reject comparisons to the racial situation in the United States, the fact remains that Canadian history, legal and nonlegal, does not support such denials.

The Commission on Systemic Racism in the Ontario Criminal Justice System (1995: 52) noted that racism has "a long history in Canada." Racism was, the commissioners said,

> fundamental to relationships between Canada's First Nations and the European colonizers ... [and] it has shaped immigration to this country and settlement within it.... European empires of the 16th and 17th centuries used racial difference to justify exploitation of the people, land and resources of other societies ... [and] the imperial powers also used these meanings to justify enslaving

African peoples and transporting them to the Americas.

It is indisputable that the legacy of slavery still plagues both Canada and the United States. The Commission on Systemic Racism in the Ontario Criminal Justice System, like many inquiries, task forces, royal commissions and the like that came before it, concluded that not only was racism still entrenched in Canadian society, but that "the practices of the criminal justice system tolerate racialization" (1995: 410). The Commission concluded that Black men, women and male youths were over-represented in the prison system; Whites charged with the same offences are more likely to be released by the police and are less likely to be detained following a bail hearing, and White accused were more favourably treated even though they were more likely than Black accused to have a prior criminal record or a more serious one.[1] The Commission also found that, in drug cases, White accused were twice as likely to be released by police than Black accused, and that differential treatment found at the policing stage of the process was subsequently duplicated during the court process. In addition, the Commission found that Black and other Canadians believe that Blacks are disproportionately the victims of police violence. Many perceive the courts to be unfairly biased against Black persons and feel there is a serious under-representation of Blacks and other people of colour on juries and among court personnel, lawyers and judges.

Similarly, the American-based National Association of Criminal Defence Lawyers (NACDL) wrote in its publication, *NACDL Legislative Policies*: *Racism in the Criminal Justice System* (1997: 1), that

> one of the most daunting yet crucial challenges facing American society today is racial bias in our criminal justice system. The racially disparate impact of America's criminal justice system belies our nation's constitutional requirement of equal justice under the law.... Beyond that, it is exacerbating the alienation experienced by African-American and other minority citizens, increasing racial tensions and accelerating the fragmentation of our society.

Black Americans endure differential treatment in the enforcement of drug laws, pretextual police stops as motorists, and disparate prison and death penalty sentences. The problems of all-White juries in criminal and civil cases and the under-representation of Black Americans among judges and lawyers are also found in the Black Canadian experience.

The criminal justice system is not the only culprit, however. Law in all its manifestations—in substance (whether it be criminal law, family law, constitutional law or other areas of civil law), in procedure and in interpretation—has been and, to varying degrees, continues to be an instrument that contributes to and maintains racial inequalities, divisions and tensions in both Canada and the United States.

There are of course differences between the two countries, particularly in the legal protection afforded Black citizens.[2] While Black Canadians have suffered racial discrimination in its many forms, such as exclusion from juries, segregation in public housing, and in voting, education, public transportation, churches, jobs, policing and so on (Walker 1997: 125), Canada historically did not have constitutional or statutory mechanisms similar to those in place in the United States that enabled Black Americans to litigate to seek civil rights and freedom from racial discrimination. Specifically, the foundations for American civil-rights litigation were the Civil War amendments to the U.S. Constitution (the Thirteenth, Fourteenth and Fifteenth amendments) and a myriad of federal civil-rights statutes that authorized civil lawsuits by victims of discrimination, such as the *Civil Rights Act of 1964,* the *Voting Rights Act of 1965* and the *Fair Housing Act of 1968* (Davis and Graham 1995, cited in Aylward 1998: 1).

In contrast, the Canadian federal government did not pass the *Canadian Bill of Rights* with respect to matters under federal jurisdiction until 1960, and basic human rights were not constitutionalized so they would apply to all levels of government until 1982 with the passing of the *Canadian Charter of Rights and Freedoms*. Notably, the equality section, section 15(1), of the *Charter* did not come into force until 1985. Although human rights legislation had been passed in all Canadian jurisdictions by 1977, except in Quebec, the enforcement of Canadian human rights legislation is confined to specialized tribunals. Human rights legislation is itself problematic because the vast majority of race-based human rights complaints never even reach the board of inquiry stage within the human rights process, even when the racial minority complainant would like the case to proceed. And the fact that jurisdiction over human rights complaints has been assigned exclusively to human rights tribunals has meant that there is no direct recourse in Canada to the civil courts for redress, seriously limiting the legal options available to address racism and the limitations of human rights commissions.

In recent years, Canadian and American scholars of colour have produced an increasing volume of legal and other academic literature that criticizes and challenges the so-called objectivity of laws and the inability of conventional legal doctrines and strategies to deliver justice for Black citizens. Critical Race Litigation is the practical application of Critical Race Theory. It requires legal practitioners and social activists, Black and White, to take a Critical Race position on any case involving a Black client and to either work collectively on precedent-setting cases involving race or to litigate race issues when they work alone to represent a Black client.[3]

Quite often, theory is divorced from the practice of law. On the one hand, many legal theorists have been accused by legal practitioners, those in other disciplines, and social activists of only talking among themselves, using convoluted and archaic language that makes their ideas virtually inaccessible to not only the layperson but also to the legal practitioner. On the other hand, those who practice law often apply theory without fully understanding how it should work in practice, or they shy away from canvassing the theoretical bases of their legal arguments, trusting instead to the abstract and neutral form of legal analysis traditionally taught in law schools. This can limit or cut off new legal avenues which may be open to their clients. This book is designed to bridge the gap between Critical Race theory and practice.

Chapter 1 details the beginnings of the Critical Race Theory movement, which originated with American Black scholars and other scholars of colour and eventually expanded to include Canadian theorists who were disillusioned with or critical of existing legal discourse which had ignored the legal and historical realities of people of colour. This chapter also discusses the relationship between the Critical Race Theory and the Critical Legal Studies movements, as well as the relationship between Black Critical Race Theory and Critical Indigenous Theory.

Chapters 2 and 3 deal with the wedding of theory and practice and detail the emerging body of Critical Race Litigation in the context of criminal and constitutional law in Canada and the United States. From the American cases of Rodney King (1991) and O.J. Simpson (1995) to the Canadian cases of *R.* v. *Parks* (1993) and *R.D.S.* v. *The Queen* (1997), these chapters explore the similarities between the Canadian Black and American Black experiences, the legal and constitutional remedies available to Black clients and the effectiveness of these remedies in redressing the subtle forms of discrimination perpetuated by law.

Chapter 4 addresses pressing issues for legal practitioners, social activists and others. When is race an issue in a case? How do you "spot the issue" and how do you frame it in litigation? This chapter also looks at specific issues involving race such as jury selection and possible *Charter* challenges to the existing human rights system.

Chapter 5 takes up ethical and practical considerations. For example, are representative juries a goal to strive for? Should "race" be raised in all cases involving a Black client, regardless of its relevancy? What guidance do the Canadian Bar Association and provincial Bar society codes of professional conduct provide? How valid are the arguments put forth by critics of the O.J. Simpson and Rodney King cases that focusing on representative juries leads inevitably to "jury nullification," that is, the phenomena of Black or White juries ignoring the law in a particular case in favour of either a discriminatory or socially desirable outcome? This chapter deals with the tough choices legal practitioners and others involved in this area of law may have to make, such as the difficult ethical choice between the interests of a particular client and those of the community or society as a whole. Chapter 5 also identifies extralegal strategies which may be employed by legal practitioners and social activists to advance goals initially identified in the context of litigation. Such strategies may include focusing media attention on issues, political lobbying, coalition building and intervention by other affected groups in particular cases to broaden the public interest and remedy in a given case. In some cases "controlled civil disobedience" may be an appropriate extralegal strategy. Finally, Chapter 5 introduces implications of Critical Race Litigation outside the criminal law context, considering, for example, its potential relevance to civil law.

Chapter 1

Critical Race Theory

The Birth of A Theory

Legal Liberalism and the Critical Legal Studies Movement

In legal discourse, one of the most traditional and standard methods of analysis employed by legal scholars has been that of "Legal Liberalism," with its emphases on the rule of law, formalism, neutrality, abstraction and individual rights. This method of analysis was traditionally thought to allow theorists to analyse legal concepts such as liberty, property, rights and so on in a liberal mode with emphasis on dispassionate discourse and linear logic, "with no connection to what these concepts may mean to real people's lives" (O'Byrne 1991: 1). For a long time this abstract standard of jurisprudential discourse went virtually unchallenged, and it is still the main methodology used in legal discourse and in the law itself today (O'Byrne 1991: 1).

In 1977 in the United States, a group of radical legal scholars, who were generally left-leaning White male professors within the legal academy, began to attack the tenets of Legal Liberalism. These Critical Legal Studies (CLS) theorists severely criticized five basic and interrelated tenets of Legal Liberalism: the rule of law, formalism, neutrality, abstraction and individual rights. What follow are brief and generalized descriptions of Legal Liberalism and the Critical Legal Studies movement. This analysis provides a foundation for an analysis of the relationship between the Critical Legal Studies movement and the subsequent birth of Critical Race Theory (CRT).

The Rule of Law and the CLS Critique

The concept of the rule of law, which is the most basic underlying tenet of Legal Liberalism, suggests that governments should be bound by known principles or laws without distinction in their application to particular individuals or groups, or, as Andrew Altman describes this principle, "there is to be a single set of authoritative norms that apply equally to all citizens" (1990: 22). Critical Legal theorists have insisted, however, that the rhetoric of the rule of law is used by the more powerful to oppress the less powerful in society and to maintain the existing political, social and economic status quo (A. Altman 1990: 15).[1]

Thus proponents of the Critical Legal Studies movement have challenged the liberal concept of the rule of law by contending that the rule of law is a "myth."[2] The Critical Legal Studies movement challenged this basic tenet of liberal legal philosophy by contending that the rule of law is simply not possible in a situation where the kind of individual freedom endorsed by liberal philosophy reigns (A. Altman 1990: 13).

The rule of law, Andrew Altman argues, plays a central role in the theories of liberal thinkers because it is judged to be a necessary institutional mechanism for securing the prevailing values cherished by liberal tradition, which are individual liberty and those values connected with it, which he lists as tolerance, individuality, privacy and private property (1990: 10). Altman contends that a social situation where the kind of individual freedom endorsed by the liberal view prevails would be characterized by

> a pluralism of fundamentally incompatible moral and political viewpoints.... The establishment of the rule of law under the conditions of pluralism would require some mode of legal reasoning that could be sharply distinguished from moral and political deliberation and choice. There would be a sharp distinction between law on the one hand and morals and politics on the other. Without such a distinction, judges and other individuals who wield public power could impose their views of the moral or political good on others under the cover of the rule of law.... [This] would destroy the rule of law and the liberal freedom it is meant to protect. Thus the liberal view requires that legal reasoning—that is, reasoning about what rights persons have under the law and why—be clearly distinguished from reasoning about political or ethical values. Legal reasoning is not to be confused with deciding which party to a case has the best moral or political argument (1990: 13–14).

Altman (1990: 14) goes on to say that the position of the proponents of the Critical Legal Studies movement, however, is that it is precisely this kind of legal reasoning that is impossible in a setting of moral and political pluralism (that is, with more than one set of political and moral values) and, as a result, the division between law and politics disintegrates, and legal reasoning becomes equivalent to deciding which party in the case has the best moral or political argument. Altman notes that one of the leading scholars in the CLS movement, Duncan Kennedy, makes this point more bluntly when he states:

> Teachers teach nonsense when they persuade students that legal reasoning is distinct, *as a method for reaching correct results,* from ethical or political discourse in general.... There is never a "correct legal solution" that is other than the correct ethical or political solution to that legal problem (quoted in A. Altman 1990: 10).

Hence, the rule of law envisioned by the liberal theorist (that is, a form of legal analysis that is separate and distinct from political and moral analysis) does not and cannot exist, because it is impossible to separate moral and political choices in a pluralistic society. Critical Legal Studies theorists argue that it is thus all too easy for decision-makers—judges and others in power—to impose their own political and moral views on the rest of society.

Formalism, Neutrality, Abstraction and the CLS Critique

The doctrine of "formalism" (legal analysis) espoused by legal liberalists is based upon the premise that legal rules "form a consistent and complete whole from which the answer to any legal question can be logically deduced simply by discovering the applicable rule and applying it to the facts of the case" (A. Altman 1990: 79). Liberal theorists argue that legal rules and the doctrine of *stare decisis* (judges following precedent and deciding like cases alike) can and do provide determinate legal results. Critical Legal Studies theorists, however, decry the existence of legal determinacy and argue simply that the law contains too many contradictions to be able to "produce" determinate results and that all law "is political and ... no amount of theorizing on its objective and neutral quality can alter its fundamental character" (O'Byrne 1991: 9). Commentators have noted that the CLS rejection of legal determinacy has merely embodied the critique of Legal Liberalism which predated it—that of the Legal Realism movement, which held that, because one could come to opposite conclusions through creative use of ambiguities of law and statutes in applying any legal rule or principle, legal rules were by nature indeterminate (Cook 1990: 988).

The concept of "neutrality" embodied in Legal Liberalism relies upon the contention that principles and laws are not based on any particular group's conception of moral right or good. Andrew Altman notes that this concept of neutrality must depend upon "arrangements ... calculated to insure that no single group or fixed coalition can gain lasting control of the power of government" (1990: 76). Additionally, the legal liberalist's concept of neutrality contends that once the appropriate political process has settled on some "normative" rule or principle, that is, some form of social consensus determined by those governed, then there must be, as Altman puts it, "neutrality in adjudication," that is,

> the rule is interpreted and applied by public officials in a way that is insulated from the influence of any fresh assessment of the contending normative views.... The political arena is the one in which the contending views are to be assessed and weighed, and some settlement is interpreted and applied without any new assessment or weighing of the contending normative views.... *Legal neutrality* is the form of neutrality that is embraced by liberals who insist upon a separation of law and politics (1990: 76).

However, the CLS theorist attacks the concept of neutrality by arguing that (1) the most dominant and powerful groups in society control the definition of the political concept of the good based on ideologies of domination and propertied interests, and (2) that legal neutrality is no less illusory, because most judges are from the dominant group in society and bring to the process of legal interpretation their own cultural and political biases.

The concept of "abstraction" embodied in the methodology of Legal Liberalism is based upon the proposition that law should operate at a high level of abstraction that excludes consideration of social context. Legal liberalists argue that

> the liberal conception of the rule of law requires that public and private power be regulated by norms that are generalizable across situations and can be applied in a regularized, predictable manner. This again requires that certain aspects of a case be deliberately disregarded in the name of predictability... Where institutions cannot presuppose that all officials share the same set of background moral, religious, and political ideas, the authoritative norms that they lay down cannot regularly call for highly context-sensitive judgments without threatening the regularity, predictability, and perhaps even the stability of the system (A. Altman 1990: 192).

If the law did not operate at an abstract level, Altman argues, legal reasoning could not be clearly distinguished from unconstrained moral inquiry and political choice. CLS theorists, however, reject the notion that law can and should treat human beings as abstractions. Altman notes that Karl Klare, a leading Critical Legal Studies theorist, claims that one of the "enormous problems" with liberal theory is its "erroneous belief that it is possible to treat the individual as an abstraction, apart from the entire texture of his or her social life" (1990: 189).

The Critical Legal Studies theorist demands that "abstraction" be replaced by "contextualized law." This reform, CLS theorists argue, is necessary because the Legal Liberalist insistence on abstraction "obscure[s] and falsely sanitize[s] human problems, [but considering] social context ... we can choose to tell different stories by meeting head on the social situation inherent in a given case" (O'Byrne 1991: 19).

Individual Rights and the CLS Critique

Finally, Legal Liberalism places great emphasis on individual rights. Richard F. Devlin, in an article which maps the progression of legal theory in Canada, notes that:

> liberalism advocates that the state and law should strive to pro-vide the citizen with as much space as possible to pursue her own self-interests (liberty); that each person should have the equal right to pursue such interests without formal restraints because of their identity, be it on the basis of their race, gender, class or ability ... [although] the key function of law is to play a facilitative role, that is, to provide mechanisms for social interaction (1991: 29).

The example Devlin uses to demonstrate the dual function of the law as a means to protect individual rights and referee social interaction is in the area of contract law. Contract law, he observes, has as its main function making free commerce easier so as to allow individuals to obtain wealth and to "therefore pursue their own conception of the good," but he also points out that another purpose is to intervene and regulate the situation when the individual right to pursue the "good" conflicts with or infringes upon other individuals' rights, whether it be an infringement of their rights to "liberty," "equality" or some other recognizable right (Devlin 1991: 29).

Critical Legal Studies theorists make their strongest attacks on the liberal concept of individual rights and the notion that the function of law is to facilitate a "neutral" outcome. Liberal theory would have it that

> the courts must enforce the boundaries articulated by the Consti-tution that define the spheres of privacy [individual rights] within which the collective cannot intrude.... This enforcement requires a delicate balancing between individual rights and duties. The apparatus of liberal rights mediates the relationship between our-selves and others. A liberal discourse of abstract rights and duties purports to map out the borders of these private spheres of au-

tonomy and to set the conditions under which they may be justifiably disregarded (Cook 1990: 1006).

Critical Legal theorists argue that the problem with this concept of neutrality and dispassionate adjudication "is that those in power draw the line between public and private to preserve the distributions of wealth and power that limit transformative change and preserve hierarchies directly or indirectly benefiting them" (Cook 1990: 1007). Anthony E. Cook points out that, while the question for the legal realist was to ensure that judges and lawyers do not make decisions in a vacuum but make informed decisions with the aid of social science data, the focus of Critical Legal theorists has been on "the values and beliefs that provided the backdrop against which research was conducted and judicial choices were made" (1990: 989). In other words, according to Cook, CLS has

> challenged the accepted values of classical liberalism by undermining the interpretations of private property, individual rights, equality of opportunity, meritocracy, and governmental power that sustain and reproduce oppressive hierarchies of wealth and power. Although liberalism purports to effect a neutral reconciliation between individual freedom and the collective restraints needed to preserve that freedom, CLS suggests that such neutrality is inherently illusory. Through structured argumentation based on manipulable legal categories, the legal system legitimates a status quo characterized by vast inequalities of wealth and power (1990: 989).

Consequently, the Critical Legal Studies movement rejects out of hand the doctrine of rights analysis because of its role in legitimating and maintaining the inequitable power imbalances in society. Here is how Richard Delgado sums up this aspect of the CLS critique of Legal Liberalism:

> Rights, a special kind of rule, receive particularly harsh criticism from Critical Legal Scholars.... Rights legitimize society's unfair power arrangements, acting like pressure valves to allow only so much injustice. With much fanfare, the powerful periodically distribute rights as proof that the system is fair and just, and then quickly deny rights through narrow construction, nonenforcement, or delay. Rights, Crits [Critical Legal theorists] argue, are never promulgated in genuinely important areas such as economic justice. They protect only ephemeral things, like the right to speak or worship. When even these rights become threatening, they are limited (1987: 4).

Deconstruction and the CLS Critique

Many Critical Legal Studies theorists deconstruct or "trash" the tenets of Legal Liberalism and legal rules and principles, denouncing both the use and usefulness of legal doctrine (especially rights doctrine) to effect meaningful social change. The vision held by the Critical Legal theorist is one of "Utopia," where hierarchies do not exist, there are no class differences and there are no legal rules and principles governing the interaction between community members. In the CLS vision, the concept of individual rights is replaced by the concept of an "interdependent community." Delgado explains it this way:

> For CLS, rights reinforce a soulless, alienating vision of society made up of atomized individuals whose only concern is to protect their own security and property. Crits argue that rights are alienating since they force one to look at oneself and others as isolated rights-bearers ("I got my rights") rather than as interdependent members of a community, and make it impossible for us even to imagine what a nonhierarchical society founded on cooperation and love would be like (1987: 4).

Critical Legal Studies is a complex and multifaceted theoretical movement. At the risk of oversimplification, it can be said, however, that the CLS movement came about because of the view held by many theorists that the discourse of Legal Liberalism maintains and legitimates the status quo and co-opts the oppressed into accepting it. Cook asserts that the Critical Legal Studies movement is seeking

> to understand why people acquiesce in the social systems that oppress them.... CLS scholars purport to show that our social-political world, from which law is inseparable, is of our own making. Just as there is nothing determinate, necessary, or natural about the application of legal rules, the way we live and relate to others is also a matter of choice (1990: 990).

American and Canadian Black scholars and other scholars of colour were attracted to the Critical Legal Studies movement because it challenged the objectivity of laws that have oppressed people of colour. While scholars of colour applauded the CLS movement's skepticism about the idea that law can produce determinate results free from reference to values, politics or historical conditions, they also believed that the Critical Legal Studies movement ignored the realities of people of colour. As Kimberlé Crenshaw argues:

> The Critics' [Critical Legal Studies theorists'] principal error is that their version of domination by consent does not present a realistic picture of racial domination. Coercion explains much more about racial domination than does ideologically induced consent. Black people do not create their own oppressive worlds moment to moment but rather are coerced into living in worlds created and maintained by others. Moreover, the ideological source of this coercion is not liberal legal consciousness, but racism (1988: 1356–57).

Scholars of colour were also attracted to CLS because of its messages that legal concepts are "manipulable" and that the law serves to legitimate existing "maldistributions" of wealth and power, but they criticized it for its lack of analysis of the role racism plays and for its inability to go beyond "trashing" to the crucial next stage of "reconstruction" (Matsuda 1987: 341). As a result of these and other criticisms, many scholars of colour rejected the Critical Legal Studies movement and began their own movement known as Critical Race Theory.

The Critical Race Theory Movement

Thirty legal scholars of colour attended the tenth National Critical Legal Studies Conference held on January 7, 1986, in Los Angeles, and six presented papers on the topic of racism and the law.

It was clear that many legal scholars of colour felt alienated from existing legal discourse (Matsuda 1996: 49). This alienation is not surprising, given the fact that people of colour, particularly Black people, have been historically excluded from the legal academy. In the United States, law schools began implementing affirmative action admissions policies in the mid-1960s, but the record of American law schools in hiring and promoting Black scholars has been dismal. In 1983, for example, only two persons of colour were full-time faculty members at Harvard Law School, out of sixty-four (Kennedy 1990: 1757).

As noted by Kennedy, "one must remember that the litigation struggle against de jure [sanctioned by law] segregation was primarily a struggle against segregation in *education*, and that prior to *Brown* v. *Board of Education* [*of Topeka*, 1954, 347 U.S. 483], the desegregation of state law schools was a major locus of controversy" (1990: 1753). In 1975, students of colour at American law schools, particularly at U.C. Berkeley's Boalt Hall School of Law, formed the Coalition for Diversified Faculty. This coalition filed a lawsuit alleging discriminatory hiring practices, and its members boycotted classes and held rallies and sit-ins to protest not only discriminatory hiring practices but the discriminatory denial of tenure to faculty of colour. In 1990 at Yale Law School, students boycotted classes and called for a national protest and nationwide strike of students against segregated law faculties. Because of the current debate in the United States on affirmative admissions policies, the passage of Resolution SP1 by the Regents of the University of California in 1995 and of Bill 209 in 1996 (which together restrict the ability of all public universities in California to practice race and gender based affirmative action), students of colour at U.C. Berkeley's Boalt Hall School of Law began a National Faculty and Student Diversity Coalition which engages in legal and extralegal activities to improve the diversity of both faculty and students in law schools across the United States. Sit-ins, rallies and guerrilla actions were reported at Boalt, Stanford, Harvard and Columbia (Matsuda 1996: 59).

This student activism encouraged faculty of colour to articulate the role race plays in law. Critical Race Theory originated among the Black and other scholars of colour who attended the tenth National Critical Legal Studies Conference in 1986 in Los Angeles. These scholars of colour not only felt alienated from existing legal discourse but felt that existing legal discourse (including Critical Legal Studies discourse) was alienating to all people of colour. What, asked the founders of the Critical Race Theory movement "does Critical Legal Studies have to offer racial minorities in their quest for social justice?" (Delgado 1987: 1). The search for an answer to this question led to a theoretical movement based on the oppression of people of colour which is unprecedented in jurisprudential discourse. Richard Delgado, one of the founders of the Critical Race Theory movement, who attended the 1986 conference, explained the failure of CLS discourse in this way:

> Although CLS purports to be a radical theory, minorities have not flocked to it. And CLS has not paid much attention to minorities, not placing racial questions on its agenda until this year, ten years after its formation as a legal movement.... The CLS negative program contains elements that repel and in fact threaten minorities. These elements include: (i) disparagement of legal rules and rights, (ii) rejection of piecemeal change, (iii) idealism, and (iv) use of the concept of false consciousness (1987: 3).

As mentioned, American and Canadian Black scholars and other scholars of colour had been attracted to the Critical Legal Studies movement because it challenged the objectivity of laws that oppressed people of colour. Scholars of colour had also applauded that movement's skepticism that law can produce determinate results free from reference to values, politics or historical conditions. However, scholars of colour believed that the CLS movement ignored the realities of people of colour because it "portrayed those who use legal doctrine, legal principles, and liberal

theory for positive social ends as either co-opted fools or cynical instru-
mentalists" (Matsuda 1987: 341).

Critical Race Theorists' Critique of the Critical Legal Studies Movement
One of the major weaknesses of the Critical Legal Studies movement for
people of colour was its failure to recognize that the minority experience
of "dual consciousness" was capable of accommodating "both the idea of
legal indeterminacy as well as the core belief in a liberating law that
transcends indeterminacy" (Matsuda 1987: 333). This failure was problematic for scholars of colour because, as Matsuda notes:

> The dissonance of combining deep criticism of law with an aspirational
> vision of law is part of the experience of people of colour ... these
> people have used duality as a strength, and have developed strat-
> egies for resolving this dissonance through the process of appro-
> priation and transformation.... The law, as critical scholars rec-
> ognize, consists of language, ideals, signs, and structures that
> have material and moral consequences. Transforming this kind of
> system into one's own has a long tradition in the Black commu-
> nity (1987: 333).

Although scholars of colour were attracted to the CLS movement because
of its messages that legal concepts are "manipulable" and that law serves
to legitimate "maldistributions" of wealth and power, they criticized its
inability to go beyond "deconstruction" (or "trashing") into the next vital
stage of "reconstruction." Delgado argues that the CLS movement is unre-
alistically idealistic:

> Crits [Critical Legal theorists] argue that the principal impedi-
> ments to achieving an ideal society are intellectual. People are
> imprisoned by a destructive system of mental categories that
> blocks any vision of a better world. Liberal-capitalist ideology so
> shackles individuals that they willingly accept a truncated exist-
> ence and believe it to be the best available. Changing the world
> requires primarily that we begin to think about it differently. To
> help break the mental chains and clear the way for the creation of
> a new and better world, Crits practice "trashing"—a process by
> which law and social structures are shown to be contingent,
> inconsistent and irrationally supportive of the status quo without
> good reason (1987: 9).

Critical Race theorists like Delgado ask us to imagine what the lot of
minorities would be if the CLS "trashing" succeeded and all laws were

repealed. Delgado doubts that the lot of minorities would improve because the forces that hold back people of colour "are not largely mental, legal, nor even political. What holds us back is, simply, racism—the myriad of insults, threats, indifference, and other 'micro aggressions' to which we are continually exposed" (1987: 10).

Critical Race theorists also argue that the Critical Legal Studies movement poorly serves the needs of people of colour because the "Utopian" society it envisions would see decision-making "decentralized." Rules would be set by community members and would be open to constant renegotiation (Delgado 1987: 14). Because Blacks and other people of colour have not been recognized as equals, it is unlikely that they could "merge" into this community of negotiation to confront problems. In other words, as Delgado (1987: 313) points out, there is no guarantee under the CLS vision of "Utopia" that racism would not resurface within the community.

Critical Race theorists criticize the Critical Legal Studies movement for not examining the role of racism in law and society and for not articulating a vision of how it can be eliminated. Delgado argues that

> if racism were to surface in a CLS-style Utopia, there would be no rules, rights, federal statutes, or even courts to counteract it.... The costs of moving to a utopian society would be borne by minorities, since dismantling of formal structures would initially lead to an increase in racist behaviour.... Utopian society would empower whites, giving them satisfaction currently denied, and disempower minorities, making life even less secure than it is today.... If we jettison rules and structures, we risk losing the gains we have made in combatting racism.... The CLS program exposes minorities to an increased risk of prejudicial treatment (1987: 16–17).

With respect to the CLS critique of rights discourse, Critical Race theorists note that people of colour see rights differently. While CLS theorists generally categorize rights as oppressive, alienating and mystifying,

> for minorities, they are invigorating cloaks of safety that unite us in a common bond. Instead of coming to grips with the different function of rights for the two groups, Crits insist that minorities adopt their viewpoint, labelling disagreement on our part false consciousness or a lack of political sophistication (Delgado 1987: 7).

The difference here results from the CLS call to abandon rights discourse altogether because it merely legitimates and maintains inequitable power imbalances in society; Critical Race theorists acknowledge that legal discourse and, in particular, rights discourse are indeterminate but suggest that they are nevertheless essential in the struggle for racial equality (Brooks and Newborn 1994: 2).

Critical Race Theory was designed to confront subtle forms of discrimination perpetuated by law and to challenge and expand rights analysis. Delgado points out that

> Critical Race Theory sprang up with the realization that the civil rights movement of the 1960s had stalled and needed new approaches to deal with the complex relationship[s] among race, racism, and American law. Derrick Bell and others began writing about liberalism's defects and the way our system of civil rights statutes and case law reinforces white-over-black domination (1993: 744).

Instead of "trashing," CRT has offered solutions from its inception. It has also challenged the ability of conventional legal strategies to deliver justice, while recognizing that law can and must be used in the battle against racism.

The Basic Tenets of Critical Race Theory
This book focuses on the Black/White paradigm of Critical Race Theory, first, because I am a Black Critical Race theorist and, secondly, because a devastating anti-Black racism exists in Canada. The growing body of Critical Race Theory developed by Aboriginal people and non-Black peoples of colour unfortunately cannot be adequately addressed in this single volume. For example, the strong relationship between Critical Race Theory and the growing body of "Critical Aboriginal Theory" has led to the development of an impressive array of litigation and scholarly literature. As a Black Canadian Critical Race theorist, I recognize that a Black/White paradigm does not deal with the concerns of all peoples of colour and Aboriginal peoples. There are commonalities, however, to which this book speaks. Critical Race Theory and its methods provide a medium to express divergent experiences, to search for and bring out the meaning of "race" and racism in the law and to provide a critical understanding of law.[3]

At the heart of Critical Race Theory is the thesis that legal discourse has not appropriately taken account of the social reality of race and racism and has ignored the fact that law "is both a product and a promoter of racism" (Matsuda 1996: 22). Racism is a distinct phenomenon that has permeated the legal and nonlegal history of American and Canadian society. Most Critical Race theorists are critical of both Legal Liberalism's and the Critical Legal Studies movement's refusals and/or hesitancies to recognize the unique historical relationship between law and racism (Cook 1990: 986). Law, Critical Race theorists argue, "is born of racism and gives birth to racism. Law thus becomes a locus of struggle. Struggle can change law, and law can aid struggle" (Matsuda 1996: 52).

Thus, most proponents of Critical Race Theory embrace the concept of "historical race" (the history of a particular group's racialization in a given society) which allows Blacks and other scholars of colour to examine legal issues through the prism of historical racism, based upon the recognition that race-based subordination was legitimated by law in the past. As Alex Johnson notes, "Historical-race focuses on how the racial group's history affects current issues" (1994: 838). Kushnick (1998) has written that, "Blacks have struggled since the days of slavery, from their resistance on the slave ships that brought them to the Americas, to the slave uprisings and individual slave resistance, to their resistance to the reestablishment of the plantation economy, through to the system of *de jure* or legal segregation known as Jim Crow which existed in both the United States [and Canada]."[4]

Kushnick notes that Black people were struggling against segregation prior to the emergence of the Civil Rights Movement in the 1950s and 1960s:

> The struggle escalated in the 1950s, particularly after the *Brown* decision. The *Brown* v. *Board of Topeka* decision of 1954 overturned the 1896 *Plessy* v. *Ferguson* decision [163 U.S. 537] which had declared "separate but equal" to be constitutional and held that *de jure* [Jim Crow] segregation was unconstitutional. *Brown II* [*Brown* v. *Board of Education of Topeka,* 1955, 349 U.S. 294] was the 1955 enforcement decision which ordered implementation of the 1954 decision on the basis of "all deliberate speed." What should have been the crowning glory of the NAACP's ... strategy of litigation and lobbying, in practice, turned out to be the beginning of a new phase of black struggle (1998: 65).

Critical Race theorists bemoan the fact that while the Civil Rights Movement may have produced real and substantial results, they were not longlasting. In the U.S., reversal of many of the legal reforms instigated by the Civil Rights Movement is continuing. Kushnick notes:

> This repeal of what may be termed the Second Reconstruction is proceeding in much the same manner as the reversal, a hundred years ago, of the First Reconstruction reforms that followed the

American Civil War. In both cases, the executive and judicial branches of the federal government worked together in an increasingly racist, popular and intellectual culture to turn the clock back (1998: 142).

Critical Race theorists such as Mari Matsuda, Richard Delgado, Derrick Bell and others emphasize that Blacks need to re-examine total reliance on rights remedies which

> do little more than bring about the cessation of one form of discriminatory conduct that soon appeared in a more subtle though no less discriminatory form.... Civil rights advocates must replace it [racial equality ideology] with an approach that recognizes the real role of racism in our society and seeks to deflect and frustrate its many manifestations (Bell 1992a: 1.17).

The civil rights activists of the 1950s and '60s employed a strategy of seeking formal, legal equality through litigation and legislation. Their strategies produced varied and sometimes limited victories in areas such as desegregation in education, housing, public accommodations, employment, voting rights and the administration of justice. The goal of American anti-discrimination law has been one of "formal equality," which entitles everyone to participate in what Allen Freeman terms the "game of equal opportunity" (1988: 350). All Americans, regardless of race, are to have equal legal status. The goal, according to Brooks and Newborn, is for American society to become "racially symmetrical," that is, to become a society where the law treats all groups, including historically excluded groups, in the same manner without reference to race and prefers "racial integration over racial separation; hence, formal equal opportunity incorporates two policies: colorblindness and racial mixing" (1994: 796). Colour-blindness forbids governments, courts and society from taking race into account and forbids race-based decisions. However, as Critical Race theorists and others have pointed out, "In order to get beyond racism, we must first take account of race. There is no other way" (Lopez 1996: 176). Lopez also points out that:

> Color-blind constitutionalism has been widely criticized.... In order to get beyond racial beliefs, we must first be race-conscious. This is the basic flaw of color-blindness as a method of racial remediation. Race will not be eliminated through the simple expedient of refusing to talk about it. Race permeates our society on both ideological and material levels (1996: 176–77).

The major concern regarding colour-blindness that Critical Race theorists have identified is that, because it is forbidden to talk about race, the United States Supreme Court has been able to strike down government actions that have been aimed at ameliorating the conditions of groups or individuals who have been disadvantaged because of race (affirmative action), because these laws refer explicitly to race, and the colour-blind doctrine does not permit this. This doctrine has also allowed the U.S. Supreme Court to uphold state action that has a clearly racist intent or effect because such action is couched in race-free language and because proof of "intent" to discriminate is required under American civil-rights law. The discriminatory effects of government action are not deemed to constitute discrimination under the U.S. Fourteenth Amendment. For example, Lopez notes that:

> In *Presley* v. *Etowah County Commission* (1992) [502 U.S. 491], ... the Court found no Voting Rights Act violation where White commissioners in two Alabama counties greatly diminished the decision-making authority of each individual county commissioner immediately after the election of the first Black, because they did so without ever directly mentioning race. In one county, the commissioners shifted the newly integrated commission's duties to an appointed administrator. In the other, the power of the individual commissioners was transferred to the commission as a whole voting by majority rule. As in these counties, White power is easily and now perhaps principally maintained without any overt reference to race. And as in these cases, color-blindness renders such power maintenance unassailable. Rejecting all talk of race would produce comparable effects across society. Under race-blindness, the language necessary to remake racial ideology could not be used, since such language would necessarily refer to race. Meanwhile, race-blindness would not challenge the continuation, extension, and innovation of new patterns of discrimination, so long as these patterns did not explicitly make distinctions on racially impermissible bases (1996: 179).

Critical Race theorists are concerned that the Civil Rights Movement has become stagnant and that many of its gains have been reversed by the doctrine of colour-blindness and the requirement that intent be proved under the Fourteenth Amendment. A person who alleges a state or federal law is discriminatory must prove the existence of a discriminatory animus behind the law before it can be struck down as unconstitutional. Proof of intent must be made even if the effect of the law is clearly to exclude Blacks. If the person is unable to prove that the law was passed with a discriminatory intent to exclude Blacks, the law will not be struck down as being racially exclusionary simply because it has a discriminatory effect. Because such a law is "neutral" on its face and does not refer explicitly to a racial classification, it will be held to be nondiscriminatory (Brooks and Newborn 1994: 804).

The "New Approach" of Critical Race Theory

Although many Critical Race theorists recognize the need to challenge and expand existing rights analysis and find a new approach that goes beyond the strategies employed by the Civil Rights Movement, they also embrace the pragmatic use of law as "a tool for social change and the aspirational core of law as the human dream of peaceable existence" (Matsuda 1996: 22). Therefore, Critical Race Theory, unlike Critical Legal Studies, consists of "criticism tempered by an underlying descriptive message of the possibility of human social progress" (Matsuda 1996: 22).

In brief, the dominant themes of Critical Race Theory are:

1. the need to move beyond existing rights analysis,
2. an acknowledgement and analysis of the centrality of racism, not just the White supremacy form of racism but also the systemic and subtle forms that have the effect of subordinating people of colour,
3. a total rejection of the "colour-blind" approach to law, which ignores the fact that Blacks and Whites have not been and are not similarly situated with regard to legal doctrines, rules, principles and practices,
4. a contextual analysis which positions the experiences of oppressed peoples at its centre,
5. a deconstruction which asks the question, How does this legal doctrine, rule, principle, policy or practice subordinate the interests of Black people and other people of colour? and, ultimately,
6. a reconstruction which understands the "duality" of law, recognizing both its contribution to the subordination of Blacks and other people of colour and its transformative power.

Critical Race Theory is also committed to exploring alternatives to discriminatory law and to offering solutions that go beyond "symmetrical" equality and include "asymmetrical" equality, or affirmative action, to ameliorate conditions of disadvantage.[5]

Critical Race methodology requires a deconstruction of legal rules, principles and policies and it challenges the so-called "neutrality" and "objectivity" of laws that oppress Blacks and other people of colour.

Deconstruction is designed to confront subtle forms of discrimination perpetuated by law. Critical Race Theory attempts to expose the ordinariness of racism and to validate the experiences of people of colour, which are important bases for understanding laws that perpetuate their disenfranchisement (Matsuda 1987: 346–47). Matsuda et al. note that, "as critical race theorists we adopt a stance that presumes that racism has contributed to all contemporary manifestations of group advantage and disadvantage along racial lines" (1993: 73). The questions asked by Critical Race theorists are: Does the legal doctrine, legal rule, principle or practice at issue subordinate and discriminate against people of colour? Are "race" and racism an issue? If the answers are yes, should the issue be litigated or should some other strategy be employed?

Critical Race Theory also employs "narrative," or storytelling. Narrative functions in a number of ways. It can allow lawyers and others to "tell the story" of their clients and the Black experience of racism and subordination in a non-ahistorical way. Narrative can debunk the myths of neutrality and objectivity by placing emphasis upon the confrontational nature of an encounter—between a Black youth and a White police officer who represents the state, for example—in its social and historical context of racial discrimination. Thus, narrative allows the lawyers representing, for example, a Black youth charged with assault of a police officer, or a Black youth who is the victim of excessive use of police force, to "tell the story" of the racial antagonism between the police and the Black community at that location in Canada at the time of the encounter. Narrative can also be a way to understand and interpret judicial opinions in order to deconstruct the "racial" and other ideologies that may underlie them.

The final stage in Critical Race methodology is reconstruction. What are the alternatives (if any) to the existing doctrine, legal rule, principle or practice that will advance the cause of Black people? What harm or benefit to the Black client and/or community might result from the adoption or nonadoption by the courts or the legislature of these changes?

Critical Race Feminism

American Black feminists and other feminists of colour have also started a new legal genre known as "Critical Race Feminism" because mainstream feminism has overlooked the fact that White supremacy and dominance affects women of colour. Critical Race Feminism has been described as "a movement which is not yet fully organized or distinct, but part of the evolving tradition that originated with Critical Legal Studies, culminating in the Critical Race Theory genre" (Cleaver 1997: 35).

There is no universal feminist theory, but rather there are a number of theories. All mainstream feminist theories, however, have gender oppression at their core. "Feminist legal scholars challenged law's deeply inscribed patriarchy, showed that gender and sex roles are constructed, not natural, and named and condemned such practices as sexual harassment in the workplace, spousal abuse, and violent pornography" (Delgado 1993: 744).

Black feminist scholars have attempted to point out the shortcomings of mainstream feminist theories in addressing the oppression of both race and gender when these issues intersect. Gender discrimination, say Critical Race feminists, is only one of the barriers to full participation that women of colour face. Black women, like Black men, are also oppressed by racism and classism. During the Civil Rights Movement and at other times, Black women have fought for Black liberation. As Kathleen Cleaver observed, "We could see how these conflicts arising from sexism within our community were subordinate to the overwhelming violence of the domination imposed on our community by the armed representatives of the state" (1997: 35). Though there is no doubt that Black women are further oppressed by sexism, as Cleaver notes:

> Eliminating gender discrimination in itself does not remove the contortion blighting the lives of women whose colour, race, national origin, or economic marginalization causes them such pain. ... Until White feminists discover how to see the insidious way that racism constricts the lives of millions of women, they cannot oppose it. Worse, they may blindly fail to perceive how their ancestry positions them to benefit passively from racism's perpetuation, and remain oblivious to the racialized nature of gender (1997: 39).

Critical Race Feminism argues that mainstream feminist theory has failed to deal with Black women's realities of racism, sexism and classism, or with White women's own part in this oppression.[6] An examination of mainstream feminist theory and, in particular, contemporary feminist legal scholarship clearly shows that this failure has manifested in the almost complete absence of analyses which go beyond gender and patriarchy to consider the impacts of racism, sexism and classism on women of colour.

Liberal feminist theory has been able to see analogies between racism and sexism but, according to Critical Race feminists, has been unable to develop a framework that encompasses both (Herbert 1989–90: 271). Socialist feminist theory focuses on the issue of class and gender without focusing on the "racism of class." Louis Kushnick (1998) argues, for example, that because institutional racism determines resource allocation (of goods and services) and opportunities (including education, employment and the like), Whites get privileged access. This kind of inequality, he argues, maintains the class system by

> inculcating and reinforcing a race consciousness rather than a class consciousness among the white working class.... One has only to look at the history of "race riots"—pogroms—against people of colour in times of economic and political crisis, for example, the race riots ... and the current escalation of racial violence among unemployed and alienated whites" (1998: 47).

Socialist feminism, while articulating the effects of class on White women, fails to examine the intersection of race and class on women and men of colour. The ruling class, as Kushnick notes, expends a great deal of effort to separate race from class, both intellectually and politically, and he notes that White working-class racism incorporates and maintains the racist ideology of the ruling class (1998: 46). And radical feminism, which has as its primary focus the concept of patriarchy and which emphasizes gender relations, or sexual oppression, as the most crucial form of oppression, has denied the commonality of oppression that Black women have with Black men. In contrast, Angela Harris (1994) has examined the issue of rape in order to demonstrate the commonality of oppression between Black women and Black men. She demonstrates that mainstream feminists such as Katherine McKinnon have failed to explore what rape means to Black women and men. Harris shows that, for Black women, rape is a more complex phenomenon and an "experience as deeply rooted in colour as in gender" (1994: 15). She points out that, as a legal matter, rape did not even exist for Black women during slavery, because at that time the rape of a Black woman by any man, White or Black, was not a crime. This lack of legal protection for Black women against the crime of rape continued, as rape laws were seldom invoked to protect Black women because these women were considered to be "promiscuous" by nature (Harris 1994: 16).

Harris notes that for Black males and females, "rape signified the terrorism of Black men by White men, aided and abetted, passively (by silence) or actively (by 'crying rape'), by White women" (1994: 16). Harris also argues that this aspect of rape is not purely historical but has a contemporary basis. She cites reports by Susan Estrich and others which show that, between 1930 and 1967, 89 percent of the men executed for rape in the United States were Blacks. A 1968 study of rape sentencing in one state showed that, in all of the fifty-five cases where the death penalty had been imposed on Black men, the victims had been White, while 47 percent of all Black men convicted of assaults on Black women had been released on probation.

Similarly, Paul Kivel notes that

at times, White women's groups have supported attacks against the African-American community in the name of [White] women's safety. In the late nineteenth century the National American Woman's Suffrage Association refused to take a stand against lynching and mob violence.... It did not support the organizing of chapters of Black women because it did not want to jeopardize White southern support for White women's right to vote," and it argued that if White women could vote, it would buttress the supremacy of the White race against the demands of Black people (1996: 62).

Kivel states that the "disproportionate criminalization and punishment of Black men for violence against White women continues today" (1996: 62). There are many examples in contemporary mainstream feminist legal scholarship where the writers have ignored the issues of race in their analysis of criminal and other areas of law. If "race" or "racism" are discussed at all, it is done in passing, with no real analysis of the differences in how the law impacts on women of colour and White women. These differences are particularly acute in the procedural area of sentencing and are demonstrated by the disproportionate representation of Black women and other women of colour in the criminal justice system.

Summary

Critical Race Theory originated with Black and other scholars of colour who attended and presented critical papers at the tenth National Critical Legal Studies Conference held in Los Angeles in 1986. It also originated as a response to the continuing activism of students of colour in American law schools against the discriminatory hiring and promotion practices of these White-dominated institutions. This student activism encouraged faculty of colour to articulate the role that race and racism play in law.

The failure of both Legal Liberalism and the Critical Legal Studies (CLS) movement to place racial questions on the legal agenda left scholars of colour skeptical of the state of existing legal discourse. Although theorists of colour were attracted to the CLS movement because it challenged liberal concepts of the "neutrality" and "objectivity" of law and because it recognized the fact that law legitimates existing "maldistributions" of wealth and power, in the end Critical Race theorists rejected it because of its refusal or inability to recognize the central role that race and racism play in law and because of its failure to give credit to the experiences of people of colour. Critical Race theorists disagreed with the CLS view of rights discourse and with its rejection of law as a tool against oppression and subordination. Critical Race theorists also criticized the CLS movement's inability to go beyond "trashing" to the next stage of reconstruction.

Critical Race Theory considers what the lot of minorities would be if the CLS "trashing" succeeded and all laws were repealed, and on this basis it rejects the CLS vision. Critical Race Theory argues that although rights discourse is indeterminate, it is still essential to the struggle for racial equality. Law now contributes to racial injustice but must also be used in the battle against it. The Civil Rights Movement that began in the 1960s has stalled and civil rights gains are being systematically diminished. Critical Race Theory therefore calls for new approaches to deal with the complex relationships among race, racism and law. Deconstruction and reconstruction go hand in hand in the struggle for racial equality. Colour-blindness and ignorance of the central role of racism in society are rejected by Critical Race theorists, for whom race-consciousness is an overriding theme, and new solutions to old problems call for a redistributive approach to law. Critical Race scholars have "also challenged law's dominant mode of detached impartiality, offering in its place scholarship that is more contextualized and based on Narrative and experience" (Johnson 1994: 819).

The work of American Critical Race scholars was to have a significant impact on the birth of a Critical Race Theory movement in Canada.

An International Movement

Canadian Critical Race Theory

> "Many ethnic and racial groups in Canada have been victims of direct and explicit discrimination in the past. Today, discrimination persists in forms more difficult to discern such as stereotypes, assumptions and singular viewpoints. It manifests itself as systems, practices, policies and laws that appear neutral, but that, under close inspection, have serious detrimental consequences for members of ethnic and racial communities."
> —Peter Rosenthal (1989–90)

The growth of Critical Race Theory began in Canada during the 1980s. Following along the same theoretical lines as American Critical Race theorists, scholars of colour in Canada began to articulate their dissatisfaction with Canadian legal discourse which, like its American counterpart, had failed to include an analysis of the roles that race and racism have played in the political and legal structures of society. Like American theorists of colour, Canadian Critical Race theorists knew that issues of race permeated the legal landscape. In one respect, however, Canada's history of racism presented more serious problems than that of the United States. In the United States, most observers would acknowledge that racism exists; the controversy is over the role that law plays in its maintenance and perpetuation. In Canada, it is hard even to reach this issue because of pervasive denial of the very existence of racism in Canadian society.

It has been said that the image Canadians wish to portray to the world is one of racial and cultural tolerance, of Canada as a mecca for the oppressed of the world. If racism is a problem at all in Canada, these image-makers insist, it is an "aberration," merely the action of a few misguided individuals that should not reflect on Canadian society as a whole. Some White Canadians point to the "welcome" given to fugitive slaves from the United States who came north through the Underground Railroad, and to the fact that in 1985 Canada was the first nation to implement a *Multiculturalism Act.*

However, a dichotomy exists between Canada's public and international image as an "egalitarian" society free from the racism that plagues the United States and the actual racial reality in this country. James Walker, for example, reveals the discrepancy between Canada's "national dream" and its reality of racial inequality and notes that "left as undisturbed illusion, the dream can perpetuate inequality by denying the very existence of racial disadvantage" (1997: 344). In Canada, as Constance Backhouse noted after canvassing historical jurisprudence, there are many examples of "judicial support" for racial segregation such as *Loew's Montreal Theatres Ltd.* v. *Reynolds* (1919, 30 Que. B.R. 459), *Franklin* v. *Evans* (1924, 55 O.L.R. 349 [H.C.]), and *Rogers* v. *Clarence Hotel* (1940, 55 B.C.R. 214 [C.A.]). Similarly, Walker, in his book *"Race," Rights and the Law in the Supreme Court of Canada,* notes that in virtually every area in which "Jim Crow" existed in the United States, such as churches, housing, jobs, restaurants, public transportation, sports and recreation, hospitals, orphanages, prisons, asylums, funeral homes, morgues and cemeteries, "African Canadians experienced exclusion and separation from mainstream institutions, amounting to a Canadian version of 'Jim Crow'" (1997: 125).

In 1995, for the first time in Canadian legal history, a text, entitled *"Racial Discrimination": Law and Practice* (and published by Carswell with research funding assistance provided by Justice Canada), focused on discriminatory practices in the Canadian system, "as manifested in federal and provincial law and policy" (Mendes 1995: 1-1). The text adequately covers the "present-day forms of discrimination and the legal mechanisms available to change these discriminatory patterns" (Mendes 1995: iii). The publication of this text is an initial response to concerns which have been raised by Canadian Critical Race theorists. However, it is just a beginning, and the authors of the text explain that various important domains could not adequately be covered, including "issues specifically affecting Canada's First Nations peoples, such as the right to self-governance, [and] the experiences of black and other ethnic communities with Canadian courts and the criminal justice system in general (Mendes 1995: iii)."

The text provides an analysis of race relations in Canada that does not deny or attempt to erase the historical reality of racism in this country. It equips us with an historical account of the institution of slavery in Canada, which was the "first institution whose very existence was governed by a distinction based on race" (Mendes 1995: 1-3). Beginning with the pre-Confederation period, the authors proceed through Confederation to the post–World War II period. The text informs us that both Blacks and First Nations people were enslaved in New France, which practised slavery under "provisional approval" until 1709 when it received full approval by France. Thus, the first Black slave to arrive in Canada directly from Africa (for whom there is an adequate record) was Oliver Le Jeune, in 1628, but as Winks points out, slavery had been present in Canada at least since 1607 (Winks 1971: 1-23). Under British rule, slavery began to flourish. The Mendes text on racial discrimination notes that, "under French governance, slaves had been purchased in small numbers and thus no large-scale slave market had developed in Canada as it had in the United States. In contrast, under British control, the number of slaves increased and slavery became more exclusively imposed on black individuals" (Mendes 1995: 1.II.B.). During this period, the largest contingent of Black slaves arrived in Canada during the American War of Independence in 1775, when United Empire Loyalists were encouraged to migrate to Canada and the British granted them permission to bring their slaves along. Following the war, more White Loyalist emigrants brought their slaves with them. Free Blacks were also encouraged, by promises of land grants, to join the British forces and ultimately to migrate to Canada. Most of these Black Loyalists settled in Nova Scotia. However, the land grants they were promised were either never received or were of such poor quality as to be incapable of providing subsistence to the Black settlers. Consequently, the Mendes text informs us that

> the legacy of slavery in Canada consigned the black migrants to a labouring and service role at the lowest level and for the lowest wages.... They were also resented and attacked by these same white workers, who perceived the black workers as having taken their employment opportunities. Black citizens were similarly segregated or excluded from churches and schools. Many of the stereotypes later applied to black persons developed from this

early marginalization (1995: 1.II.B.)

Hence, Canada's free Black population dated back to the American Revolution, and by the "first decade of the 19th century, approximately 3,000 people of African origin were held as slaves in what is now Canada, their status duly noted in the legal documents of the times." Historians note that in 1808 the Nova Scotia Assembly was debating a Bill for "regulating Negro Servitude" (Walker 1997: 124).

Other major migrations of Blacks into Canada occurred during the War of 1812, when about two thousand Black fugitives from slavery in the United States arrived in Nova Scotia in 1813 and increasingly more Black fugitives settled in what was then Upper Canada. "In 1832, there were approximately 300 blacks living in Amherstburg and several hundred living in London. By approximately 1850, the numbers had increased to 800 and 500, respectively" (Mendes 1995: 1.III). After the United States enacted the *Fugitive Slave Act* in 1850, thousands of fugitive slaves fled to Canada. It is estimated that by 1860 the number of Blacks in Upper Canada had increased to approximately 40,000 (Mendes 1995: 1.III).

The institution of slavery lasted in Canada for close to two hundred years.[7] It was not as economically viable in Canada as it was in the United States, however, and slavery was abolished throughout the British Empire in 1883. But the abolition of slavery did not end discrimination and anti-Black racism in Canada. "Whether in Canada or in the United States, most black citizens would continue to face various forms of discrimination" (Mendes 1995: 1.II). After Confederation the legacy of slavery continued to impact on Black Canadians, and the constitution of the new Canada enacted in 1867 did not protect Blacks or other racial minority groups against discrimination. James Walker, in his historical account of the Canadian legal systems' treatment of racism, and others who have studied the problem of racism in Canada have documented the "substantial extent of racial segregation in Canada" which was rampant particularly in education and employment (1997: 124). Walker notes with respect to education:

> The most significant area of separation, at least in legislative terms, was in education. In Nova Scotia the *Education Act* of 1836 permitted local commissioners to establish separate schools for "Blacks or people of colour." ... Ontario's *Common School Act* of 1850 allowed 12 or more heads of families to request a separate black school ... in practice 12 white family heads could request separate schools for black children. Under this legislation segregated education was imposed in most Ontario districts with a sizeable African-Canadian population (1997: 128).

Nor was school segregation confined to the 1800s. Segregation provisions remained on the books until the mid-1960s and de facto forms of segregation still exist to some extent today. Walker also notes that employment discrimination was widespread, "encompassing the civil service as well as the private sector," and public transportation and accommodation were also segregated (1997: 128).

Walker also puts Canadian racism in its contemporary context. He notes that surveys of racism in Canada in the 1980s and 1990s indicate that there are

> objective data illustrating the survival of "race" as a meaningful factor in Canadian life.... Racial antagonism continued to provoke harassment, vandalism and assault. In 1993, according to B'nai B'rith, there were more "hate crimes" than in any year since records began in 1981, with Jews and African Canadians the most frequent victim groups. More indicative of Canadian reality were census data from 1981, 1986 and 1991 revealing that "visible minorities," and especially African Canadians, had consistently lower-than-average incomes and higher levels of unemployment. Even when qualifications, experience and regional factors were considered, Canadians of African and Asian origin earned less than white Canadians in comparable circumstances. ... A national survey of 672 employment recruiters in 1987 reported that 87 percent of corporate recruiters and 100 percent of employment agencies received implicit requests to discriminate by "race" when selecting personnel; these requests were actually fulfilled by 73 percent of the corporate recruiters and 94 percent of the private agencies. A series of tests run by the Canadian Civil Liberties Association in the 1980's and 1990's into employment agencies showed a consistent 80 percent willing to "screen" applicants according to racial requests.... Racial discrimination was widely reported in housing as well, and in one 1986 test of apartment rentals in Toronto more than 40 percent of applications were denied on apparently racial grounds. Perhaps most insidious of all, studies by the Toronto Board of Education showed that black school children were streamed into "basic" courses at a rate more than double that for white children (1997: 339).

Walker's conclusion, already painfully obvious to racial minorities and Critical Race theorists in Canada, was that "race" was still a significant factor in Canada that determined where racial minorities "could live, what they could study in school, [and] how they could earn their living ... [and] despite profound changes in the law, the 'remedial' phase in rights policy beginning around 1980 had limited impact upon 'race relations' in Canada" (1997: 339). In addition to the data unearthed by Walker, there are numerous task force and royal commission reports and other studies related to the existence of racism in Canadian society.[8]

The leading legal authority on the existence of anti-Black racism in Canada is the 1993 case of *R. v. Parks* (84 C.C.C. [3d] 353 [Ont. C.A.]). In this case, the Ontario Court of Appeal held that the accused Black man, who was charged with the murder of a White victim, should be allowed to challenge jurors for racial prejudice because of the overwhelming evidence of anti-Black racism in Metropolitan Toronto and Canada. Justice Doherty relied on his own research into the existence of racism in Canadian society and found "an ever-growing body of studies and reports documenting the extent and intensity of racist beliefs in contemporary Canadian society, many deal[ing] with racism in general, others with racism directed at black persons" (*R. v. Parks* at 366). Additionally, the Commission on Systemic Racism in the Ontario Criminal Justice System was directed in 1992 to make "anti-Black racism" the focal point in its inquiry into systemic racism.

Like their American counterparts, historically, Blacks have been excluded from the profession of law in Canada. For example, the Royal Commission on the Donald Marshall Jr. Prosecution (1989) recognized this exclusion when it made Recommendation 20, addressing the issue of legal careers for visible minorities. The royal commission recommended that the government, the Nova Scotia Barristers' Society and the Dalhousie Faculty of Law cooperate in the development of a program to identify, recruit and support qualified visible-minority students aspiring to legal careers. Prior to the Marshall Inquiry, there were only seven Black lawyers in the entire province of Nova Scotia, most of whom were not practising law, primarily because of the colour barrier they faced in the profession. The first native-born Black Nova Scotian to graduate from Dalhousie Law School was James Robinson Johnston in 1898, but the next, George Davis, did not graduate until fifty-four years later, in 1952. This lack of Black legal representation in Nova Scotia and Canada has seriously undermined the Black community's ability to attack issues of racism in a legal framework and has retarded the advancement of rights doctrine in the context of race under the *Canadian Charter of Rights and Freedoms*.

Canadian law schools only began to address the education of substantial numbers of minority students in the late 1980s. Formal programs to ameliorate the conditions of groups disadvantaged because of race or colour only began to emerge in law schools at that time. The past failure to address the problem of student diversity has placed an enormous burden on the few minority faculty in Canadian law schools. As a result of this late start, the pool of minority candidates for faculty hiring is very small. Some Canadian law schools are attempting to address the issues of faculty and student diversity simultaneously, while others are still debating whether to address them at all. Most Canadian law schools have no First Nations people or persons of colour on their faculties (Aylward 1995: 470).

Those few Canadian scholars of colour, however, began writing about the impact of race and racism on Canadian law in the 1980s and the early 1990s. For example, in 1994, Professor Joanne St. Lewis wrote a critical piece on *Racism and the Judicial Decision-Making Process* in which she defined "racism" in the judicial context as

> an attitude in the judicial decision-making process which assumes the inherent superiority of the values of the dominant cultural/racial group and the concomitant inferiority of another cultural/racial group. The issue of racism is fundamentally about power of the mass and the shared belief system; the power to shape reality in accordance with one's values; the power to give voice to or to silence the diversity of others; the power to rewrite history and to develop legislation which meets the socioeconomic imperatives of the majority (1994: 15).

In 1994 another Canadian Critical Race theorist, Esmeralda Thornhill, noted that:

> Our arsenal of legal devices is sorely in need of repair when it comes to Racism and racial discrimination. The Index to Canadian Legal Periodical Literature—the last time checked—still comported no category or heading labelled "Racism" or "Racial Discrimination," thus from the outset, incontrovertibly, limiting the body of doctrine available to practitioners and to the Courts to help them assess Racism. We have no published collection of case commentaries assembling decisions involving incidents with racial overtones or [any] other similar published body of doctrine (1994: 8).

In 1993 the *Canadian Journal of Women and the Law* published a thematic volume entitled *Racism ... Talking Out,* the first of its kind in Canadian legal publication history.[9] The editorial in this volume stated that, "despite the growing recognition of the centrality of race and racism to feminist analysis of law, there remains a dearth of such scholarship within legal feminism" (C.J.W.L. 1993: v). This was the first Canadian legal publication to respond to the call for inclusion by scholars of colour.

The editorial also recognized a "profound imbalance" in legal publishing, in that "the voices of Women of Colour and Aboriginal women have not been heard. Empowering this group to speak out on issues of race and racism is a precondition to any serious effort to foster race-conscious feminist analyses of law" (C.J.W.L. 1993: v). Contributions to this volume on racism by Black, Aboriginal and other women of colour included critical race analyses addressing the following topics:

- A "general conspiracy of silence and denial [and] the prevalence of Racism in Canadian Legal Culture" (Thornhill 1994: 2).
- "Canadian [human rights] tribunals [which] largely ignore the racial and gender identity of both complainants and respondents" (Duclos 1993: 25).
- "Practices which focus on racism without addressing sexism [that] create a hierarchy of oppressions. Instead, what is required is a reframing of the issues so that racism and sexism are seen as interlinking oppressions which contribute to the invalidation of Islam and the marginalization of Muslims" (Khan 1993: 52).
- "Differential immigration policy [that reinforces] black nurses' subordination within a racialized and gendered nursing labour force" (Calliste 1993: 85).
- "The lack of studies and statistics to support a systemic racial discrimination claim" (Carasco 1993: 142).
- "Under-representation of Aboriginal Peoples in the English common law tradition ... [and] the failure to address the representation of Aboriginal Peoples in the civil law tradition" (Monture-OKanee 1993: 121).

The "invisibility" of Canadian racism and its impact on the law is also illustrated in the work of most White Canadian feminist scholars. Examples of the deficiency of mainstream feminist analysis (of the substance and the procedure of criminal law) can readily be seen in the scholarship of mainstream feminists such as Boyle et al. (1991). I will illustrate this problem by using examples drawn from a "Forum on *Lavallee* v. *R.: Women and Self-Defence*" (1991), organized by Christine Boyle and others to provide a feminist critique of a 1990 Supreme Court of Canada decision where a woman was acquitted of second-degree murder with respect to the death of her common-law partner on the basis of self-defence. Various mainstream feminist writers suggest that, on the whole, this Supreme Court of Canada decision seemed to be in the best interest of women. The majority of the Court held that expert psychiatric evidence was admissible to assist the jury in understanding the battered woman syndrome, in order to determine the reasonableness of the accused woman's belief that killing her batterer was the only way to save her life. These feminist writers note that the Supreme Court of Canada decision changes the configuration of the self-defence doctrine and recognizes that legal doctrines (such as reasonableness) have been historically based on a male model and therefore may not meet the needs of women. They suggest that the adoption by the Supreme Court of Canada of a "reasonable battered woman" standard for self-defence is demonstration of "the Court's openness which may have benefits and costs for women" (Boyle et al. 1991: 23).

Critical Race theorists go further, however, and highlight the absence in mainstream feminist analyses of a recognition that the "reasonable person" standard was not only based on a male model but on a White male model. For this reason, it not only failed to meet the needs of White women, but it continues to ignore the realities of women and men of colour, since the *Lavallee* v. *R.* case ([1990] 1 S.C.R. 888 [S.C.C.]) did not address the issue of colour, even though Ms. Lavallee was a Metis woman.

Boyle et al. examined the implications of the *Lavallee* decision for other defences and concluded that "the non-narrow, contextual approach that is taken in *Lavallee* with respect to both the construction of reasonableness and the issue of the need for imminent danger opens the door to the dramatic reconstruction of other defences which may have disadvantaged women.... The *Lavallee* approach would apply to any defence, whenever reasonableness is in issue" (1991: 25–26). The authors then went on to examine other defences, such as provocation. In this context they concede that the issue of gender was not the only one relevant to women, and reasonableness and factors such as culture, race, age, class, religion and sexual orientation may also be relevant. The defence of provocation also has a "reasonableness" requirement, in that the provocation must be sufficient to deprive the ordinary person of self-control. Historically, in provocation, the legal concept of the ordinary or "reasonable" person was one of normal temperament and average mental capacity (read *White male*). However, in the British case of *R.* v. *Camplin* ([1978] 2 All E.R. 168 at 721 [H.L.]), Lord Morris held that "if the accused is of particular colour or particular ethnic origin and things are said which to him are grossly insulting, it would be utterly unreal if the jury had to consider whether the words would have provoked a man of different colour or ethnic origin—or to consider how such a man would have acted or reacted."

Mainstream feminists point out that in 1985, in the pre–*Lavallee* environment of *R.* v. *Hill* (51 C.R. [3d] 97 [S.C.C.]) the Supreme Court of Canada also held that other factors such as age and race, as well as gender, may be relevant in determining what a reasonable person would do when provoked. They also note the fact that the majority in *Hill* did not make it a mandatory requirement that the trial judge in such cases explicitly tell the jury what attributes they should consider (Justice Dickson emphasized in *Hill* [at 116] that the jury, in applying their common sense to the factual determination of the objective test, would quite naturally and properly ascribe such characteristics to the "ordinary person"). Although mainstream feminists consider this aspect of *Hill* unfortunate because the admission of the expert evidence presented in *Lavallee* demonstrated how the so-called "common sense" of a jury may lead to an erroneous conclusion, they only explicitly discuss bias in relation to the risk that a decision-maker who is male, or who has internalized a male perspective on the world, would be unable to comprehend the issue of provocation from a female perspective. They do not consider the implications of a failure to explicitly instruct about issues of race. In other words, they never ask the question, What are the implications for a Black person who may be provoked by repeated racial slurs?

Important arguments can be made concerning racism and provocation. Peter Rosenthal (1989–90) argues that because of the psychological damage caused by racial harassment and racist propaganda, it is appropriate to use the criminal law to limit the harm it causes. A racial taunt, says Rosenthal, "has certain features that distinguish it from other kinds of insults. It attacks an aspect of the victim that she or he cannot change. Furthermore, this aspect encompasses the entire person as a human being and not only attacks the person directly, but also her family and social contacts, which give the victim no place to turn for solace (see Rosenthal 1989–90: 118).[10]

The mainstream feminist scholars who participated in the *Lavallee* symposium ignored the fact that it may be doubly difficult for any decision-maker who is White or has internalized a White perspective on the world to see the issue from a Black woman's or man's perspective. They fail to recognize this crucial racial element and do not discuss it anywhere in their analyses. This is only one example of how White feminist scholars generally fail to address the issue of the Black woman's status in a racist society. In this case, mainstream feminists made no attempt to analyse the implications on women of colour of the defence of self-defence, the battered woman syndrome, or the defence of provocation.

How might *Lavallee* be adopted to take account of the relevance of race to the legal concept of reasonableness? I will give one example. In addition to the issues discussed above, the Court in *Lavallee* also concluded that an "imminent attack" is not necessary in all cases for self-defence to succeed. This finding is also relevant to provocation, because the requirement of "suddenness" in the defence of provocation is equivalent to the "imminent danger" requirement for self-defence. What implications does this have on the defence of provocation, where the provocation offered must have been such as to deprive the "ordinary" person of the power of self-control and the provocation must have been "sudden"? Critical Race theorists would argue that the cumulative impact of continual and prolonged racial harassment upon Black and other people of colour is similar to that of long-term spousal abuse upon women. If expert evidence can be introduced to provide a context for relief from the "immediacy" requirement in self-defence for battered women, should expert evidence be admitted to address the cumulative effect of months or years of abuse and prolonged racial harassment on Black women, men and other people of colour by society, with a view to reinterpreting the "suddenness" requirement with respect to provocation and racial insults?

As can been seen from this collection of work by scholars of colour, Canadian Critical Race theorists are seeking new approaches to deal with the complex relationships among race, racism and Canadian law. Because of the tendency in Canada to "erase" the history of racism, Canadian Critical Race theorists have a much more daunting task than their American counterparts in deconstructing the role racism plays in law.

Summary

The exclusion of Blacks and other people of colour from the Canadian legal academy has led to a serious under-representation of legal scholars of colour, which in turn has led to a slower development of Critical Race Theory in Canada. However, the historic pattern of exclusionary legal scholarship by White authors is being challenged by those few Critical Race scholars who have managed to challenge the existing status quo, bringing a new dawn of deconstruction of legal rules and reconstruction of principles and policies from a Critical Race perspective. As we shall see, the Critical Race Theory movement in Canada and the United States has the potential to have a profound effect on the way we see race, racism and the law.

Chapter 2

American Critical Race Litigation: Wedding Theory and Practice

Criminal and Constitutional Law: American Critical Race Cases

"Nobody listens," said Sandra Bankhead, a community activist in Los Angeles, following the riots in that city in 1992, which resulted in part from the "not guilty" verdict handed down by an all-White jury in the case of four White police officers accused in the beating of Black motorist Rodney King. She continued:

> Yes, there's unemployment. Yes, there's police brutality. But, you know, the bottom line is the sense of hopelessness, the stereotypes, and the prejudicial actions that have been going on since that first slave boat came across the ocean (Gibbs 1996: 62).

Rodney King and two of his friends had been out on the town having a few drinks after work. King was employed and out of prison on parole following a conviction for a 1988 robbery of a grocery store, which had gained him only two hundred dollars. He had received a two-year sentence at the California Correctional Centre and, having served one year, had been out on parole just a few months. On the evening of March 2, 1991, while King and his friends were driving towards the freeway, they heard a police siren behind them.[1] King did not stop for the California Highway Patrol but led them on a high-speed chase on the freeway. The two California Highway Patrol officers called for backup and were joined in the chase by twenty-three Los Angeles Police Department (LAPD) officers and two security officers from the school district. King left the freeway and pulled over to the side of the road. He was ordered out of the car, along with his two friends. By now many people are familiar with the horrific scenes of LAPD officers beating Rodney King which were captured on video by a citizen, George Holliday, who had been among the crowd of spectators standing behind a fence which divided an apartment building from the freeway. Jewelle Taylor Gibbs describes what happened to King next and what the video camera picked up:

> A large black male [was] surrounded by a cordon of police officers who had pushed him to the ground; while one officer shot darts from a taser gun to stun him, three others used their batons to beat him all over his body and their feet to kick him and stomp him. They shot him with an electronic harpoon and then dragged him around the ground by the long wires and hogtied him like a steer, all the while cursing him and shouting racial epithets (1996: 30).

The video camera showed the police officers administering a total of fifty-six blows and six kicks to Rodney King. Four White LAPD officers were charged by the state with assault with a deadly weapon and excessive use of force (*People* v. *Powell et al.,* 1991, 232 Cal. App. [3d]). Medical experts testified that the injuries King suffered were so severe that fluid and tissue from his eye socket and brain had dropped down into his crushed sinus cavities (Levenson 1994: 519). The police officers were ultimately acquitted in State Court by an all-White jury after the trial was moved from racially diverse Los Angeles to predominately White Simi Valley in Ventura County as a result of a defence motion for a change of venue. Although two of the four police officers were eventually convicted in 1993 in Federal Court (*U.S.* v. *Los Angeles Police Department,* 1993, 883 F. Supp. 769) of violating King's constitutional rights under colour of law,[2] the acquittal in State Court of the four White police officers for the beating of an unarmed Black man set off the worst racial riot in U.S. history.[3] More than forty people were killed, more than two thousand people were injured and there was over a billion dollars in property damage (U.S. Senate Special Task Force 1992: 10–11). In spite of the racialized nature of the beating and the response, in both the state and federal trials the issue of race was kept out of the proceedings.

Black Americans have persistently sought equality under the law and freedom from discrimination. The main mechanism by which Black Americans hoped to achieve this goal was a civil rights strategy. This strategy allowed them to litigate for equal rights through a host of constitutional and statutory enactments designed to "detect and punish breaches of the principle of formal equal opportunity" (Delgado 1990: 1393). However, despite gains in the quest for equality, racism has remained a consistent and intractable problem throughout American history, resulting in great disadvantages and inequalities for Blacks. To understand why race and racism continue to "re-emerge" in modern cases such as the Rodney King case (*People* v. *Powell et al.,* 1991, 232 Cal. App. [3d]) and the O.J. Simpson criminal case (No. BA097211 [Cal. S.Ct] 1994, 1995 WL S16132), and the reasons why traditional civil rights discourse has not offered workable and lasting solutions to the problem, we must first understand how race and racism came to be part of the foundation of American culture. Further, we must also comprehend the view put forward by Critical Race theorists that a new strategy, one that goes beyond traditional civil rights law, must evolve to adequately confront the problem.

Race and Racism in American Culture

Slaves in the United States were regulated by legislation known as the "Slave Codes"[4] under which all aspects of their existence were determined. They had no access to the courts, could not enter into contracts, own property or vote, among other things. In 1863, Abraham Lincoln gave freedom to the slaves when he issued the *Emancipation Proclamation,*[5] and six months after the end of the Civil War in 1865 the United States abolished the institution of slavery for good by ratifying the Thirteenth Amendment to the Constitution. The Southern states responded to the Thirteenth Amendment by enacting the "Black Codes" which were merely a reassertion of the Slave Codes under a new name.[6] The Black Codes were designed to keep the former slaves in political, legal, social and economic bondage (ACLU 1996: 2). In an attempt to reform the system, Congress passed new laws and constitutional amendments which invalidated the Black Codes. These reforms (known as the "First Reconstruction") included the *Civil Rights Act of 1866* and the Fourteenth Amendment to the Constitution in 1868.

The Fourteenth Amendment's purpose was to strengthen the *Civil Rights Act of 1866* and to allow for the application of the Constitution's Bill of Rights (which had initially applied only to the federal government) to all state and local governments. Thus, the Fourteenth Amendment "conferred citizenship upon all persons born in the United States, and forbade the states from depriving any person of 'life, liberty or property without due process of law,' or denying to any person 'equal protection of the laws'" (ACLU 1996: 2). Passage of the Fifteenth Amendment in 1870 conferred upon former slaves the right to vote. The promise of these reforms was never realized, however. The First Reconstruction (an attempt to confer upon Black citizens constitutionally protected rights) was resisted by the Ku Klux Klan and other White supremacist and segregationist groups who employed methods of intimidation such as the beating and lynching of Blacks. These actions were further bolstered by the Supreme Court of the United States, which, in response to pressure from former slaveholders and other segregationists, narrowly interpreted the *Civil Rights Act of 1875,* holding that it did not bar discrimination by private individuals "such as hotel owners, theatre proprietors etc." (ACLU 1996: 5). This interpretation by the Supreme Court made possible both the introduction of segregation laws (de jure, or legal, segregation) in the South known as the "Jim Crow laws," and less formal, or de facto, segregation in the North. Blacks were separated in all areas of public services, including education, housing, hotels and the like, and no legal remedy was available at that time.

The Supreme Court of the United States was ultimately required to rule on the constitutionality of Jim Crow laws in 1896. In *Plessy* v. *Ferguson* (163 U.S. 537) a Black man had refused to leave the first-class section of a Louisiana train and had been arrested and convicted of breaching segregation laws. The Court decided in *Plessy* that the segregation laws did not violate either the Thirteenth or Fourteenth Amendments of the U.S. Constitution because former slaves or descendants of slaves were not citizens of the United States and had no rights which a White man had to respect, thereby recognizing the "separate but equal doctrine." The "separate but equal" doctrine asserted that separation of the White and Black races was not unconstitutional so long as the separate facilities and services provided to Blacks were "equal" to those provided to Whites. Following this decision, even more restrictive and discriminatory segregation laws were passed and the Southern states instituted measures to deny Blacks the vote. Mob lynchings, beatings and the burning of Black homes and churches were measures used against anyone who opposed or otherwise displeased the champions of American apartheid.

In response to these restrictive laws and the measures used to enforce them, W.E.B. Du Bois and others met in Niagara Falls, Ontario, in 1905 and subsequently formed the National Association for the Advancement of Colored People (NAACP), which began to make demands for equality in all areas, especially in education. By 1921, according to the ACLU, the civil rights movement became a "fixture in the American landscape." Following World War II, the NAACP began bringing cases to the courts, and in 1946 the United States Supreme Court struck down segregation in interstate bus travel, holding it to be unconstitutional (ACLU 1996: 6). In the 1950s and 1960s the Civil Rights Movement, guided by Dr. Martin Luther King Jr. (as well as the NAACP's legal attacks on the "separate but equal" doctrine), made significant gains in the fight for desegregation. For example, in 1954 the Supreme Court of the United States declared in *Brown* v. *Board of Education* (347 U.S. 483) that "in the field of public education the doctrine of 'separate but equal' has no place. Separate educational facilities are inherently unequal.... Any language in *Plessy* v. *Ferguson* contrary to this finding is rejected" (Davis and Graham 1995: 166n4).

The *Brown* decision led to further attacks by the NAACP and the Civil Rights Movement on other patterns of government-legislated segregation, such as segregation at public parks, beaches, sporting events, hospitals, public accommodations and other public facilities. While the NAACP was attacking segregation in the courts, Dr. Martin Luther King Jr. and his followers were using nonviolent measures such as sit-ins, Freedom Rides, the Montgomery bus boycott, voting drives and other measures to protest segregation in all its manifestations. These efforts were often met by violent resistance, including beatings, murder, burnings and imprisonment. In response to the demands made by civil rights activists and the growing civil unrest, Congress passed a new *Civil Rights Act* in 1964 which declared private, as well as government, acts of discrimination unlawful. Title II of the Act prohibited discrimination based on race in privately owned facilities open to the public, such as hotels and swimming pools, Title VI prohibited discrimination in federally funded programs and Title VII prohibited discrimination in employment in the public and private sectors (ACLU 1996: 7). Congress also passed the *Voting Rights Act* in 1965. In 1968, shortly after the assassination of Dr. Martin Luther King Jr., Congress passed the *Civil Rights Act of 1968*, the most far-reaching civil rights legislation to date, and the *Fair Housing Act*, which prohibited discrimination in the sale, financing and advertising of housing. These measures came to be known as the "Second Reconstruction," or the second attempt by the U.S. government to bring equality to its Black citizens. Notably, the United States Supreme Court

> upheld the new laws as legitimate exercises of the Congressional will to undo past [racial] injustices.... [The Court] struck down discriminatory laws and practices as well as designed new and creative remedies intended at least to lessen the effects of 300 years of slavery, and 100 years more of pervasive [legal] racial discrimination (ACLU 1996: 8).

These legislative and constitutional reforms provided foundations that enabled Black Americans to litigate to seek civil rights and freedom from racial discrimination. Former U.S. Supreme Courts sometimes struck down discriminatory laws; however, the Court has had a checkered history in this regard. In more recent years, the Court has substantially reduced its support for civil rights. Spann states that, "in reviewing the work of the Court during its infamous 1988–89 term, *U.S. Law Week* reported a series of civil rights decisions by a conservative majority of the United States Supreme Court making it easier to challenge affirmative action programs and more difficult to establish claims of employment discrimination highlighted the 1988–89 term's labour and employment cases. [There were] seven decisions handed down that term alone that adversely affected minority interests"(Spann 1993: 2). Spann also notes that many of the decisions issued by the Court since 1985 were subsequently overruled by Congress in the *Civil Rights Act of 1991*. But these legislative reversals, Spann (1993: 1) observes, came only "after a bitter political debate that was characterized most strongly by the racially divisive political opposition mounted against the proposed legislation by the Bush Administration."

Critical Race theorists contend that there is an assumption in the United States that Americans are no longer racist (in contrast to the assumption held in Canada that Canadians never were). This big lie, argue Critical Race theorists, allows Americans to declare that they have triumphed over racism in the face of all evidence to the contrary (Lawrence and Matsuda 1997: 6). This assumption that Americans have triumphed over racism is reflected in the doctrine of colour-blindness adopted by the courts, as well as in the policy of formal equal opportunity which permeates current American civil rights ideology. The colour-blind approach assumes that racism no longer exists and demands that there be no government decision-making based on race. However, the doctrine of colour-blindness, as Critical Race theorists as well as some dissenting justices on the United States Supreme Court point out, ignores the social reality of racism.

> White racism has made "blackness" a relevant category in our society. Yet colour-blindness seeks to deny the continued social significance of the category, to tell blacks that they are no different from whites, even though blacks as blacks are persistently made to feel that difference (Aleinikoff 1991: 1087).

The concept of "formal equality opportunity," the argument goes, is logical because once colour-blindness disallows all categorizations based on race, all persons in society will have an identical opportunity to succeed (Aleinikoff 1991: 1088). This doctrine is assailed by Critical Race theorists because it presupposes that racism has been eliminated in American society and because it ignores historical, as well as current, disadvantages that racism has inflicted on Blacks.

The combined policies of colour-blindness and formal equal opportunity have allowed the Supreme Court to repudiate civil rights gains in most areas. In support of the claim that the United States Supreme Court, as well as the Federal Courts, have gradually been chipping away at civil rights gains, Critical Race theorists point to cases such as *Regents of the University of California* v. *Bakke* in 1978 (438 U.S. 265) and *Hopwood* v. *State of Texas* (861 F. Supp. 551) in 1996.

In *Bakke* the U.S. Supreme Court dealt with the issue of affirmative action in the context of admissions to a medical school. Allan Bakke was a White male applicant who claimed that he was the victim of "reverse" discrimination because the University of California had rejected his application to its medical school in favour of minority students under its affirmative admissions program, which set aside sixteen of its one hundred seats for minority applicants (Ross 1990: 553). These minority students, Bakke claimed, were less qualified than himself. His claim was based on the Equal Protection Clause of the Fourteenth Amendment which prohibits states from depriving any person of life, liberty or property without due process of law, and from denying any person the equal protection of the law (Davis and Graham 1995: xviii). The Fourteenth Amendment had become the primary legal foundation in the Black American's fight for justice. However, the *Bakke* decision turned this amendment on its head and set back the Black struggle for equality.

The trial court agreed with Bakke, and held that the University of California's affirmative action program was unconstitutional because it violated the Equal Protection Clause of the Fourteenth Amendment and ordered the university to admit him. As Lawrence and Matsuda point out, "by the time the *Bakke* case reached the U.S. Supreme Court, in 1978, many white Americans were ready to hear the argument that affirmative action was nothing more than discrimination in reverse" (1997: 51). The Supreme Court in *Bakke* divided 5–4 on the issue of whether or not affirmative action constituted "reverse discrimination." The majority concluded that although the admissions process might take account of race, a quota system such as the one used in this case either violated Title VI or denied White applicants their constitutional right to equal protection (Ross 1990: 560). The justices therefore reached a "compromise" decision which held that all racial classifications were "suspect" but justified if they were necessary to achieve a "compelling state interest." They concluded that societal discrimination (past racial discrimination) was not a sufficiently compelling interest to justify racial classifications but noted that "a court, a legislature, or a government agency could consider race in order to remedy specifically identified past discriminatory acts that were in violation of the law" (Lawrence and Matsuda 1997: 51).

The decision in *Bakke* opened the door for educational institutions to opt out of introducing affirmative action programs to combat the effects of discrimination; only those institutions truly committed to equity need feel compelled to implement such programs. Critical Race theorists argue that

> none of America's least advantaged citizens was a winner in the *Bakke* case. The Court had, by the slimmest of margins, declared that affirmative action was permissible in certain narrow circum-

> stances, but there was no guarantee that those who ran America's universities and businesses would choose to continue these programs, which had only just begun to bring equal opportunity to minorities and women (Lawrence and Matsuda 1997: 53).

Further, the decision ignored the continuing role of "race" and racism in the United States. As Derrick Bell points out, by holding that an affirmative action policy is unconstitutional because it "reversely" discriminates against Whites, the Court ignores "which race has been denied entry for centuries into academia.... By introducing an artificial and inappropriate parity in its reasoning, the Court effectively made a choice to ignore historical patterns" (1992b: 369). Had a Critical Race Theory approach been taken in the *Bakke* case, Bell argues, the Court would have examined the social context, especially the reality of racism and its consequences. This examination would have taken account of the segregation of Blacks in education, and the under-representation of Blacks and other minority students in the medical school and all other institutions of higher education. A Critical Race Theory stance would have enabled the Court to consider the reasons for this exclusion, such as racism in the public school system and the use of standardized tests to evaluate all applicants by "White" cultural and experiential standards, and the lack of minority role models in these institutions. Had the Court taken these factors into consideration, Bell argues, the Court "very well may have decided *Bakke* differently" (1992b: 369).

The major lesson of the *Bakke* decision, from a Critical Race Theory perspective, is that judges can use rights analysis to protect the rights of Whites over those of Blacks while denying that Whites are not an historically disadvantaged group in American society and that some amendments to the Constitution were specifically designed to guarantee equality for Blacks in the face of active oppression for the advantage of Whites. As Bell notes, "by reasoning that race-conscious policies derogate the meaning of racial-equality, a judge can manipulate the law and arrive at an outcome based on her world view, to the detriment of blacks" (1992b: 376).

The Supreme Court in *Bakke,* Critical Race theorists Lawrence and Matsuda (1997) contend, also failed to address the most critical constitutional question posed in America today: Does the Constitution of the United States require a neutral, colour-blind stance that will maintain the existing inequities of opportunity, or does it require an active and fundamental reconstruction of a world shaped by race, gender, and class privilege? In other words, does the Constitution require affirmative action in the broad sense in the form of positive remedial measures, such as representative juries, to guarantee equality of outcome?

A case in which the United States Supreme Court might have given a definitive answer to this question but refused to do so was the 1996 *Hopwood* v. *State of Texas* case (861 F. Supp. 551). Four White applicants to the University of Texas Law School sued the school when their applications for admission were rejected. The four claimed that the law school's affirmative action program violated their constitutional right to equal protection. This program, they argued, amounted to "reverse discrimination." The Federal District Court disagreed with them and held that the affirmative action program was in fact constitutional because it was designed to remedy the ongoing effects of discrimination in "primary, secondary, and higher education in Texas" (Lawrence and Matsuda 1997: 54). This decision was, however, overturned by the Federal Court of Appeals for the Fifth Circuit, which held that the affirmative action program did in fact constitute "reverse discrimination." The Supreme Court declined to hear a further appeal based on a procedural defect, which enabled it to avoid the constitutional question regarding affirmative action posed by the case. Consequently, the Appeals Court decision stood, and the three states covered by the Fifth Circuit—Texas, Louisiana and Mississippi—were affected by it. In practical terms this means that affirmative action programs have been held to be unconstitutional by lower courts, but no decision on the matter has yet been made by the highest court in the land, resulting in not just an uncertainty in the law, but in a setback to the Civil Rights Movement's attack on entirely White institutions.

Critical Race theorists condemned the Fifth Circuit's decision in *Hopwood* because it did not take a contextual approach to the issues raised by the case but instead used rights analysis to elevate the rights of Whites over those of Blacks. Lawrence and Matsuda illustrate this point by emphasizing the fact that the Court in *Hopwood* disregarded the history of racism and past discrimination in the State of Texas:

> Texas is a state with an active Ku Klux Klan and regularly reported hate crimes against people of colour; a state that admitted Blacks to its law school only when it was forced to do so by the United States Supreme Court in 1950; a state where a licensed attorney once said ... we like our dirt black and our people white ... [where] until the mid-1960s, a Texas Board of Regents policy prohibited Blacks from living in or visiting white dorms (1997: 55).

Because these realities were ignored by the Court in *Hopwood* through a process of historical reconstruction, "Blacks and Mexican Americans became 'favoured minorities' and whites became victims of racial discrimination" (Lawrence and Matsuda 1997: 55). As in the *Bakke* case, Critical Race theorists have concluded that the critical question of the meaning of the Equal Protection Clause and whether or not it requires an active and fundamental reconstruction of American society was left unanswered, while the critical and hard-fought civil rights gains of Blacks had been decimated under the guise of equal protection.[7] The Court has also rolled back civil rights gains in affirmative action and employment discrimination cases, for example, in 1998 in *City of Richmond* v. *J.A. Crosen Co.* (448 U.S.). This case struck down the affirmative action plan of the City of Richmond, Virginia, which had allowed set-asides for Black contractors, because the plan constituted "reverse discrimination" under the Equal Protection Clause of the Fourteenth Amendment. The Supreme Court based this result on the premise that the Constitution requires all governmental racial classifications to be subject to strict scrutiny even when they are designed to remedy past discrimination. Davis and Graham (1995: 359) point out that the Court in the *Crosen* case failed to take into consideration the history of racial discrimination in the historical capital of the Confederacy.

Legislatures in the United States have also been incrementally rolling back the hard-earned gains of the civil rights era.[8] By 1996, according to Lawrence and Matsuda (1997), anti–affirmative action legislation had been introduced in Congress and thirty-five states. Nor are the reversals limited to the area of affirmative action in education and employment discrimination. Significant reversals have also occurred in voting rights, desegregation in schools, housing discrimination, jury selection and racial discrimination in death penalty cases, to name a few other contexts (Davis and Graham 1995: 359–82).

While the U.S. Supreme Court, Federal Courts, and state and federal legislators roll back the civil rights gains of the 1950s and 1960s, objective data continues to show that in the United States (as in Canada), "race" has survived as a meaningful and significant factor in society. Lawrence and Matsuda, after canvassing a large number of reports and studies, conclude that:

> Racism is alive and well in America.... [R]ecent polls confirm what we know from experience: racist attitudes persist in the 1990s. The most recent decade has also seen a significant rise in the number of hate crimes motivated by racial bias.... Racist hate groups such as the Ku Klux Klan have witnessed an alarming increase in membership.... Blacks had more than a 50 percent chance of being discriminated against when seeking housing and ... African Americans were rejected for home loans at twice the rate of whites.... Schools are becoming more segregated than

ever ... and stark disparities are evident when the incomes of African Americans and white households are compared, and disparities in incarceration and mortality rates between Blacks and whites also indicate the continuing impact of racism (1997: 71–73).

The doctrine of colour-blindness has promoted the myth that racism is no longer a factor in American society. If the law says that you cannot talk about race or make decisions based on race, the logic goes, then racism no longer exists because it has been effectively eradicated by a colour-blind policy. If racism doesn't exist, no positive measures are necessary to combat it. Additionally, colour-blindness requires that Whites and Blacks be treated the same and thus "white racism is subjected to the same scrutiny as efforts aimed at ameliorating the effects of racism" (Bell 1992b: 369).[9]

However, because of the adoption of this colour-blind stance, the issue of "race" continues to dominate the American social and legal landscape, but the law forbids addressing it head on. This truism was never more apparent than in the state and federal trials of the four White police officers accused of beating Rodney King, where the issues of race and racism were avoided.

The Rodney King Case

In the 1991 state trial of the four LAPD police officers accused of beating Rodney King (*People* v. *Powell et al.,* 1991, 232 Cal. App [3d]) the prosecution did not introduce evidence of "racial animus" on the part of the officers, nor did they present the overwhelming historical and contemporary evidence of racism within the LAPD. The prosecution also did not appeal the decision of the State Court to move the trial from a racially diverse venue to the predominately White venue of Simi Valley, where it was inevitable that the officers would be judged by an all-White jury. The state prosecutors, who were influenced by racial stereotypes of the aggressive Black man, did not put King on the stand because they did not consider him a sympathetic witness. Further, the prosecution did not adequately challenge the defence's attempt to put King on trial by presenting irrelevant evidence of his past behaviour and by attacking his character. As well, the prosecution did not challenge defence assertions that no racial epithets had been used by the White police officers, despite video-audio evidence and eyewitness testimony to the contrary. The prosecution also did not challenge the defence's portrayal of King's injuries as trivial. In spite of the facts that King had not been charged with any offence (such as drunk driving or resisting arrest), no trace of PCP (angel dust) had been found in King's system, contrary to police statements to that effect, and eyewitness and video evidence clearly proved that racial slurs had been used by the police officers, the jury acquitted them. "The all-White jury, which was convinced that 'race' was not an issue, allowed the defence lawyers to persuade them that Rodney King was beaten by four White police officers while seventeen other police officers looked on simply because he refused to stop moving when he had been ordered to do so" (Gibbs 1996: 30).[10]

The erasure of race from the state trial of the four police officers accused of beating Rodney King, and the racial riots which followed, prompted the NAACP Legal Defence and Education Fund to make the following statement, which fairly sums up the prevailing attitude of Black Americans toward the Rodney King case and the justice system in the United States:

> The anger ignited by this verdict among African-Americans was based on the well-founded belief that people of colour are consistently denied equal justice in our courts. (A recent poll shows that 81 percent of African-Americans believe that the judicial system is racially biased.) In the Rodney King case, the first assault on simple justice was, of course, the beating itself. The second occurred when this racially charged case was moved to a nearly all-white community. That change of venue had precisely the same discriminatory effect as practices that were once used to exclude African-Americans from juries when Jim Crow ruled much of this land. The final assault on justice was the verdict. The jurors, none of whom were African-American, apparently were unable to see a person of colour like King as anything other than a threat, as opposed to a helpless human being who was mauled by officers of the law.... While outrageous, the verdict and the racism that infected it were hardly aberrations. Indeed, the perception among many African-Americans that there are two systems of justice—one for whites and one for people of colour— is not a result of one jury's decision in Simi Valley. That perception is based on a host of racial inequities in our legal system (NAACP 1992: 62).[11]

The riots that followed the not-guilty verdict in the Rodney King state case were reminiscent of the racial riots that rocked the Watts area of Los Angeles twenty-seven years earlier, in 1965, which had been in part precipitated by the brutality of three White California Highway Patrol officers who had encountered a young Black male, Marquette Frye, and tried to arrest him for drunk driving (Gibbs 1996: 13). Following the 1965 Watts riots, a commission had been appointed by the governor of California. The McCone Commission submitted its report in December 1965. Ironically, the McCone Report identified police misconduct and brutality as one of the causes of the Watts riots. Similarly, one month following the beating of Rodney King (and a year before the trial and acquittal of the four White police officers), another independent commission, the Christopher Commission, was appointed by the Mayor of Los Angeles to investigate the Los Angeles Police Department. And one year after the acquittal in State Court of the four police officers accused of the beating, a second independent commission, the California State Assembly Commission, was appointed to investigate the causes of the riots. Both commissions documented a pervasive pattern of misconduct, harassment and excessive use of force at all levels of the LAPD (Gibbs 1996: 79). The Christopher Commission, headed by Warren Christopher, who had been vice-chair of the McCone Commission, found that forty-four police officers had numerous complaints of excessive use of force against them but had never been disciplined by the department. The Commission also found that nearly six thousand officers had been involved in "use of force" reports between 1987 and 1991 alone. The problem of police misconduct was "not an exception or an aberration; it was systemic, an old 'family secret' in the LAPD" (Gibbs 1996). Gibbs notes that the Christopher Commission documented

> the pervasive attitudes of racial bias within the Los Angeles Police Department in a survey showing that one out of four police officers admitted both the existence of racial prejudice within the department and its relationship to the use of force against minorities. Police messages on the MDTs [mobile digital terminals] were full of racial epithets, negative characterizations of minorities with derogatory and dehumanizing stereotypes, and offensive jokes and threats about killing them or burning and destroying their communities (Gibbs 1996: 81).

The California State of Assembly Commission tabled its report one year after the riots and concluded, as had the McCone Commission before it, that "police brutality was ... symptomatic of a much deeper, more pervasive, and more intractable pattern of racial discrimination, persistent poverty, and urban decay in Los Angeles" (Gibbs 1996: 84).

Sadly, the race issue in the Rodney King case was also not addressed by the U.S. federal government when it stepped in after the riots and charged the four police officers with violating King's civil rights. In 1993 the four police officers, Sergeant Stacey Koon and Officers Lawrence Powell, Timothy Wind and Theodore Briseno, were charged with wilfully violating the constitutional rights of Rodney King.[12] Two of the four police officers who beat King were acquitted in Federal Court, and two were convicted but only received sentences of thirty months and a waiver of any fines for offences which usually carried, as a maximum, ten years of imprisonment and a $250,000 fine (*United States* v. *Los Angeles Police Department*, 1993, 883 F. Supp. 769).

Under Title 18 of U.S. federal civil rights statutes, sections 241 and 242,[13] federal prosecutors can seek an indictment for a violation of civil rights in cases of police misconduct. Unlike state charges, which can include a myriad of criminal law offences such as aggravated assault, assault with a deadly weapon and even murder, federal charges are limited to the single charge of a violation of civil rights, which requires a high standard of proof of intent to violate the rights of another. Section 241 of Title 18 prohibits conspiracies to deprive a person of his or her civil rights, and section 242 prohibits persons acting under colour of law (such as police officers) from violating a person's civil rights (see Levenson 1994: 552). To prove a violation under either section, federal prosecutors must meet a legal burden of proof that state prosecutors do not have to meet for many other criminal charges. Federal prosecutors had to prove that the defendants wilfully and intentionally deprived Rodney King of his civil rights. Additionally, section 242 of Title 18 has been interpreted by the courts to mean that violations under it may be prosecuted in alternative ways:

> The first half of the statute permits prosecution of any violation of an inhabitant's constitutional rights regardless of whether there was a racial motive for the offence [*United States* v. *Classic,* 313 U.S. 299, n.10 (1941)].... The second half of the statute makes it an offence to punish or penalize an individual more harshly on the basis of that person's race. Because the prosecution in the federal King beating trial did not want the burden of proving racial animus, it chose to indict the defendants under the first half of the statute only (Levenson 1994: 607–8).

The prosecutors in the federal case chose not to pursue a violation of Rodney King's rights based on race and, once again, the race issue was not addressed by the court. Some analysts argue that if the federal prosecution had shown that the four White police officers had had a racial motive in violating King's rights, it would have been easier to prove that they wilfully committed civil rights violations (Levenson 1994: 608). Critical Race theorists, however, deconstruct the intent requirement and argue that the requirement of proof of an intentional or wilful violation of an individual's civil rights contributes to the continuing subordination of Blacks and is the main failure of rights discourse.[14] The requirement of a proof of specific intent to violate particular federal rights will perhaps flush out only the most shocking violations (although the burden is so high on the party required to prove intent that even the most egregious violations often go unpunished), leaving the more subtle cases of discrimination and racism undetected.

Additionally, enforcement of the civil rights statutes has been problematic. The reason for this lack of enforcement is attributed, as Derrick Bell notes, to the fact that

> where blacks allege harm, the responsibility for the racial injustices is [quite often] not [just] the blatantly illegal acts of a few policemen but reflects policies authorized or condoned by the entire police force, often enough in conjunction with the full law enforcement establishment, [and] the judicial response is listless, procedural, and unresponsive (1992a: 5.10).

As mentioned, two of the four police officers who beat Rodney King were acquitted in Federal Court; Sergeant Koon and Officer Powell were convicted but only received sentences of thirty months and a waiver of any fines[15] (Gibbs 1996: 186). In handing out these lenient sentences to the two officers, Federal District Court Judge Davies held that Rodney King's misconduct contributed significantly to provoking the police officers' behaviour. Judge Davies held this in spite of the fact that no charges were ever laid against King and the video clearly showed the brutal beating to which he had been subjected. The sentences handed down by Judge Davies were appealed to the Ninth Circuit Court of Appeal, which reviewed the decision and in 1994 (*United States* v. *Koon,* 34 F. [3d] 1416) rejected the discretionary departures from the Sentencing Guidelines by the District Court. However, in the same year the United States Supreme Court on appeal (*Koon* v. *U.S.,* 116 S.Ct. 2035 at 2039) held that the departure from the Sentencing Guidelines based on King's misconduct was valid, as was the departure based on the police officers' high susceptibility to abuse in prison and the fact that the police officers were subjected to successive state and federal prosecutions.

The Black community was fully cognizant of a double racial standard when they contrasted the treatment of the four White police officers accused of beating Rodney King with that of the four Black men involved in the beating of White motorist Reginald Denny in the wake of the Los Angeles riots. The four Black defendants were charged with the very serious offences of attempted murder and aggravated mayhem. These charges carried life sentences, while the four police officers had only been charged by the state with assault, and by federal prosecutors with violation of Rodney King's civil rights. Defence lawyers in the Denny case

accused the District Attorney of racially discriminatory prosecution policies, and the community was outraged when it learned that the prosecution had petitioned for the removal of a Black judge who had originally
been randomly assigned to the Denny case and had been replaced by a
White judge (Gibbs 1996: 96). In contrast, the prosecutors in the cases of
the four police officers had not suggested that the White judges in these
cases might suffer from racial bias. And both state and federal charges
against the police officers carried much less severe penalties.

Two of the Black men in the Denny case, although acquitted of the
more serious charges, were convicted of simple mayhem and sentenced to
eight years in prison, compared to the thirty months meted out to the
White police officers. Paul Harris notes that the Black men accused of
beating Reginald Denny were sent to Pelican Bay, "California's notorious
high-tech, maximum security prison where conditions are so bad that a
federal judge held that it had violated the cruel and unusual punishment
prohibitions of the Constitution," while the two White police officers
finally convicted in the Rodney King beating were sent to an institution
reserved for those convicted of committing white collar crimes (1997:
189).

Further enraging the Black community was the treatment Rodney
King received from the jury in the civil trial. King subsequently sued the
police officers and the city of Los Angeles in the civil courts. More than
three years after the beating, a civil jury found Sergeant Koon, Officer
Stacey Powell and the Los Angeles Police Department liable for damages
for the injuries suffered by King and for violation of his civil rights.
However, King was only awarded compensation (monetary damages designed to restore the injured party to his former state), and the jury refused
to award punitive damages (a remedy in civil law designed to punish
wrongdoers and to serve as a deterrent to others) against the officers.

The significance of the Rodney King case for Critical Race Theory is
that the failure to confront the race issue at both the state and federal
levels confirms the argument that relying on the current system and its
colour-blind doctrine and rules to provide justice for people of colour is
neither effective nor acceptable. The failure of the justice system and the
inadequacies of traditional rights analysis in protecting the interests of
people of colour exacerbates and reinforces racial oppression. Critical
Race theorists point out that the Rodney King case clearly illustrates that
the American legal agenda continues to be dominated by the race issue in
spite of the myth of colour-blind justice. Most importantly, this case
vividly demonstrates the need for new legal strategies to force the courts
to recognize that issues of race require not avoidance but direct confrontation if we are ever to guarantee justice for people of colour.

I would argue, more specifically, that a Critical Race Litigation strategy is needed. Such a strategy would require commitments by lawyers and others to take a Critical Race Theory position on any case involving a Black client, and to either work collectively on precedent-setting cases involving race or to litigate race issues when they individually represent a Black client. Critical Race Litigation is the practical application of Critical Race Theory and is the next vital step in race discourse. Critical Race Litigation requires a stance that puts the issue of race and racism in society and law squarely on the litigation agenda.

Gibbs observes that Blacks in the United States are fully aware that colour-blind justice is a myth:

> The Black folks [of Los Angeles] might not have all understood their civil rights guaranteed by the Constitution or the complexities of the legal process, but they fully understood that justice in Los Angeles was not colorblind—from the cop on the beat to the judge on the bench, justice in L.A. was coloured white ... and it was that visceral understanding that fuelled their anger at the jury that exonerated the police assailants of Rodney King in April 1992 yet also aroused their empathy with the jury that acquitted O.J. Simpson of two brutal murders in October 1995 (1996: 21).

As Critical Race theorists explain, "We [have] to force the courts to ask the race question, much as feminists have required the courts to ask the woman question.... Only by denying the importance of the race question is it possible for twelve non-black jurors to conclude that no crime was committed by those four officers despite the neutral video record" (Culp 1993: 209). The Rodney King case is an example of a situation which cried out for the use of a Critical Race Litigation strategy (but instead avoided it at all costs). The case exposed the significance of race in constitutional and criminal law and the dangers of avoiding it to maintain the "myth" of colour-blindness. On the other hand, the O.J. Simpson case confirmed the importance of race consciousness and moved the courts and society, however reluctantly, toward a better understanding of the role that race plays in law.

Applied Critical Race Theory

The O.J. Simpson Criminal Case

> *"I never again would unhesitatingly trust my client's fate to the system's basic fairness"* —Johnnie L. Cochran Jr. (1996: 140)[16]

The race question did not just emerge in the Rodney King case. Critical Race theorists and others argue that racism has historically pervaded the administration of justice in America (and Canada) and still does. The reason sections 241 and 242 of Title 18 of the United States Constitution were enacted was to combat both established and arbitrary White violence against Blacks (Bell 1992a: 5.1). As Davis and Graham point out, the Rodney King beating and the subsequent trials of the four White police officers merely validated what Black Americans knew from experience to be true, but many White Americans have denied, namely, that Blacks are treated unequally and more brutally than Whites in the American criminal justice system (1995: 397). While many Whites have argued that what happened to Rodney King was an aberration, Black Americans argue that they experience excessive use of force against them by police officers and other forms of police harassment on a regular basis. Davis and Graham point out that police use of excessive force is a nationwide problem and not one confined to California (and, as we shall see later in this book, it is a nationwide problem in Canada as well):

> Less than sixty days after the Rodney King beating verdict, six police officers in New Jersey were suspended from the force without pay because they admitted to lying about a shooting in which a seventeen-year-old unarmed Black youth suspected of car theft was seriously wounded, and approximately four and one-half months after the Rodney King beating verdict, more than 2,000 police officers participated in an unruly demonstration at city hall in New York City to protest a proposal by Mayor David Dinkins to create an independent civilian agency to investigate misconduct by police officers. Some of the shouts by the police officers were racially derogatory.... Fewer than seven months after the verdict in the Rodney King beating case, it became abundantly clear that some police officers were continuing to use excessive force. Malice Green was beaten to death in Detroit by two white plainclothes police officers who had a history of complaints.... The persistent pattern of brutality against blacks is illustrative of the significance of race in the administration of

criminal justice.... Failure to seriously address these problems openly and honestly has created a societal time bomb capable of a violent eruption at any moment (1995: 406).

Nor is the problem of excessive use of force by police against Blacks and other people of colour the only racial problem in the administration of justice in the United States. The problem is far-reaching and includes other forms of police misconduct such as planting and falsifying evidence, police perjury,[17] and inappropriate and pretextual vehicle stops of Black motorists (also known as the offence of "driving while Black"), which is a form of racial profiling (police officers stop motorists based on their racial identity, which is clearly illegal, but they later offer some other pretext to justify the stop) (Davis 1977).[18] Other examples include the problem of exclusionary jury selection (the all-White jury),[19] as well as the exclusion of Blacks and other people of colour from the judiciary as defence lawyers, prosecutors and court staff,[20] the racist enactment and enforcement of drug laws[21] and discriminatory enforcement of the death penalty,[22] to name but a few.

The race question was addressed head on in the O.J. Simpson criminal case (BA097211 [Cal.S.Ct.] 1994) when Black lawyer Johnnie Cochran took a Critical Race Theory position and implemented a Critical Race Litigation strategy in defence of his client. On June 13, 1994, Nicole Brown Simpson and Ronald L. Goldman were found stabbed to death outside her home in Brentwood, Los Angeles. O.J. Simpson, Nicole Brown Simpson's ex-husband and former football hero and Heisman Trophy winner, was eventually arrested and charged with the murders.

Johnnie Cochran practiced Critical Race Litigation in *Simpson* by acknowledging and analysing the centrality of racism in the case. The White supremacist form of racism exhibited by Detective Mark Fuhrman was central to the case, as were the systemic and subtle forms of racism with which the criminal justice system was infected. The defence lawyers rejected, and asked the jury to reject, a colour-blind approach which ignores the fact that Blacks and Whites have not been historically and are not now "similarly" situated with regard to legal doctrines, rules, principles and practices. The defence took a contextualized approach to the case and urged the jury to do the same. This contextualized approach positioned the experiences of Black people within the criminal justice system, particularly at the policing end of that system, at the centre of the analysis. As Cochran points out in *Journey to Justice* (Cochran and Rutten 1996), the defence did not argue that there was a "conspiracy" of Los Angeles police officers to "frame" O.J. Simpson. Rather, it argued that Detective Fuhrman, a virulent racist, had planted the blood on O.J.'s Bronco and the bloody glove evidence at Simpson's residence in order to implicate him in the crime, and that a "blue wall of silence" was at work to protect Fuhrman. Dershowitz (1996) explains that the "blue wall of silence" is a code that forbids one police officer from testifying against another, and requires police officers to "back up" a fellow police officer even if they know he is lying. Dershowitz also notes that "the Christopher Commission [which investigated the LAPD following the beating of Rodney King] ... found such cover-up behaviour to be a real problem [and] every objective study of police perjury has come to the conclusion that police perjury is widespread and condoned" (1996: 54–55).

The defence lawyers in the O.J. Simpson criminal case explicitly addressed the issue of racism by alleging that LAPD Detective Mark Fuhrman, motivated by hatred of Blacks and interracial couples, transported a bloody glove from the crime scene at the Bundy residence, where Nicole Brown Simpson and Ronald L. Goldman had been murdered, to O.J. Simpson's residence in Rockingham in order to frame Simpson, a Black man, for the murders. Fuhrman was the detective who discovered most of the evidence which implicated Simpson in the murders, including the critical "bloody glove" found at the Simpson residence which was a match for one found at the murder scene, and the blood evidence found on Simpson's vehicle. Detective Fuhrman testified at the *Simpson* trial that he had not used the racial epithet "nigger" in the past ten years. The Fuhrman Tapes revealed, however, that he had used this racial epithet at least forty-one times. The tapes also revealed eighteen examples of situations where Fuhrman admitted he either participated in or was willing to participate in misconduct such as the use of deadly or excessive force in making arrests, acts of revenge against those suspected of killing a police officer, manufacturing probable cause for arrest, cover-up of unlawful use of force, a belief in the necessity for police officers to lie, revenge against those who opposed the choke hold, willingness to testify in court to events he had not personally witnessed, coercing statements from suspects and pretextual automobile stops.[23]

Cochran wanted to introduce evidence of thirty of the incidents where Detective Fuhrman used racial epithets, and eighteen examples of misconduct contained in the audio tapes Fuhrman had made in preparation for a screenplay, as proof of Fuhrman's racial animus and willingness to fabricate evidence. The Court refused to allow all of the racial comments made by Detective Fuhrman to be admitted into evidence and excluded all of the incidents where Fuhrman admitted to "misconduct" (Rosenburg 1995: 1).

Judge Ito did, however, permit the defence lawyers to put three witnesses on the stand to testify to the racist attitudes of Detective Fuhrman which they had experienced first-hand, including witness Katherine Bell, who was able to testify not only to Fuhrman's racial animus but also to the fact that he had engaged in misconduct by lying in the context of a pretextual stop in order to pull over a car containing an interracial couple (Rosenburg 1995: 1).

Further evidence of Detective Fuhrman's racial bias and misconduct was contained in legal documents he had filed in 1981 in support of a disability claim against the LAPD.[24] In these documents, Fuhrman admitted to psychiatrists that he had an extreme hatred for Blacks and other racial minorities. He also described incidents of brutality against people of colour (Cochran and Rutten 1996: 250). Judge Ito excluded all but two excerpts of the evidence contained in the Fuhrman Tapes of the use of racial epithets. He also excluded all the evidence contained in the tapes of police misconduct and racial animus, holding that its probative value was outweighed by its prejudicial effect. Rosenburg argues that Judge Ito was concerned about the particular negative inferences that the jury might have drawn if it were to hear all the racial and misconduct comments on the tapes, including the inferences:

1.   That Detective Fuhrman was not merely a "casual" racist and a boor who liked to use racially abusive language to shock his friends and acquaintances, but that he had a true hatred of African Americans.
2.   That Detective Fuhrman, by his own account, had in fact committed many illegal acts and successfully covered them up, sometimes with the assistance of other police officers.
3.   That the combination of (1) and (2) made it plausible that Detective Fuhrman had a motive to plant the glove or other evidence in order to assist in convicting O.J. Simpson and that the fact that the exact means by which he did so has not been discovered does not necessarily negate the inference. We might call this third inference the "racial bias/evidence planting" inference (1995: 4).

Under the circumstances, Rosenburg (1995) and Critical Race theorists argue that the racial animus/evidence-planting inference was not an irrational one for the jury to draw.

Rosenburg concludes that the Court was "willing to allow the jury to hear only 'weak' evidence that would link racial bias with actual evidence planting but was not prepared to allow 'strong' evidence such as the fact that Fuhrman was willing to break the law in significant ways according to his own statements contained in the tapes, or that he had a racial animus and was violent towards Blacks and other people of color" (1995: 4).

The defence recalled Detective Fuhrman to the stand to impeach his credibility after the jury heard the two excerpts from the tapes that Judge

Ito had allowed into evidence. Out of the presence of the jury, Fuhrman asserted his right not to incriminate himself under the Fifth Amendment to the United States Constitution in order to avoid answering questions regarding the inconsistencies in his previously sworn testimony with regard to his use of racial epithets, and to avoid answering questions regarding the alleged planting of evidence.

In addition to the problems of the racial animus and misconduct of Detective Fuhrman, there were serious questions about the way the search of the Simpson residence came about. Detectives Vannatter and Lange conducted a warrantless search, later claiming on a sworn search warrant affidavit that they believed Simpson and others at his residence might have been in danger, rather than the truth, which was that the officers suspected O.J. Simpson of the crimes at that early stage of the investigation (if Simpson was a suspect at that stage, the officers would have required a search warrant to effect a search of his residence). Even though Judge Ito did not exclude the evidence found as a result of the warrantless search pursuant to the evidence rules, he did say that Vannatter had "acted with reckless disregard for the truth" (Cochran and Rutten 1996: 272). The defence also made much of the fact that even though Vannatter had taken a blood sample from Simpson downtown and should have labelled it and put it in the evidence room there, he had transported the vial of blood with him to the Simpson residence. There were allegations that since there was some blood missing from the vial, this blood had been used to contaminate the socks found in Simpson's bedroom, as well as the Bronco and other areas. And some of the evidence handled by the criminalists (forensic scientists) had been mishandled or contaminated in the labs. Johnnie Cochran summed it up this way: "The criminalists' ignorance and incompetence, the detectives' habitual sloth and deceit, Fuhrman's racism, and the prosecutors' ambitions had come together with terrible effect" (Cochran and Rutten 1996: 276).

The jury in the O.J. Simpson criminal case, comprising nine Black female jurors, two White jurors and one Latino juror, unanimously acquitted O.J. Simpson of all charges in the deaths of Nicole Brown Simpson and Ronald L. Goldman on October 3, 1995. The differing reactions of the Black and White communities to the acquittals further laid bare the racial rift in the United States that the Rodney King case had exposed. Because the jury was predominately Black, much criticism was directed at them and their verdict, which many Whites categorized as a "racist" one.

Many Whites alleged that the predominately Black jury participated in race-based "jury nullification" (the act of acquitting a defendant despite evidence and law that support a conviction). Jurors in these circumstances "vote their conscience."[25] In the case of race-based jury nullification, the argument goes, Black jurors ignore the facts and the law in individual cases and acquit a defendant whom they believe to be guilty in order to prevent the unfair and discriminatory imprisonment of more Blacks by a racist criminal justice system.

Most Blacks and, indeed, the jurors themselves in interviews given after the verdicts,[26] argued that the not-guilty verdict was the product of reasonable doubt and not the product of jury nullification as some Whites have insisted. In other words, the jury did not acquit O.J. Simpson despite a belief that he was guilty. Instead, they believed that the prosecution had not proven its case beyond a reasonable doubt as required by law. The combination of a racist policeman, the possibility of evidence tampering and the hint of a police cover-up raised a reasonable doubt in the mind of the jurors as to the guilt of the defendant. This reasonable doubt was entertained not just by the Black jurors but also by the White and Latino members of the jury, because the verdict was a unanimous one.

Critical Race theorists argue that Blacks and Whites view the world differently. Black Americans, given their experience with police misconduct and brutality, are more likely to entertain the thoughts that there are racist police officers and that police officers sometimes lie. Johnnie Cochran noted that Black and White America remain "two nations." We have, he said,

> very different experiences with many of our public institutions. In White neighbourhoods in Los Angeles ... the police department is largely benevolent, a helpful presence ... but ... the LAPD has for generations behaved much differently in the city's predominantly minority neighborhoods. There is a long history of abusive, unpunished, even officially sanctioned misconduct.... That history has left African American Angelenos with a well-founded skepticism about police misconduct (Cochran and Rutten 1996: 362).

White America accused the defence in the *Simpson* case of playing the "race card" in its litigation strategy. They point to Johnnie Cochran's closing statement to the jury—"Stop this cover-up"—as proof that he was asking the jury to participate in race-based jury nullification. However, Critical Race theorists argue that the defence was merely presenting a contextualized analysis to the jury. The defence placed Blacks at the centre of the analysis and trusted that the jury, composed primarily of African Americans, would find it easier to accept and understand evidence of police misconduct, and therefore would be less willing to reject out of hand the possibility that police do sometimes lie.

Notwithstanding the belief that the jury based its decision on the prosecution's failure to prove its case beyond a reasonable doubt as it was required to do, some Critical Race theorists have argued that, even if the jury in the O.J. Simpson criminal case had practised jury nullification, this would have been a legitimate exercise of political power. They point to historical and contemporary instances of White jury nullification (for example, the acquittal of the four White police officers accused of beating Rodney King by an all-White jury in spite of videotaped evidence of police brutality and the racist legacy of the LAPD). These Critical Race theorists argue that there is a moral case for the use of jury nullification by Blacks in America based on the inherent racial bias in the criminal justice system. Butler (1995: 725) points out that some commentators have noted a double standard in the analysis of the appropriateness of nullification, depending upon which group is engaging in it, and he is concerned about the racial implications of critiques of jury nullification.

Alan Dershowitz notes that:

> It is fair to ask why so much more criticism has been directed against black jurors (and blacks in general) for "closing their minds" to the possibility that Simpson might be guilty, than against whites for closing *their* minds to the possibility that the police might have planted evidence against him.... This observation led *Los Angeles Times* reporter Andrea Ford to ask why the media did not do stories "trying to explain why whites were so overwhelmingly certain of his guilt?" Why were blacks, rather than whites, cast as the people whose position needed explaining? ... Several white journalists were "equally outraged" at the implicit assumption that black open-mindedness was more "irrational" than white closed-mindedness (1996: 124–25).

In addition to the schism between the position of Black and White Americans with respect to the verdict, the O.J. Simpson criminal case also exposed the existing gulf between the White mainstream feminist movement and Critical Race Feminism. Mainstream feminists were outraged by the not-guilty verdicts because of the issues of spousal abuse the case presented. The prosecution's theory of the case was that Nicole Brown Simpson had been the victim of prior spousal abuse, which ultimately led to her death and the death of her friend Ronald Goldman. For White feminists the important issues in the case were not "race" and police misconduct but "gender" and spousal abuse. They pointed to the fact that there were nine Black women on the jury who acquitted O.J. Simpson, as proof that the jury was racially biased and had allowed "race" to triumph over gender.

Gibbs notes that many leaders of women's organizations and "celebrity feminists" talked to the media, denouncing the verdict as a "vindication" of spousal abuse. However, she notes that

> it became apparent that there were at least two subtexts underlying their strong rhetoric. For one thing, apparently none of these leaders had ever before come forward in defence of a black female victim of domestic violence whose partner had been tried and exonerated for murder, so they seemed to be directing their message toward white women with a metamessage that targeted yet another black male as the stereotypical brute (1996: 221).

Once again, mainstream feminism had failed to address the oppression of race, gender and class when they cross-sect each other.

Black feminists, and indeed most Blacks, were aware of and concerned about spousal abuse, but they also knew and were concerned about the history of police brutality in the Black community and the lynching of Black men accused of raping or even speaking to White women. Dershowitz (1996: 127) also points out that the White woman on the jury said that the case, for her, turned more on the racial bias of the police than on the prior spousal abuse of the defendant.

Clearly America was suffering from cognitive and racial dissonance which was exposed by the Rodney King case and further accentuated by the O.J. Simpson criminal case. The defence lawyers in *Simpson* directly confronted the issues of race raised by the case and forced the court to consider the race question. America did not like the answer it received.

The Rodney King case showed the fallacy of attempts to erase the issue of race from criminal proceedings, and the racial injustices perpetuated by the justice system upon this Black man brought into stark relief the historical and contemporary role of race in American society. The Rodney King beating and its aftermath set a course in which the issue of race and the role it plays in law could no longer be avoided. The defence lawyers in the *Simpson* criminal case followed that course by implementing a Critical Race Litigation strategy in defence of their client that could arguably alter the condition of "colour-blind" justice in America forever.

American Critical Race Theory and the Rodney King and O.J. Simpson cases combined with uniquely Canadian factors were also to have a profound impact on the developing Critical Race Theory and Critical Race Litigation strategy and race consciousness in Canada.

Summary

A Critical Race Litigation strategy is one that requires lawyers and others to take a Critical Race position on any case involving a Black client and to either collectively work on precedent-setting cases involving race or to litigate race issues when they individually represent a Black client. Critical Race Litigation is the practical application of Critical Race Theory and is the vital next step in race discourse. It requires a stance that puts the issue of the role race and racism play in society and law squarely on the litigation agenda. It requires a contextualized approach to a case that positions the experiences of Black people at the centre of the analysis.

Black Americans have persistently sought equality under the law and freedom from discrimination. Despite a host of constitutional and statutory enactments which allowed Blacks in the United States to litigate for equal rights and equal protection under the law, "race" has remained a consistent and intractable problem in American society.

Many Critical Race theorists believe that the current United States Supreme Court has substantially reduced its support for civil rights. There is a widely held assumption in the United States that Americans are no longer racist. This assumption is reflected in the doctrine of colour-blindness adopted by the courts, as well as in the policy of formal equal opportunity which permeates current American civil rights laws. The doctrine of colour-blindness, however, ignores the social reality of racism. While the United States Supreme Court, the United States Federal Courts, and state and federal legislators roll back the civil rights gains of the 1950s and 1960s, objective data continues to show that in the United States (as in Canada), race has survived as a meaningful and significant factor in society. Because of the adoption of a colour-blind stance, the issue of race continues to dominate the American social and legal landscape but is prohibited from being addressed.

Issues of race continue to re-emerge in modern cases such as Rodney King and O.J. Simpson, but traditional civil rights discourse does not offer workable and lasting solutions to the problem. However, a new strategy, a Critical Race Litigation strategy, that goes beyond traditional civil rights law is emerging to confront the problem.

The Rodney King case exposed the significance of the race question in constitutional and criminal law and the dangers of avoiding the question in order to maintain the "myth" of colour-blindness. The O.J. Simpson criminal case confronted the courts with the race question head on. The criticism levelled at the lawyers who took a Critical Race Litigation strategy in that case and at the predominately Black jury which exonerated him further highlights the existing gulf between Black and White society in the United States, as well as the gulf between White mainstream feminists and Critical Race feminists. But the lasting legacy of these cases is that the issues of race and racism and the role they play in society and law can no longer be ignored. These cases have also had a profound impact on the developing Critical Race Theory and an emerging Critical Race Litigation strategy in Canada.

Chapter 3

Canadian Critical Race Litigation: Wedding Theory and Practice[1]

Criminal and Constitutional Law: Canadian Critical Race Cases

On Monday, May 4, 1992, hundreds of Metropolitan Toronto police officers watched as an angry mob of about one thousand Black and White youths and young adults attacked bystanders and police and smashed windows at about one hundred stores in downtown Toronto following a peaceful demonstration organized by the Black community. This peaceful demonstration and the resulting riot came in the wake of the verdict in the Rodney King case and the ensuing Los Angeles riots and were fueled by yet another shooting of a Black man, Raymond Lawrence, on May 2, 1992, in Toronto by a White police officer (Downey 1992). Racial unrest in Canada has not been confined to Toronto or to protests over the Rodney King verdict. Rioting has also occurred in other Canadian cities over the years, including Halifax and Montreal.

There has been an ongoing and growing dissatisfaction with the state of relations between the police and racial minority communities in both Canada and the United States. These relations have resulted in numerous claims of excessive use of force against the police in many jurisdictions in Canada. Many of the claims of excessive use of force by police have involved shootings of Black Canadians in Toronto and Montreal and have included accusations that these shootings were racially motivated. Claims that police use excessive force and racial slurs against Blacks have also been made in Nova Scotia and other Canadian jurisdictions. While the doctrine of "colour-blindness" has promoted the myth that racism is no longer a factor in American society, the same doctrine has promoted a prevailing myth in Canada that racism was never a factor in Canadian society.

Many Canadians have clung to the myth that Canada is not really a racist country. The veracity of this myth is often supported by a self-serving distinction between Canada and the United States.... Canadian history has provided much clear evidence that belies the non-racist myth ... [still] this myth took on a life of its own.... Attention should be paid to the myth of a non-racist Canada ... it is not a harmless one ... it has caused direct, extensive, and iniquitous consequences to individuals, groups, and society as a whole ... hence, the really debilitating result of the pervasiveness of the myth has been the frustratingly slow and inadequate response of Canadian governments, institutions, and other organizations to racist laws, policies, and practices (Brown and Brown 1996: 48–49).

Many commentators have recognized that the perception Canada has of itself as an egalitarian society devoid of a history of racism does not reflect reality (see, for example, Walker 1997: 3, and Mendes 1995: 1-1). James Walker, a social historian, looked at historical legal cases where race and law intertwined, and he explored the historical role of the Supreme Court of Canada in the perpetuation of the Canadian myth. To do this, Walker selected four Supreme Court of Canada cases that involved four separate minority groups, spanning the years 1914, 1939, 1950 and 1955. The cases he selected for examination included *Quong Wing* v. *The King* (1914, S.C.R. 440 [S.C.C.]), involving a Chinese Canadian who was charged under a Saskatchewan statute preventing Chinese men from employing White females; a case involving a Black Canadian, *Christie* v. *York Corp.* ([1940] S.C.R. 139 [S.C.C.]), who was refused service in a tavern because of colour; a case involving a Canadian Jew, *Noble and Wolfe* v. *Alley* ([1951] 92 S.C.R. 64 [S.C.C.]), who was denied the right to purchase a cottage because of a restrictive covenant preventing owners from selling to Jews; and a case involving a Trinidadian of East Indian ancestry, *Narine-Singh* v. *Attorney General of Canada* ([1955] S.C.R. 395), who was excluded through the Immigration Act from Canada because he was of the "Asian race." Walker maintains that the cases present a challenge to the Canadian image of a tolerant and racism-free country:

> The four case studies suggest a startlingly different reality. Many of the restrictions in genuinely racist societies apparently had a Canadian counterpart, including features for the protection of women of the dominant class, employment and other economic disadvantages, limited access to land and services, legalized segregation and even the legal definition of citizens by "race." ... Race was a legal artifact and in the process of its formulation, the

Supreme Court of Canada was a significant participant, legitimating racial categories and maintaining barriers among them. Even in *Noble* v. *Wolf,* the Court allowed the respondents' argument—that racial discrimination was both morally and legally acceptable—to pass without contradiction, and declined to confirm the appellants' assertion that racial distinctions were contrary to public policy. None of the seven judges in the case commented on discrimination per se or its legality, so that the law already established on racial discrimination, for example by the *Quong Wing* decision, [where the discriminatory Saskatchewan statute was upheld as being within the jurisdiction of provincial powers] and [the] *Christie* [decision, where racial discrimination was found to be not immoral or damaging and the discriminatory conduct was upheld on the doctrine of freedom of commerce], was not affected. Then in *Narine-Singh* the Supreme Court positively upheld the legality of "race" as a discernible factor in Canadian public policy. The widespread existence of a racial paradigm in Canada and a legal role in its fashioning are two of the observations one might take from the examined cases (1997: 302).

If one could pinpoint the exact moment in legal history when the courts were most supportive of and responsible for the perpetuation of racist ideology in the United States, it would be when the United States Supreme Court handed down the *Dred Scott* decision (*Dred Scott* v. *Sandford*, 1857, 60 U.S. [19 How.] 393). In Canada, it would be the moment in 1940 when the Supreme Court of Canada handed down the *Christie* decision.

The *Dred Scott* case is considered one of the most controversial decisions ever issued by the United States Supreme Court. In 1846, a Missouri slave named Dred Scott sued for his freedom in court, claiming he should be free since he had lived in a free state for a long time prior to his master's death. Dred Scott lost the case when the United States Supreme Court handed down its decision in 1857, with Chief Justice Taney declaring (at 393) that "Dred Scott was not a citizen of Missouri within the meaning of the Constitution of the United States, and not entitled as such to sue in its courts.... Colored men had no rights which the White man was bound to respect."

The Supreme Court of Canada held in the *Christie* case in 1939 that even though Blacks were discriminated against in almost all public services, including employment, housing, education and recreation, and even though the situation of "Jim Crow" made life no better for Blacks in Canada than it did for Blacks in the United States, discrimination was legal in Canada absent any "positive" law forbidding it. Discrimination was not contrary to good morals or public order. Some would argue that the *Christie* decision was merely reflective of its times and that, although the case may somewhat tarnish the "myth" that Canada is a tolerant country without a racist past, it has no bearing on the present time when racism has been eliminated by human rights codes and equality is guaranteed by the Canadian Constitution. Critical Race theorists and others point out, however, that "despite these important [legal] achievements, racism is still entrenched in Canadian society" (Commission on Systemic Racism 1995: 52).

Also significant to the present discussion is the role of precedent (a legal doctrine which specifies that previously decided cases comprise an authority for deciding future cases) in the Canadian common law tradition. Using *Christie* as precedent, in 1981 the Supreme Court of Canada in *Bhadauria* v. *Seneca College of Applied Arts and Technology (Board of Governors)* ([1981] 2 S.C.R. 181 [S.C.C.])—a case in which a South Asian woman attempted to sue a college in civil court on the basis that it had denied her employment because of her race and ethnic origin—held that her lawsuit should be dismissed because there was no common law right to sue for discrimination. The court held that the common law route had been "foreclosed" or circumvented by the introduction of human rights legislation, and that the proper recourse for those claiming discrimination was through that regime. Walker noted that in the *Bhadauria* case:

> Laskin implied that the [Human Rights] Code had *created* rather than *recognized* the right to freedom from discrimination, lending retroactive approval to *Christie* v. *York* which occurred before human rights codes existed in Canada.... *Christie* [had] survived [yet] another test (1997: 180, emphasis added).

The Supreme Court of Canada in *Bhadauria* relied upon precedent as justification for severely limiting access to the courts by those claiming discrimination, once again denying Black Canadians equality under the law. Canadian and American Critical Race theorists point out that:

> Through the doctrine of precedent, the law is rooted in the past. It becomes difficult to envision a racism-free jurisprudence when the law relies upon concepts derived from a time when chattel slavery existed, women were not persons, and colonization, including the theft of Aboriginal lands, was in full force. We have not yet had an acknowledgement of this conceptual taint, much less an attempt by the courts to revitalize the law within an anti-discriminatory framework. Legal precedents cannot transcend this racist history. It is one of the primary, yet invisible, obstacles

within the legal system (St. Lewis 1996: 106).

The authors of *Racial Discrimination: Law and Practice* outline the various discriminatory practices that have been tolerated and positively promoted by law in Canada since 1867 (Mendes 1995: 1-28). They document that many ethnic and racial groups have been victims of overt and covert forms of racism. This racism took the form of prohibitions on Native voting rights; denial of education; segregation and assimilation policies; genocide of Native populations and the appropriation of Native lands. Other racial and ethnic groups toward which racist laws and policies have been directed include the Japanese (restrictions on immigration, internment during World War II, and restrictions on civil liberties) and the Chinese (including restrictions on voting rights, immigration and employment) (Mendes 1995: 1.III). The authors, however, begin their analysis of race relations in Canada with the institution of slavery, demonstrating that anti-Black racism has a long and enduring history in Canada. Moreover, one contemporary Canadian court found in 1993 that there was still overwhelming evidence of anti-Black racism in Metropolitan Toronto and Canada (*R.* v. *Parks*, 84 C.C.C. [3d] 353 [Ont. C.A.]).

Historically, Canada did not have the constitutional or statutory mechanisms that were in place in the United States and enabled Black Americans to litigate to seek civil rights and freedom from racial discrimination. The Canadian government did not pass the *Canadian Bill of Rights* with respect to matters under federal jurisdiction until 1960, and basic human rights were not constitutionalized to apply to all levels of government until 1982 with the passing of the *Canadian Charter of Rights and Freedoms*.[2] Notably, the equality section of the *Charter*, section 15(1), did not come into force until 1985. Section 15(1) of the *Charter* guarantees that:

> Every individual is equal before and under the law and has the right to the equal protection and equal benefit of the law without discrimination and, in particular, without discrimination based on race, national or ethnic origin, colour, religion, sex, age or mental or physical disability.

Although human rights legislation had been passed in all Canadian jurisdictions by 1977, except in Quebec, the enforcement of human rights legislation in the first instance is confided to specialized tribunals and there is no recourse to the civil courts for redress. Human rights legislation (more fully discussed in Chapter 4) is problematic because the vast majority of race-based human rights complaints never reach the board of inquiry stage within the human rights process, even when the racial minority complainant would like the case to proceed. As well, the fact that jurisdiction over human rights has been confined exclusively to human rights tribunals has meant that there is no recourse to the civil courts.

In addition to the lack of constitutional and statutory protection, Black Canadians have also not had visible access to a rights-based litigation organization like the American National Association for the Advancement of Colored People (NAACP), which was established to attack a number of discriminatory and racist practices and policies such as the racially based exclusion of African-Americans from juries, segregation in public housing and discrimination in voting and education in the United States. Although Canada did have chapters of the NAACP, such as the Nova Scotia Association for the Advancement of Colored People founded in 1945, these Canadian organizations were ill-equipped to conduct expensive and controversial litigation.

In Canada today, discrimination and racism exist in much more subtle forms than during the periods in which the cases considered by James Walker were decided. As the report of the Commission on Systemic Racism in the Ontario Criminal Justice System (1995: 52) has documented, today discrimination is usually found in systemic form and concealed in systems, practices, policies and laws that may appear neutral on their face but have a serious detrimental effect on people of colour.

In the United States, Black Americans who wish to challenge the constitutionality of an apparently neutral law have to prove a discriminatory intent on the part of those responsible for enacting the law or those responsible for its administration, although discriminatory effects have been recognized as a ground for relief under U.S. federal human rights legislation (Lawrence 1987: 317). In Canada, however, an "adverse effects" doctrine of discrimination has been adopted both in the context of the *Charter* and under human rights codes.

The 1976 Alberta Supreme Court case of *Alberta (Attorney General) v. Gares* (67 D.L.R. [3d] 635 [Alta. T.D.]) was one of the first cases to reject the American definition of discrimination based on intent to discriminate and to hold instead that law prohibits not just discriminatory intent but also discriminatory results. The Supreme Court of Canada followed this reasoning in the case of *Ontario (Human Rights Commission) v. Simpsons-Sears Ltd.* ([1985] 2 S.C.R. 536 at 549) and held that an intent to discriminate is not required under human rights legislation. Subsequently, the Supreme Court of Canada extended the adverse-effect test for discrimination to the *Charter of Rights and Freedoms*. In *Andrews v. Law Society of B.C.* ([1989] 1 S.C.R. 143), the Supreme Court stated that the purpose of section 15(1) of the *Charter* was to correct historical social and political inequality, rather than to achieve "identical treatment" of all individuals and groups.

Despite these significant developments, which mean that, in theory, the legal environment in Canada provides a better analytical framework for challenges to racism, the issue of systemic discrimination remains unresolved. The *Charter* has not been used extensively as a litigation tool to combat racism in Canadian society (Mendes 1995: 1-24). Additionally, in 1992, the only avenue open to Black Canadians for redress for private acts of discrimination not covered by the *Charter* (in light of the *Bhadauria* case), the human rights complaints process, was found to have an "unsettling trend" in the way it dealt with cases based on race; it was found that complaints based on race were dismissed without a hearing more often than those based on any other grounds (Mendes 1995: 2-9). Critical Race theorists and others in Canada have severely criticized human rights law and condemn it as a typically Canadian effort to maintain the myth of toleration by pretending to address intolerance while at the same time maintaining the dominant groups' "right" to discriminate.

Although Critical Race theorists condemn law as a tool of oppression, they also recognize the importance of law as a tool in the fight against oppression. When lawyers litigate race issues, they are seeking to ameliorate the legal, social and economic conditions of their Black clients and the Black community in general.

Critical Race Theory methodology requires a deconstruction of legal rules and principles and challenges the so-called "neutrality" and "objectivity" of laws that oppress Black people and other people of colour. Deconstruction is designed to confront subtle forms of discrimination perpetuated by law. The questions to be asked by the lawyer engaged in Critical Race Litigation are: Does the doctrine, legal rule, principle or practice at issue in the particular case subordinate and discriminate against people of colour? Is race an issue? If the answers are yes, should it be litigated or should some other strategy be employed? An important stage of Critical Race Litigation, and the most crucial step in transforming theory into practice, is reconstruction. What are the alternatives, if any, to the existing doctrine, legal rule, principle or practice? What harm or benefit to the Black client and/or the Black community might result from the adoption or nonadoption by the courts of this change?

Because of the historic and financial constraints on litigation by Black Canadians, there is no body of jurisprudence recognizing racial equality that can compare to the extensive jurisprudence developed in the United States after the 1954 decision in *Brown* v. *Board of Education* (347 U.S. 483). To this day, race-based litigation in Canada is impeded by the paucity of Black lawyers to conduct the litigation and the unwillingness or inability of many White practitioners to make racial arguments before the courts. This unwillingness or inability may stem from a number of factors such as conscious or unconscious racism, an inability to recognize the racial implications of a particular case, a lack of knowledge about how to challenge and deconstruct legal rules and principles which foster and maintain discrimination, total acceptance of the myth of the "objectivity" of laws, or fear that raising issues of race before the courts will disadvantage a client's case because of the courts' unacceptance or hostility towards these arguments.

For these reasons, and because the development of Critical Race Theory in Canada is very recent, there was no Critical Race Litigation in Canada until the mid-1990s. The *R.D.S.* case was the first Critical Race Litigation case in Canada to reach the Supreme Court of Canada.

Important Canadian Critical Race Cases

R.D.S. v. The Queen

On October 17, 1993, R.D.S., a Black youth, was riding his bicycle home. Subsequent events would take this Black youth, a Black female judge and the Black community of Nova Scotia and Canada on a journey that would take four years. This journey, from the street of a predominately Black neighbourhood in Halifax, would wind its way to Youth Court, through two provincial Appellate Courts and ultimately to the Supreme Court of Canada.

R.D.S. was arrested and charged with assault on a police officer in the execution of his duty, assault with intent to prevent the lawful arrest of another and resisting arrest, after he stopped to ask his cousin, who was being arrested by a White police officer on the street, the circumstances of that arrest and whether he (R.D.S.) should call his cousin's mother.

Only two witnesses testified at the trial: R.D.S. and the White police officer, Constable Stienburg. R.D.S. testified that while he was still straddling his bicycle, he spoke only to his cousin and only asked him what happened. He denied touching the police officer with his hands or his bicycle and he also denied telling the police officer to let his cousin go. R.D.S. testified that the police officer told him to "shut up" or he would be placed under arrest and that then the police officer had proceeded to put him in a choke hold and to handcuff him. He testified that both he and his cousin, N.R., were put in choke holds by the officer. The police officer testified that he had been assaulted by R.D.S., and that R.D.S. had been obstructing the lawful arrest of another person. He gave no testimony with regard to the handcuffing of R.D.S. or the choke holds the two youths were allegedly subjected to.

R.D.S. was subsequently tried by way of summary conviction and acquitted of all charges by a Black Youth Court Judge (*R.* v. *R.D.S.*, N.S. YO93-168, December 2, 1994) who, faced with making a determination based on the credibility of the witnesses, accepted the testimony of the Black youth over that of the White police officer. This acquittal provoked a fire storm of controversy and litigation which uncovered the racial tensions between the Black community and the criminal justice system in Nova Scotia and Canada.

The Crown appeal alleging an actual racial bias on the part of the only Black judge in Nova Scotia against the White police officer, and the subsequent overturning of the acquittal of the Black youth R.D.S. by the Chief Justice of the Supreme Court of Nova Scotia (*R.* v. *R.D.S.*, S.C.N.S., SH No. 112404, April 18, 1995), created the "spark" that ignited the Black community. Black lawyers across the country challenged what was interpreted as an emerging legal legitimatization of a discriminatory standard with respect to the test of reasonable apprehension of bias in judicial decision-making. This standard was being applied only to Black judges and, presumably, judges from other historically excluded groups.

As previously noted, in the United States, civil rights litigation has occurred since the 1960s. The resulting decisions have enhanced the civil rights of African-Americans through favourable substantive and procedural outcomes on many race-related issues. However, Critical Race theorists argue the need for new strategies that go beyond the traditional rights discourse. In Canada, Black lawyers and others are now beginning to take a Critical Race position for the benefit of the Black community. *R.D.S.* was the first Critical Race Litigation case explicitly arguing a race issue before the Supreme Court of Canada in the context of section 15 of the *Charter* and therefore had the potential to be precedent-setting. A growing number of Black lawyers and others in Canada are beginning to recognize that it is crucial to collectively and individually work in the area of race-based litigation and to identify and overcome oppressions in order to enhance the interests of Blacks through substantive outcomes.

The first step in Critical Race Litigation is the ability of defence lawyers to recognize when the issue of race arises, and the ability to do so depends on an awareness and acknowledgement of the existence of racism in Canadian society. The Critical Race position taken in the *R.D.S.* case was that the existence of racial discrimination and the context of the interaction between police officers and "non-White" groups in Canada is not a matter that requires evidence before the courts but is rather a matter of the common sense and experience of the judge which can be applied whenever the facts warrant. In this case, race was not a material fact that had to be proved but rather was a matter of societal context, and accordingly it did not require evidence nor the taking of judicial notice. The "reasonable person" whom the court invokes to determine whether or not a reasonable apprehension of bias arises must be aware of the fact that racial discrimination exists in Canada.[3]

In the context of the *R.D.S.* case, the Critical Race Theory method of deconstruction took the form of challenging and deconstructing: the doctrine of reasonable apprehension of bias, the reasonable person test, the myth of "neutrality" and "objectivity" in the context of judicial decision-making, the concept of formal equality, and the concept of legal reasoning as ahistorical.

The Critical Race Theory approach of narrative or storytelling jurisprudence was also employed in the *R.D.S.* case. Put to practical use, narrative or storytelling can function in a number of ways. It can allow lawyers to "tell the story" of their clients in a non-ahistorical way. In other words, in the context of the *R.D.S.* case, narrative, or storytelling, allowed the lawyers to debunk the myth of neutrality and objectivity by placing the encounter between the Black youth and the White police officer representing the state in its social and historical context of racial discrimination. Narrative allowed the lawyers representing R.D.S. to tell the story of the racial conflict between the police and the Black community of Nova Scotia, and indeed in the whole of Canada, at the time of the encounter.[4]

Police and Black Community Relations in Canada

In a report to the Commission on Systemic Racism in the Ontario Criminal Justice System in 1995, Professor H.J. Glasbeek noted that:

> Many believe that it is the criminal justice system as a whole which is racist, not just a few individual actors within it. *And there are data to support this argument* [including] the Donald Marshall inquiry's revelations that it was not just a few police persons who acted in a truly deviant way; they had the help and support of a great number of senior officials in the prosecutorial and judicial offices of the province. And a Manitoba report documented the discriminatory way in which Native peoples are treated by the criminal justice system. *Armed with this kind of authoritatively assembled evidence and supported by the evidence of the perceptions of minority groups who deal with the police on a day-to-day basis, the shootings of black persons by police officers takes on a particular significance.* It is in this context that they are characterized as manifestations of systemic racism within the police forces (1995: 8, emphasis added).[5]

What follows is a brief overview of cases, taken from Glasbeek's report, involving the shooting of Black citizens by police and the state of Black/police relations in Canada and Nova Scotia at the time R.D.S. was arrested. It is crucial to understanding the Critical Race Theory argument of "social context'" made in the case.[6]

On May 14, 1990, in Scarborough, Ontario, Marlon Neil, a sixteen-year-old Black youth, was shot and seriously wounded by a White Metropolitan Toronto police officer after Neil refused to get out of the car he was driving. Neil was travelling at 54 kilometres per hour in a 40-kilometre-per-hour zone. Constable Rapson, on radar duty, spotted the car and chased it after the car sped away. The police officer eventually stopped the car, and Neil locked the car and refused to get out. The police officer fired three shots at the car at a distance of six feet. The Black teenager was hit by two bullets which entered his back. One broke a rib and entered his esophagus and spine.

A witness indicated that the teenager had held his hands out with the palms up shortly before the officer fired the three shots. The witness stated that the teenager appeared to be "frightened and confused" and the police officer appeared to be "angry and losing his patience" (Downey 1991: A12). The White police officer later claimed that he thought the teenager was armed.

The Black youth testified that he slowed down when he passed Constable Rapson's radar trap, but that he sped up again when he saw something in the police officer's face. The White police officer was charged with attempted murder, criminal negligence causing bodily harm and aggravated assault. He did not take the stand during the trial. A sworn statement, in which he said he thought he saw a black shiny object in the front seat of the car that he took to be a weapon, was allowed into evidence. The youth was in fact unarmed. The police officer also said in his "sworn statement" that the teenager told him to "Back off or you're dead meat." Because the police officer did not take the stand during his defence, this "sworn statement" was not subject to cross-examination. The defence called no other witnesses. The Crown argued that Constable Rapson's statement explaining why he shot Marlon Neil was "filled with deliberate falsehoods" (Hampton 1991: A12). An all-White jury returned a verdict of not guilty and cleared the White Metro Toronto police officer of all charges.

Metropolitan Toronto Police Association president Arthur Lymer said the verdict sends out a message that a jury will support the police. In this and other cases of police shootings of Blacks, both before charges have been laid and after, dozens of Metro Toronto police officers, together with the president of their union, have gone on the defensive and often crowded into the courtroom in support of their comrades.

In one such case in Toronto, after a charge of manslaughter was laid against White police officer David Deviney in the shooting death of a Black man, Lester Donaldson, police briefly worked to rule to protest the charge. At a closed meeting of Metropolitan Toronto's Police Association, seven thousand members met to "weigh strategy in seeking to have the charge against Constable Deviney withdrawn" (Appleby 1989: A10). Metro Toronto police received many calls of support from the public, and a group backing the police, Citizens Opposed to Police Slander, was formed. Toronto's Black community charged that the shooting had racial over-tones. Twenty-five-hundred police officers demonstrated, claiming that the charge of manslaughter laid against the police officer was only a political response to the vocal Black community, and they demanded the resignation of then Attorney General Ian Scott. This police shooting of a Black person in Ontario and the subsequent acquittal of Police Officer Deviney by an all-White jury followed on the heels of five other incidents in Toronto of Black citizens being shot by White police officers in less than two years (Claridge 1994).

One of these five incidents involved the case of a Metro Toronto police officer, Constable Cameron Durham, who had stopped a car in which Sophia Cook, a Black woman, was a passenger. Ms. Cook was shot by the police officer after he stopped the vehicle and the two male occupants fled the car. Constable Durham was charged with careless use of a firearm in the shooting of Ms. Cook. Both the driver and the other male passenger were Black. Sophia Cook had accepted a ride with the men while she was waiting for a bus (it was later determined that the car she was riding in was stolen). Sophia Cook was left partially paralyzed as a result of this shooting. Again, the White police officer in this case was tried and acquitted by an all-White jury consisting of seven men and five women. The twelve jurors had all been screened for potential racial prejudice during the selection process. This selection had resulted in the rejection of four Black members of the jury panel but not of any White jurors.

Also reported by Glasbeek (1995) is an earlier 1979 incident, the Albert Johnson case, involving a White Metro Toronto police officer shooting a Black citizen in his own home. In this case, Metro Toronto police officers Inglis and Cargnelli had responded to an anonymous tel-ephone call telling them that there was a disturbance at the Johnson residence. Two or three police cars were dispatched. Inglis and Cargnelli drove to the lane at the back of the house. There was no disturbance. A neighbour told them that Albert Johnson had been "noisy" earlier but had left. Johnson was expected to return because he had promised to help this neighbour with a chore. When Albert Johnson returned on his bicycle, he asked the police officers what they wanted and if they had a warrant. When he was told they did not have a warrant, he raced to his back door and closed it.

Constables Inglis and Cargnelli went to the front door, where a third police officer was standing. The police officers decided that everything was all right and left, walking down the back of the residence. They claimed that at this point Albert Johnson started shouting insults at them. However, these claims were contradicted by neighbours who said they heard no shouting. The police officers testified that they believed that Albert Johnson might harm someone, so they broke into the house through the back door. Even though family members present at the time testified that the police officers encountered no disturbance, the police officers told Albert that they were arresting him for causing a disturbance. He told them he had done nothing wrong and refused to go with them.

The police officers later testified that Albert threw a pot of peas cooking on the stove at them. However, other witnesses said the pot fell over during the struggle. One of the police officers hit Albert over the head with a metal flashlight a couple of times. Albert managed to free himself and ran upstairs to his bedroom. The police officers stayed downstairs. Albert came to the top of the stairs holding his daughter. The police officers testified that they thought he was going to throw her down. Mrs. Johnson took the child. The police officers then testified that Albert threw a bottle of disinfectant at one of the officers. They then claimed he was coming down the stairs with what looked like an axe but turned out to be a lawn-edger. They testified that Inglis shot at Johnson and missed, and then shot a second time, killing Johnson. A child witness for the prosecution said that Albert Johnson was coming down the stairs calmly, not menacingly, and was in a kneeling position when the police officer shot him. However, this child's testimony was excluded at trial because of claims of coaching by adults. Again, two White police officers were acquitted of manslaughter by an all-White jury. This was the first manslaughter charge to be laid against Metro Toronto police officers for a shooting death of a Black citizen.

At the trial of these police officers for manslaughter, as in all of the other cases, the victim's character became the main issue. In this case, Albert Johnson's many altercations with the police and the number of times the police had been called to his house were treated as relevant evidence by the court. Moreover, the Crown's theory in prosecuting the officers was that racism was irrelevant to the case. It was evident that the issue of racial motivation on the part of the White police officers in the shooting death of Albert Johnson was not an issue the White Crown prosecutor was prepared to argue because of an inability or an unwillingness to acknowledge the existence of racism in Canadian society or in the provision of policing services. Since the Crown pursued a manslaughter charge rather than a second-degree murder charge, the intent or racial motivation of the accused police officer was not in issue, because proof of intent is not a requirement for a conviction for manslaughter. However, as Professor Glasbeek noted in his analysis of this case, with regard to the failure of the Crown to develop the issue of racial motivation, and to the admission of evidence concerning the victim's character, "this accused-favouring evidence was admitted without regard to its [racial] context" (1995: 118). Had the Crown pursued the issue of race, Glasbeek argues:

> Evidence that Albert Johnson's strange and allegedly violent anti-police behaviour was, to the police officers' knowledge, in large measure due to police harassment would have become relevant. ... Contextualized evidence of this kind might have been admissible because it would have tended to prove a fact in issue, namely, that the confrontation was the result not just of one domestic disturbance involving a known person but due to a personal, perhaps racist, animus towards an unusual, unemployed black man who was somewhat mentally ill (1995: 118).

Glasbeek also notes that some of the evidence the Crown could have offered to show racist animus on the part of the police would have included information such as the fact that on May 12, 1979, Johnson had been arrested in his house after having several squad cars chase him for having driven through a red light on his bicycle. On this occasion, police had broken his door and ripped his arm through the opening, causing serious injury. His resistance during this event had, according to police, forced them to shackle him and take him to the hospital for his injuries. Glasbeek also notes that on June 11, after this event, it was Johnson who had been charged with assaulting a police officer.

Further evidence the Crown could have offered to show racial motivation by the police was that on June 19, 1979, Albert Johnson had been charged with reading his Bible aloud in a park. He was later acquitted of this charge. Then on July 12, 1979, Johnson had been charged with having a dangerous weapon in his possession. This turned out to be a six-inch stick he was using to exercise the arm the police had injured during his arrest on May 12, 1979. Also, a neighbour had heard a police officer call Johnson a "nigger" on a previous occasion. When Johnson had been hospitalized as a result of his injuries in the May 12, 1979, incident, he had filed a racial harassment complaint with the Ontario Human Rights Commission (Glasbeek 1995: 120) and the Metro Toronto police department was aware of this filing at the time of Johnson's death.

Racial tensions were again high across Canada, and particularly in Ontario, following the shooting death of Wade Lawson, a seventeen-year-old Black teenager, in 1988. He was killed by two White Peel Regional Police officers, Constable Anthony Melarani and Constable Darren Longpre, who fired six shots at him while he was sitting behind the wheel of a stolen car fastened in by his seat belt. Angry demonstrations over police racism occurred. Again the White police officers were acquitted by an all-

White jury. Following the acquittal, the spokesmen for the Black Action Defence Committee[7] stated that "The trial of these police officers was a farce. If we can't get justice from the Courts, maybe it is time that our committee began to think of ways of getting justice for ourselves" (Sarick 1992: A1).

Questions of race were avoided not only during the Lawson trial, discussed above, but also in the other police-shooting and excessive-use-of-force cases. In spite of this, headlines in Canadian newspapers increasingly recognize that each new shooting by White police officers of a Black Canadian or other racial minority group member demonstrates the presence of a recurring problem. The phenomenon of police shootings and other forms of excessive use of force by police on Blacks and other racial minorities is not confined to Metropolitan Toronto. As one *Globe and Mail* editorial noted:

> Toronto is not the only Canadian city where relations between the police and visible minorities have ended in violence in recent years. In Halifax, relations between the police and the city's black community have been strained in the wake of allegations that the police have used excessive force against blacks. In Montreal, six men—three blacks and three hispanics—have been killed by police in the past five years.... Although white persons have been shot by police officers in the carrying out of their duties, even Arthur Lymer, president of the Metropolitan Toronto Police Association, says that "the number of blacks shot in such incidents is 'out of proportion' to their share of the population" (1992a: A14).

On May 9, 1992, "reverberations from the King verdict blended with anger at yet another police shooting of a Black man and flared into an outburst of violence and vandalism in downtown Toronto" (*Globe and Mail* 1992b: D6). During and after the Los Angeles riots, some Canadians started to ask the question, "Could it happen here?"

> Although police deny that race is a factor, police have been accused of using excessive force against blacks in a number of recent cases—including that of Marcelus Francois, the unarmed black man shot dead by a Montreal SWAT team that mistook him for someone else; and Wade Lawson, the Toronto youth fatally shot in the back of the head as he sat at the wheel of a stolen car. We have not seen major riots as a result—not yet—but blacks have made clear their anger.... As tension between police and the black community rises, other Canadians are becoming more fear-

ful about crime.... The American pattern is clear. Crime rises. Police, feeling threatened, become edgy and aggressive. Black men are picked up—or worse—just for being black. The frightened middle-class looks the other way. Could it happen here? In some ways, it already is (*Globe and Mail* 1992b: D6).

Clayton Ruby, an Ontario criminal law lawyer, stated:

Young native Canadians are shot and killed by police in Winnipeg. Winnipeg's police are overwhelmingly white. Vancouver contains a large important Asian community. But Vancouver's police are overwhelmingly white. Black youths are shot and killed in Montreal. Montreal's police are overwhelmingly white. Black youths are shot and killed by Toronto's police in alarming numbers—eight in the past four years. Toronto's police are overwhelmingly white. Yet no police officer has been convicted of any offence in connection with these shootings.... Three days ago in Toronto, a white undercover police officer shot and killed a 19-year-old black man armed with a knife.... Metro Police Chief William McCormack and Police Services Board chairwoman Susan Eng appeal for calm. Who are they kidding? Every black and native person in this country knows that the justice system will not deliver justice for them.... Again and again there is the laying of inadequate charges, the wrong charge or no charges at all. Prosecutors and police like each other.... And so with police and prosecution and courts, the message comes: white folks get justice, black folks get excuses (1992: A18).

Additionally, more recent headlines suggest that the Toronto police force exceed most police forces on the continent when it comes to police shootings of civilians (Nolan 1996: 20)[8]. For example, according to Nicole Nolan, the data shows that from 1991 to September 1996, Metro Toronto police were proportionally more likely to shoot suspects than their colleagues in many of America's most "crime-ridden cities." For example, Metro Toronto police had, in police shootings relative to homicides, a rate 53 percent higher than Washington, D.C.'s, and 88 percent higher than that of the "notorious" Los Angeles Police Department (Nolan 1996: 20).

In 1996 the Black Action Defence Committee of Toronto lobbied for a commission to examine why victims of police shootings are frequently Black. In a study of Toronto with respect to racial distribution of civilians shot by police versus racial distribution of the general population, the percentage of persons shot by police who were Black compared to the percentage of the general population was found to be 24 percent, although

Blacks make up only 7.45 percent of the general population (Nolan 1996: 20).

In Canada, criticism of police investigations into police shootings of Black civilians, and other perceived police misconduct in relation to Black citizens and other persons of colour, prompted the appointment of various task forces, royal commissions and the like to study relations between police and racial minority communities.[9] These various reports well document the police culture of loyalty and support of fellow officers, which "means that police investigations of police officers, even if properly conducted, may lack credibility" (Commission on Systemic Racism 1995: 380). The Commission on Systemic Racism also noted that in one shooting of a Black man by a Metro Toronto police officer, the initial investigation was conducted by the officer's own force, which laid no charges. It was only in response to public outcry that the case was turned over to another police force to investigate and charges were laid. Additionally, the Commission found that in one high-profile case, the police immediately released a false account of the shooting to the media. It was later determined that a police officer had lied when he told a journalist that a large knife was the knife the shooting victim had brandished at the police officer who killed him. It was later determined that the knife in question was one the police officer had had in his possession from another, unrelated investigation. However, as the Commission noted, the story was widely reported and probably was never dispelled in the minds of the public (Commission on Systemic Racism 1995: 379).

Of particular relevance to the *R.D.S.* case, the Royal Commission on the Donald Marshall Jr. Prosecution in Nova Scotia in 1989 indicated that research, as well as experience, had emphasized very significant racial discrimination at the key point of policing and the Commission's own study strongly supported this finding.

In 1991, a disturbance in downtown Halifax, which resulted when Black males had been consistently refused admittance to the city's downtown bars, again focused attention on racial tensions in Nova Scotia. This incident erupted into altercations between Blacks and Whites and subsequently led to allegations that the police used excessive force and uttered racial slurs against Blacks involved in the incident. This incident received national and international media attention. As a result of this riot, the chief of police in Halifax set up an ad hoc Incident Review Committee of both civilian and police members to "investigate the allegations of racial slurs and excessive use of force on the part of the police" (Halifax Police Department 1991; also see N.S. Advisory Group on Race Relations 1991 and Justice Canada 1992).

Although the Committee was supposed to produce a joint report, the members were unable to agree on the findings. The civilian and police members wrote separate reports. The report by civilian members of the Committee found that "the internal investigation conducted by the Halifax Police Department into allegations of excessive force and racial slurs uttered by police officers on July 19, 1991, was inappropriately handled" (Halifax Police Department 1991: 8).[10] The report by police members of the Committee stated that "the incident of July 19, 1991, was not precipitated by racial discrimination but was intended to be 'a settling of a score' by a Black community member" (Halifax Police Department 1991: 9).

Subsequently, other controversies arose in Nova Scotia with respect to interactions between police and members of Black communities in the province. In 1994 two young Black men in Halifax claimed police officers used excessive force after ordering them out of a taxi. Early in 1995 a police officer strip-searched three little Black girls in their school after a suspected theft of ten dollars. Lawyers for the children, Burnley Jones and Anne Derrick, suggested the incident was racially motivated (Saunders 1995: A17).[11]

Black/police relations in Nova Scotia also came under scrutiny in 1989 in the context of a racially motivated brawl at Cole Harbour High School in Dartmouth. Accusations of police racial motivation followed after police laid charges against more Black students than Whites involved in the incident. Eventually two Blacks were convicted, while all charges against Whites involved in the incident were dropped. In 1996, Cole Harbour High School was again the scene of a brawl involving Black and White students. The Black community accused police of racial motivation in singling out only Black teens as targets for pepper-spraying. Ultimately, five Black males were charged with obstructing a police officer. Calls for a public inquiry followed police spokesman Corporal Hubley's response that colour was not a factor in deciding whom the police would pepper-spray. To date this incident is still unresolved.

This was the state of Black community and police relations in Nova Scotia and Canada on that day in October 1993 when fifteen-year-old R.D.S. left his grandmother's house on his bicycle and encountered his cousin's arrest on his way home. Understood in this racialized social context, the arrest of this Black youth by a White police officer in a predominately Black neighbourhood and the subsequent allegation of a racial bias against the only Black judge in the province who acquitted him takes on systemic qualities and becomes racially significant.

The Critical Race Theory Significance of the R.D.S. Case
The lawyer representing R.D.S. was Black. The fact that R.D.S. was able to obtain a lawyer from his own community is quite remarkable, given the fact that at the time of his arrest and trial no Black lawyer was on staff at Nova Scotia Legal Aid and only one was in a staff position at Dalhousie

Legal Aid. Additionally, at the original trial something unique occurred: in court that day were a Black female judge, a Black male lawyer, a Black court reporter and the Black accused. As one commentator noted, it was the kind of scene the Marshall commissioners had hoped for. The trial was held before Corrine Sparks, Nova Scotia's only Black female Youth Court Judge, on December 2, 1994 (*R.* v. *R.D.S.*, N.S. YO93-168).

Historically, Blacks have been excluded from the profession of law in Nova Scotia. There has been an ongoing and continuing struggle by Nova Scotian Blacks to obtain a legal education despite segregation and oppression. Throughout most of the twentieth century, Blacks were legally segregated from the public school system in the province of Nova Scotia. From 1876, Black communities throughout the province formally organized to combat the inferior education and racial discrimination they encountered in the provincial school system. Legal segregation of Blacks in education was only officially repealed (at least on paper) in the late 1960s. In 1964 there were still four segregated school districts in the province, and differential streaming on the basis of race continues in many Nova Scotia high schools to the present day. Critical Race theorists argue that this exclusion from the educational system and the legal profession has seriously undermined the Canadian Black community's ability to attack issues of racism in a legal framework and has retarded the advancement of rights doctrine in the context of race under the *Canadian Charter of Rights and Freedoms.*

At trial before Judge Sparks, only Constable Stienburg and R.D.S. testified, and the Black judge acquitted the young offender. Her decision was based on a finding of credibility. She preferred the testimony of the Black youth over that of the White police officer. Delivering an oral judgement, Judge Sparks said:

> In my view, in accepting the evidence, and I don't say that I accept everything that Mr. S. has said in Court today, but certainly he has raised a doubt in my mind and, therefore, based upon the evidentiary burden which is squarely placed upon the Crown, that they must prove all the elements of the offence beyond a reasonable doubt, I have queries in my mind with respect to what actually transpired on the afternoon of October the 17th (at 67–68).

Following this oral judgement, the Crown attorney questioned the judge's finding of credibility in favour of the Black youth by stating that "there's absolutely no reason to attack the credibility of the officer." Judge Sparks made the following comments in response:

The Crown says, well, why would the officer say that events occurred the way in which he has relayed them to the Court this morning? I'm not saying that the constable has misled the Court, although police officers have been known to do that in the past. And I'm not saying that the officer overreacted, but certainly police officers do overreact, particularly when they're dealing with non-white groups. That, to me, indicates a state of mind right there that is questionable. I believe that probably the situation in this particular case is the case of a young police officer who overreacted. And I do accept the evidence of Mr. S. that he was told to shut up or he would be under arrest. That seems to be in keeping with the prevalent attitude of the day (at 68–69).

These remarks turned a routine acquittal of a youth on summary conviction charges into a case where the credibility of a Black judge was attacked on the basis that she had a racial bias against the police. Constable Stienburg complained about what he termed these "disparaging" remarks by Judge Sparks. Chief of Police Vince MacDonald threatened to take action against Judge Sparks in the form of a formal complaint to the Judicial Council (he never followed through), and the Crown immediately filed a notice of appeal of the acquittal of R.D.S., alleging actual racial bias on the part of the Youth Court Judge. The Crown appeal of the acquittal of R.D.S. on the ground of an *actual* racial bias on the part of Judge Sparks against the police was heard by Chief Justice Constance Glube of the Supreme Court of Nova Scotia on April 18, 1995 (*R.* v. *R.D.S.*, S.C.N.S. SH No. 112404). Chief Justice Glube did not find an actual bias based on race but held that there was a reasonable apprehension of racial bias on the part of Judge Sparks based on the comments Judge Sparks had made in response to the Crown's assertion that there was no reason to attack the credibility of the officer. Based on this finding, Chief Justice Glube ordered a new trial before a different judge. In the racial context of Nova Scotia, this meant a new trial before a White judge.

The decision by Chief Justice Glube shocked and angered the Black community across the country. In Nova Scotia, it was acutely felt for a number of reasons. First, Judge Sparks was not only the first Black judicial appointment in Canada but also the only Black judge in Nova Scotia, having been appointed to the Nova Scotia Provincial Court in 1987. The Black community celebrated Judge Sparks' personal achievement as well as its own. They viewed these achievements as one hopeful sign that the racial divide that existed in the province might be bridged. Chief Justice Glube's decision was seen as an attempt to bring down a role model of the Black community and as a warning to all Blacks to "keep their place" in the racial and social structures of the province. As one Black commentator noted:

> These events imply a pattern that recurs whenever accusations— or even suggestions—of racism are made by blacks against the legal system.... The presence of blacks and Micmacs on the bench and bar was supposed to render the legal system more responsive to the needs and circumstances of their communities. Thus far, however, the system has been more defensive than responsive (Saunders 1995: A17).

In the decision rendered by Judge Sparks, the Black community saw what they had hoped for, and what the Royal Commission on the Donald Marshall Jr. Prosecution had envisioned when it made recommendations regarding the appointment of minority judges. A Black judge had brought her life experiences to the adjudication process, and the social reality of racism had not only been recognized by that judge, but its impact on the particular case had been openly considered as relevant to the decision-making process. The Black community was also cognizant of the fact that, three years after Judge Sparks' appointment to the bench, the Royal Commission on the Donald Marshall Jr. Prosecution had recognized what the Black and Aboriginal communities had known all along, namely, that racism had played a part in Donald Marshall Jr.'s wrongful conviction and imprisonment. From the outset of their deliberations, the Royal Commission had heard allegations that the criminal justice system in Nova Scotia dealt with people differently based on their race and social standing. In recognition of this fact, the Royal Commission recommended that governments consider the needs of visible minorities by appointing qualified visible-minority judges and administrative board members whenever possible.

The Black community also astutely recognized that this decision, if allowed to go unchallenged, could have wide-ranging consequences beyond the particular case. Prior to the decision in *R.D.S.*, there had been no Canadian case in which a finding of bias on the part of a judge had been based on race (see Devlin 1995).[12] This decision potentially subjected judges of colour and women judges (and judges with disabilities, and gay and lesbian judges) to unfounded allegations and challenges for bias not before countenanced with respect to White male judges. It also meant that in Nova Scotia, Black defendants potentially would always appear before White judges in future cases because this case stood for a wider proposition that Black judges could not be unbiased when adjudicating a case involving a Black accused and a White police officer (a return to the pre-Marshall status quo). A ruling that a Black female judge was subject to a reasonable apprehension of bias based on race created the opportunity for "judge shopping" on the part of Crown attorneys (and defence lawyers in certain circumstances) based on the race of the judge.

When Chief Justice Glube's decision was rendered, the immediate reaction in the Black community was outrage and an outpouring of support for an appeal. A notice of appeal of Chief Justice Glube's decision was filed on May 18, 1995. From that point on, Black lawyers, Critical Race theorists and the Black community knew that this case was of significant import, not just to the interests of the Black youth but also to the interests of the Black community across Canada.

Three grounds of appeal were set out in the appellant's Court of Appeal factum. These were that Chief Justice Glube had erred in law in (1) overturning the acquittal of R.D.S., where the acquittal was based on findings of credibility by the Youth Court Judge, (2) finding a reasonable apprehension of bias on the part of the Youth Court Judge and (3) adopting a *formal* equality approach to the determination of a reasonable apprehension of bias, rather than, as mandated by sections 15, 11(d) and 7 of the *Charter*, a *substantive* equality approach.

In the end the Nova Scotia Court of Appeal upheld Chief Justice Glube's finding that there was a reasonable apprehension of bias (*R.* v. *R.D.S.*, 145 N.S.R. [2d] 284). Despite of the fact that the issue of race was squarely before the Court, the reported decision of the majority in the Nova Scotia Court of Appeal is devoid of any mention of race. Based on a reading of the majority decision, the reader would not know that Judge Sparks is Black. It was only in the dissenting opinion of Justice Freeman in the *R.D.S.* case that the issue of race was acknowledged. Justice Freeman said that Judge Sparks in her oral decision "only articulated what everyone present ought to have known, that the case was racially charged, and that questions with racial overtones cannot be ignored if justice is to be done" (at 292). He refused to take a colour-blind stance in the case.

The erasure of the issue of race by the majority from the *R.D.S.* decision is similar to the erasure of racial issues in the excessive-use-of-force-by-police cases, where neither the Crown prosecutors nor the defence lawyers argued the issue of racial animus on the part of the White police officers and where Crown prosecutors failed to lay appropriate charges in some of the cases. The erasure of the issue of race from the majority Nova Scotia Court of Appeal decision in *R.D.S.* is also eerily reminiscent of the historical cases, such as *Christie*, studied by James Walker, where "in court, 'race' dropped from view, but in the 'real world' ... *Christie* as precedent produced an increase in racial discrimination. The courts had not addressed Fred Christie's problem at all" (1997: 312).

The lawyer for R.D.S., who had begun by conducting Critical Race Litigation at the individual level in representation of his client, was now about to embark on an ever-broadening "collective" strategy of Critical Race Litigation. As one Critical Race theorist noted, "Law should be emancipatory and liberatory for everyone. And, although for Black people, law in Canada has so often operated against us and so seldom worked for us, law remains too valuable a tool for us ever to abandon" (Thornhill 1994: 4).

After the decision of the Nova Scotia Court of Appeal was rendered in the *R.D.S.* case, a critical decision about whether to proceed to the Supreme Court of Canada had to be made. Because this was a summary conviction of a young offender, there was no automatic right of appeal to the Supreme Court. Leave to appeal had to be sought pursuant to section 40 of the *Supreme Court Act* of 1985. A number of questions immediately arose. Would the client want to appeal to the high court? Would the legal aid service support an appeal? Where would the funding come from to launch such an appeal? Would there be interveners in the litigation (third parties who have a stake in the outcome of a case) and, if so, which ones? And, most importantly, would the Supreme Court entertain a leave application where the issue was one of race? Critical Race theorists have bemoaned the fact that the Supreme Court of Canada has maintained a "systematic" and "steadfast" refusal to take a stance on racism (Thornhill 1994: 5).

R.D.S. and his mother wanted to pursue an appeal to the Supreme Court of Canada. Thus the first hurdle was crossed. This is the most crucial issue in any Critical Race Litigation strategy: without the consent and full participation of the client, raising issues of race in litigation can be difficult, if not impossible. Issues of ethics and the best advocacy for the Black client may collide with the interest of the larger Black community in addressing legal issues of racism (this issue is more fully discussed in Chapter 5).

Issues of funding were addressed by the success of an application to the Court Challenges Program for assistance. This is a government-funded program that has as its mandate the sponsoring of *Charter* challenges to the Supreme Court of Canada and the provincial Appellate Courts.

The Supreme Court of Canada would only grant leave to appeal under section 40 if it was of the opinion that the issue involved in the case was of sufficient public importance. It was therefore necessary to convince the Supreme Court that the right of racial minority judges and indeed all judges to recognize and address issues of race was a matter of public importance.

The main reason that the appointment of Blacks and women to the judiciary was seen as an important goal was to ensure that the judiciary would reflect the experiences of a broader spectrum of society. As Madam Justice Bertha Wilson noted with respect to the appointment of women:

"Women view the world and what goes on in it from a different perspective from men; and ... women judges, by bringing that perspective to bear on the cases they hear, can play a major role in introducing judicial neutrality and impartiality into the system" (Wilson 1990: 507). Madam Justice Wilson also noted with approval Professor Griffith's suggestion that "judicial attitudes [in Canada] towards political and social issues reflect the lack of a proper understanding of the view of labour unions, minorities, and the underprivileged" (1990: 508).

Currently in Canada, there are only five Black judges at the Superior Court level and approximately twelve in Provincial Courts across the country. If these judges are to achieve the goal of bringing their "different perspective" to bear on legal issues, it is essential that they not be silenced or overruled by White judges on the basis of allegations of bias when they try to apply their knowledge and experience in addressing issues of race. This was the underlying issue that the appellants hoped the Supreme Court would recognize by granting leave to appeal in *R.D.S.* Black Canadians have called for greater diversity on the bench because they have hoped it would "enrich the law by bringing sensitivity to the lived realities of communities of colour.... The experiences of excluded ethnic communities, and therefore our issues, are simply beyond the experience of most White judges" (Issac 1997). There was, however, no precedent for judicial sensitivity of this kind to issues of race at the Supreme Court level. Critical Race theorists and the Black community were somewhat skeptical about the Supreme Court's receptiveness to race issues. However, leave to appeal to the Supreme Court of Canada was granted on May 6, 1996.

Although the lawyers involved in the *R.D.S.* case were skeptical about the Supreme Court's willingness to fully confront the issues of race raised by the case, they were determined to squarely place the issue in arguments before the Court. Lawyers involved in the *R.D.S.* case and the Black community across Canada were cautiously optimistic that the Supreme Court of Canada was ready to make a definitive statement on the existence of racism in Canadian society. This would bring Canadian jurisprudence into line with American jurisprudence on this issue and lead to a fuller recognition of racism in this country. Further, a recognition of racism in Canadian society would be in accordance with Canadian jurisprudence, which now accepts without question the existence of gender discrimination in Canadian society (for gender discrimination and feminist litigation in Canada, see Razack 1991 and 1996, and Allen and Morton 1997). It was hoped that the controversy over whether one must prove racism through the introduction of evidence of whether it can be accepted as part of the judge's general background knowledge would be settled. This recognition could provide the impetus to more effective Critical Race Litigation strategies and lead to meaningful improvements for people of colour in Canadian society, in the same way that the recognition of gender discrimination by the courts has helped women and the feminist agenda.

The Critical Race Theory methods of deconstruction, narrative and reconstruction were employed in the *R.D.S.* litigation strategy. Specifically, the litigation team's strategy was to offer the argument that the allegation of a reasonable apprehension of bias arose in this case because Judge Sparks was a Black female judge who, in adjudicating a trial of a Black accused, explicitly recognized that the case had racial overtones.[13] And as Justice Freeman, in dissent in the Nova Scotia Court of Appeal, observed, "Questions with racial overtones ... are more likely than any other to subject the Judge to controversy and accusations of bias."[14] R.D.S.'s position was that the "reasonable person," whom a court invokes to determine whether or not a reasonable apprehension of bias arises, must be aware of the fact that racial discrimination exists in Canada.

A further element of the R.D.S. team's Critical Race Litigation strategy was to use the *Charter,* specifically section 15 (the equality section) to challenge the formal notion of equality, that is, the proposition that judges must be colour-blind. The appellant argued that:

> To be capable of detecting racism, one must be conscious of colour, race, and racial interactions because s.15 was not restricted to a formal notion of equality, it was not satisfied by the notion of equality as sameness. Judicial analysis which ignores the possible racial dynamics of a situation will perpetuate racism, while a substantive notion of equality recognizes that it may be necessary to take account of race in order ultimately to discount the invidious effect of race. To be sensitive to the possible racial dynamics of a given situation, as Judge Sparks was, is not indicative of bias but rather evidence of an understanding of the real meaning of equality. Given that racism is a reality in Canadian society, racism will be perpetuated if, as the majority of the Court of Appeal's analysis demands, judges studiously ignore the dynamics of race.[15]

As soon as the decision granting leave to appeal to the Supreme Court of Canada was handed down, the litigation team encouraged rights advocacy groups to participate, particularly Black organizations, as well as coalitions consisting of other groups interested in the outcome of the *R.D.S.* case. A number of organizations filed motions for intervener status (an intervener is a person, organization or government agency authorized by a court to participate in cases to raise issues that might not be fully argued by the immediate parties) these included the Women's Legal Education and Action Fund (LEAF), the National Organization of Immigrant and Visible Minority Women of Canada (NOIVMWC), the African Canadian Legal Clinic (ACLC), the Afro-Canadian Caucus of Nova Scotia, the Congress of Black Women and the Parent Student Association of Preston, Nova Scotia. Most of the intervener organizations represented Black people, and the Supreme Court of Canada granted standing to all interveners.

For the first time in the history of this country, the Black community had rights-based organizations who not only intervened in a case but had Black lawyers to argue their positions. Also for the first time in Canadian history, four Black lawyers from across Canada argued before the Supreme Court of Canada, either as appellant's counsel or as intervener counsel. Other Black lawyers who did not actually argue the case worked on the various litigation teams, preparing factums and offering advice or encouragement to their colleagues on what could be a precedent-setting case involving race and the *Charter.* Many White lawyers also worked on the case.

The respondent Crown argued, both in its factum and orally before the Supreme Court of Canada, that the issue of the existence of racial discrimination was a disputable fact and therefore any judge who wished to take judicial notice of the existence of racism would have to inform the parties that she or he was taking such notice of its existence and then allow the parties to introduce evidence for or against the existence of racism in Canadian society. Further, the respondent argued that if race had been the issue at trial, the Crown should have been afforded the opportunity to rebut the studies supporting the existence of racial discrimination, such as the Marshall Report, by providing a literature review and viva voce (oral or live) evidence from a sociologist, psychologist or research methodologist to properly interpret the studies, examine their methodology and evaluate their reliability.[16]

Despite the respondent's efforts to persuade the Supreme Court to disregard the race and *Charter* arguments put before it by the appellant and the interveners, the lawyers for the appellant and the interveners were cautiously optimistic at the end of the arguments that the Supreme Court of Canada was now ready to pronounce affirmatively on the existence of racism in Canadian society and to state that it is a matter that can and should be acknowledged by reasonable people and judges as a matter of experience and common sense. Further, the Black community and other communities of colour, as well as women and other historically excluded groups in Canadian society, hoped that arguments of reasonable apprehension of bias based on race would no longer be available as a tool for those who prefer to maintain the status quo by silencing judges who seek to render real justice by refusing to be "colour-blind" in adjudicating cases in situations where racism is a social reality.

By a 6–3 majority, the Supreme Court of Canada allowed the appeal in the *R.D.S.* case (*R.D.S.* v. *The Queen*, [1997] 151 D.L.R. [4th] 193 [S.C.C.]) and set aside the judgements of the Court of Appeal and Chief Justice Glube, restoring the decision of Judge Sparks. The majority consisted of Justice L'Heureux-Dubé, who wrote the majority opinion, and Justices La Forest, Gonthier, Cory and McLachlin, who concurred in it. The dissenting judgement was written by Justice Major and concurred in by Chief Justice Lamer and Justice Sopinka.

In the dissenting opinion in the Supreme Court of Canada, Justice Major says (at para. 6) that "whether racism exists in our society is not the issue" and he asserts (at para. 3) that this appeal "should not be decided on questions of racism but instead on how courts should decide cases." Justice Major concluded that the trial judge in this case might be perceived as assigning less weight to the police officer's evidence because he was testifying in the prosecution of an accused who was of a different race. The issue in this case, according to Justice Major (at para. 6) was "whether there was evidence before the court upon which to base a finding that *this* particular police officer's actions were motivated by racism. There was no evidence of this presented at the trial."

In Justice Major's narrative there is once again an attempt to "erase" the issue of race by resorting to legal rhetoric. The dissenting opinion chooses not to "tell the story" of racism in Canadian society. In this respect, it is not unlike the old historical cases about which James Walker (1997: 349) writes, "The distance from the original problem remained glaringly apparent. In court, 'race' dropped from view."

Did the decisions rendered by the majority in the *R.D.S.* case further the Critical Race agenda? For the individual Black client in this case, the outcome was a resounding success. He no longer faced the prospect of a new trial and there was a recognition by at least four members of the Supreme Court of Canada that there was evidence capable of supporting a finding of racially motivated overreaction by the White police officer. Justice L'Heureux-Dubé (with Justices McLachlin, Gonthier and La Forest concurring) stated (at para. 55):

> At no time did Judge Sparks rule that the probable overreaction by Constable Stienburg was motivated by racism. Rather, she tied her finding of probable overreaction to the evidence that Constable Stienburg had threatened to arrest the appellant R.D.S. for speaking to his cousin. *At the same time, there was evidence capable of supporting a finding of racially motivated overreaction.* At an earlier point in the proceedings, she had accepted the evidence that the other youth arrested that day was handcuffed and thus secured when R.D.S. approached. *This constitutes evi-*

dence which could lead one to question why it was necessary for both boys to be placed in choke holds by Constable Stienburg, purportedly to secure them. In the face of such evidence, we respectfully disagree with the views of our colleagues Cory and Major JJ. that there was no evidence on which Judge Sparks could have found "racially motivated" overreaction by the police officer (emphasis added).[17]

Did the decision in the *R.D.S.* case reflect the objective of Critical Race Litigation by challenging and deconstructing legal rules and principles which foster and maintain discrimination? Did it challenge the myth of the "objectivity" of laws? Did it benefit the Black community? In determining the answers to these questions, it is important to note that three different sets of detailed opinions/narratives[18] were rendered by the Court. There are, however, four areas on which all six members of the majority concur: (1) the disposition of the case, (2) judging in a multicultural society, (3) the importance of perspective and social context in judicial decision-making and (4) the presumption of judicial integrity.

Critical Race theorists and feminists have challenged the so-called "neutral" standard of the "reasonable person" used in law to determine the existence of a reasonable apprehension of bias and in other contexts as well. The "reasonable person" traditionally was implicitly constructed as a White, heterosexual, able-bodied male who belonged to the dominant group by judges from the dominant group, who perceived the experiences of that group as "neutral" and "normal."[19] The Critical Race position put forward by the appellant in the *R.D.S.* case was that the "reasonable person" must be aware of the fact that racial discrimination exists in Canada. In short, the argument was that racism exists in Canadian society, therefore a reasonable person in touch with broad Canadian social reality would know of racism. A recognition of that fact can help jurists recognize and remedy the effects of discrimination.

Justice Cory (at para. 111) and all members of the majority accepted these arguments and accordingly expanded the concept of the reasonable and informed person to mean one who is also aware of the social reality that forms the background to a particular case, such as societal awareness and acknowledgement of the prevalence of racism or gender bias in a particular community. Most importantly for the Critical Race agenda, all members of the majority held what should have been obvious to all Canadian judges but, as the *R.D.S.* case demonstrates, was not, namely that:

Finally, in the context of the current appeal, it is vital to bear in mind that the test for reasonable apprehension of bias applies equally to all judges, regardless of their background, gender, race, ethnic origin, or any other characteristic. A judge who happens to be black is no more likely to be biased in dealing with black litigants, than a white judge is likely to be biased in favour of white litigants. All judges of every race, colour, religion, or national background are entitled to the same presumption of judicial integrity and the same high threshold for a finding of bias. Similarly, all judges are subject to the same fundamental duties to be and to appear to be impartial (Cory J. at para 115).[20]

With respect to the submission of the appellant and interveners that judges should be able to refer to social context in making their judgements, and to power imbalances between the sexes or between races, and to other aspects of social reality without the introduction of evidence to prove that context, Justice Cory held that each case must be assessed in light of its facts and circumstances to determine whether reference to social context is appropriate and whether a reasonable apprehension of bias arises from particular statements.

The appellant also submitted that the test for bias or a reasonable apprehension of bias requires a demonstration of "real likelihood" of bias, in the sense that bias is probable, rather than a "mere suspicion." All members of the majority agreed that this position is supported by the English and Canadian case law (Cory J. at para. 112). Therefore the majority adopted the two-fold objective test for bias set out by Justice de Grandpré in *Committee for Justice and Liberty* v. *National Energy Board* ([1978] 1 S.C.R. 369 at 394 [S.C.C.]): "The person considering the alleged bias must be reasonable, and the apprehension of bias itself must also be reasonable in the circumstances of the case" (Cory J. at para 111). The majority further held that the threshold for a finding of real or perceived bias is high:

> Courts have rightly recognized that there is a presumption that judges will carry out their oath of office.... [T]his is one of the reasons why the threshold for a successful allegation of perceived judicial bias is high.... [H]owever, despite this high threshold, the presumption can be displaced with "cogent evidence" that demonstrates that something the judge has done gives rise to a reasonable apprehension of bias.... [T]he presumption of judicial integrity can never relieve a judge from the sworn duty to be impartial (Cory J. at para. 117).[21]

And Justice L'Heureux-Dubé states:

> Before concluding that there exists a reasonable apprehension of

bias in the conduct of a judge, the reasonable person would require some clear evidence that the judge in question had improperly used his or her perspective in the decision-making process; this flows from the presumption of impartiality of the judiciary. There must be some indication that the judge was not approaching the case with an open mind fair to all the parties. Awareness of the context within which a case occurred would not constitute such evidence; on the contrary, such awareness is consistent with the highest tradition of judicial impartiality (at para. 58).

From a Critical Race perspective, the majority decisions expand the concept of the "reasonable person" to include an awareness of the social context of a case, such as societal awareness and knowledge of the prevalence of racism or gender bias in a particular community. The Supreme Court of Canada's majority finding with respect to judges' ability to refer to social context in their decision-making and whether such references raise a reasonable apprehension of bias will depend on the individual case, as well as on the requirement that a high standard for a finding of a reasonable apprehension of bias is required. The Court's articulation that this high standard applies to all judges, regardless of their race, gender or other characteristics, furthers the agenda of Critical Race theorists and practitioners. It is a move away from the historical denial of the existence of racism in Canadian society, and a move toward a recognition that the doctrine of "neutrality" and "objectivity" in judicial decision-making is a myth. The Supreme Court of Canada's recognition that the "reasonable person" in Canadian society is not unaware of the social reality of racism is also a significant advance for the Critical Race Theory agenda.

As stated earlier, in determining whether the decision in the *R.D.S.* case furthers the Critical Race agenda, it is important to note that three detailed decisions were rendered in the case: two sets of opinions within the majority and the dissenting opinion of Chief Justice Lamer and Justices Major and Sopinka. These multiple opinions leave certain issues in an unsettled state and reflect differing philosophies and/or comprehensions of Canadian social realities on the part of the various judges. Justice L'Heureux-Dubé (with Justices McLachlin, La Forest and Gonthier concurring) explicitly distinguished "neutrality" from the concept of judicial impartiality. They explicitly recognized what they term the "fallacy" of judicial neutrality. Objectivity is an impossibility, because judges, like all other humans, operate from their own perspectives. This is in keeping with the position postulated by Critical Race theorists and others that the "objectivity" and "neutrality" of laws and judicial decision-making are myths. Critical Race Theory requires a recognition that "reason and logic are not the only influences that determine judicial results" (Harris 1997). Judicial decisions may be influenced by a myriad of factors, such as public pressures, social movements and the judge's own, as well as society's, prejudices and opinions (see Harris 1997).[22]

Justices L'Heureux-Dubé, McLachlin, La Forest and Gonthier explicitly state in their opinion/narrative that a reasonable person must be taken to be aware of the history of discrimination faced by disadvantaged groups in Canadian society protected by the *Charter's* equality provisions. They recognize that the reasonable person is not only a member of the wider Canadian community, but a member of a local community, in this case the Nova Scotian and Halifax communities. Such a person, they say, must be taken to "possess knowledge of the local population and its racial dynamics, including the existence in the community of a history of widespread and systemic discrimination against black and aboriginal people, and high profile clashes between the police and the visible minority population over policing issues" (L'Heureux-Dubé J. at para. 46–47). They say that these matters are the proper subject of judicial notice (a doctrine that permits a judge to recognize the existence or truth of certain facts without the parties having to introduce evidence to prove them):

> The reasonable person must be taken to be aware of the history of discrimination faced by disadvantaged groups in Canadian society protected by the *Charter's* equality provisions. These are matters of which judicial notice may be taken (L'Heureux-Dubé J. at para. 46).

This assertion is important to the Critical Race agenda. Justice L'Heureux-Dubé and those concurring in her opinion are saying that the existence of racism in Canadian society, as well as at the local community level, is an uncontestable fact and is therefore the proper subject for the taking of judicial notice.[23]

Justice L'Heureux-Dubé and those concurring choose to "tell the story" of the widespread and systemic discrimination existing in Nova Scotia, as well as the known racial tensions between police and Black and Aboriginal people in that province. Further, they choose to "tell the story" of the existence of racism in Canadian society as a whole. It is because of this acknowledgement of contextualized and historical background that Justice L'Heureux-Dubé and the other justices concurring found that Judge Sparks' comments did not give rise to a reasonable apprehension of bias and were not "close to the line." In applying the test for a finding of a reasonable apprehension of bias, Justice L'Heureux-Dubé held (at para. 59) that Judge Sparks' oral reasons showed that she approached the case with an open mind and that in "alerting herself to the racial dynamic in the case, she was simply engaging in the process of contextualized judging which, in our view, was entirely proper and conducive to a fair and just resolution of the case before her."

Justice L'Heureux-Dubé ascribes to the fictional "reasonable person" who evaluates the possibility of judicial bias certain attributes, namely, that in addition to being informed of the circumstances of the case, he or she would also be knowledgeable about the local community in which the case arose and about the nature of judging. The reasonable person would also be knowledgeable of Canadian *Charter* values and supportive of the principles of equality set out in section 15:

> An understanding of the context or background essential to judging may be gained from testimony from expert witness in order to put the case in context ... from academic studies properly placed before the Court; and from the judge's personal understanding and experience of the society in which the judge lives and works. This process of enlargement is not only consistent with impartiality; it may also be seen as its essential pre-condition. A reasonable person, far from being troubled by this process, would see it as an important aid to judicial impartiality (L'Heureux-Dubé J. at para. 44–45).

The "reasonable person" Justices L'Heureux-Dubé, McLachlin, La Forest and Gonthier envision expects judges to undertake an open-minded, carefully considered and dispassionately deliberate investigation of the realities of each case. Moreover, judges must be aware of the context in which the alleged crime occurred. Justices L'Heureux-Dubé, McLachlin, Gonthier and La Forest assert that contextual inquiry has become an accepted step towards judicial impartiality. They recognize that neutrality and true objectivity are impossible standards, and they disagree with Justices Cory and Iacobucci, who assert that references to social context are not appropriate in making determinations of credibility as long as the judge strives for impartiality and decides the issues with an open mind.[24]

Justices L'Heureux-Dubé, McLachlin, Gonthier and La Forest also would not limit reference to social context to situations where expert evidence has been introduced or academic studies have been placed before the court, but say instead that an understanding of the context or background essential to judging may also be gained from the judge's personal understanding and experience of the society in which he or she lives and works, and that "judges' own insights into human nature will properly play a role in making findings of credibility or factual determinations" (L'Heureux-Dubé J. at para. 40). This, they say, is not unfettered but balanced by the fact that judges must make factual determinations and findings of credibility "only after being equally open to and considering the views of all parties before them" (L'Heureux-Dubé J. at para. 40).

What appears to be the essential difference between the two majority judgements is that Justices Cory and Iacobucci would seem to prefer to limit *explicit* judicial consideration of social context to situations requiring expert evidence and would prefer that judges refrain from making *explicit* reference to it in cases of assessment of credibility. Justice Cory puts it this way (at para 132):

> In *Parks* and *Lavallee*, for instance, the expert evidence of social context was used to develop principles of general application in certain kinds of cases. These principles are legal in nature and are structured to ensure that the role of the trier of fact in a particular case is not abrogated or usurped. It is clear therefore that references to social context based upon expert evidence are sometimes permissible and helpful, and that they do not automatically give rise to suspicions of judicial bias. *However, there is a very significant difference between cases such as* Lavallee *and* Parks, *in which social context is used to ensure that the law evolves in keeping with changes in social reality, and cases, such as this one, where social context is apparently being used to assist in determining an issue of credibility* [emphasis added].

While Justice Cory agrees that judges should be able to refer to social context in making judgements and that any issue of a reasonable apprehension of bias which may arise as a result must be dealt with on a case-by-case basis, he appears to limit the concept of social context to certain situations where expert evidence was adduced with respect to the social context. However, he draws a distinction between those circumstances and the use of reference to social context to assist in the determination of credibility.

At first glance Justices Cory and Iacobucci appear to take a more narrow approach to the issue of social context in judicial decision-making than their colleagues, Justices L'Heureux-Dubé, La Forest, Gonthier and McLachlin. But it is also apparent on a closer reading of Justice Cory's opinion that he is not saying that reference to social context should *never* be made to assist in the determination of credibility. In paragraph 130 of his opinion he says that:

> When making findings of credibility it is obviously *preferable* for a judge to *avoid* making any comment that *might* suggest that a determination of credibility is based on generalizations rather

than on the specific demonstrations of truthfulness or untrustwor-
thiness that have come from the particular witness during the
trial. It is true that judges do not have to remain passive, or to
divest themselves of all their experience which assists them in
their judicial fact finding ... yet judges have wide authority and
their public utterances are closely scrutinized. Neither the parties
nor the informed and reasonable observer should be led to believe
by the comments of the judge that decisions are indeed being
made based on generalizations [emphasis added].

Justice Cory does, however, concede that in some circumstances it may be
acceptable for a judge to acknowledge racism in society in evaluating
credibility, for example, with respect to the motive for overreaction:

In some circumstances it may be acceptable for a judge to acknowledge that racism in society might be, for example, the
motive for the overreaction of a police officer. This may be
necessary in order to refute a submission that invites the judge as
trier of fact to presume truthfulness or untruthfulness of a cat-
egory of witnesses, or to adopt some other form of stereotypical
thinking. Yet it would not be acceptable for a judge to go further
and suggest that all police officers should therefore not be believed or should be viewed with suspicion where they are dealing
with accused persons who are members of a different race (at
para. 132).

It is apparently under this latter exception, and taking into consideration that "cogent evidence" was required for a finding of a reasonable
apprehension of bias, that Justice Cory allowed the appeal. He says that
although Judge Sparks' remarks are "unfortunate" and "unnecessary" (at
para. 158) and "close to the line" (at para. 152) when viewed in isolation,
it was important to remember that it is necessary in cases where a reasonable apprehension of bias is alleged to read all the comments in the
context of the whole proceeding. Having done this, Justice Cory concluded (at para. 158) that a reasonable, informed person aware of all the
circumstances, would not have concluded that Judge Sparks' comments
gave rise to a reasonable apprehension of bias.

From a Critical Race perspective it is unfortunate that it appears that
Justices Cory and Iacobucci would prefer the existing status quo, namely,
that judges simply not divulge the full reasons behind their judgements.[25]
Justice Cory's approach is not consistent with the arguments put forward
in the *R.D.S.* case that section 15 of the *Charter* requires that judges
articulate in their decisions all non-legal assumptions upon which they

base their decisions. This articulation would "facilitate judicial review and guard against reliance on myths and prejudicial beliefs," the appellant and the interveners LEAF/NOIVMWC contended, and it would also ensure that "the inclusion in reasons of judgement of valid generalizations based upon well-known social facts and observations is not construed as bias."[26]

If Justice Cory's position is that it is preferable that judges remain "silent" about their reference to social context in their decision-making, it unfortunately would not further the Critical Race agenda because it does not guard against reliance on myths and prejudicial beliefs. If one does not have to articulate the basis for one's decisions, then one is not accountable. From a Critical Race perspective, Justice Cory's position is the antipode of judicial accountability. There are those perhaps who might prefer the status quo, as this commentator's statements seem to indicate:

> *R.D.S.* itself has certainly advanced the debate and heightened awareness of these critical issues. Nevertheless, it may be prudent in other circumstances for judges to use "common sense," "social context" or "judicial notice" in silence, knowing that even *unreasonable* apprehensions of bias can cause needless controversy which may bring the administration of justice into disrepute (Archibald 1988: 66, emphasis added).

This seems to ignore the test for apprehension of bias supported by the majority, including Justice Cory in the *R.D.S.* case, which requires a two-fold objective test, that is, that the person considering the alleged bias must be reasonable, and the *apprehension of bias itself* must also be reasonable. Critical Race Theory and Critical Race Litigation reject "silence" about the racism, and in particular the anti-Black racism, that spawned the *R.D.S.* case.

It is also unfortunate that in the process of addressing the issues of social context and determinations of credibility, Justice Cory seems to reintroduce the concept of judicial neutrality. He appears to endorse the principle of impartiality in paragraph 93 of his opinion where he states that, "For very good reason it has long been determined that the courts should be held to the highest standards of impartiality." However, he does goes on to state in paragraph 118 that:

> It is right and proper that judges be held to the highest standards of impartiality since they will have to determine the most fundamentally important rights of the parties appearing before them. This is true whether the legal dispute arises between citizen and citizen or between the citizen and the state. Every comment that a judge makes from the bench is weighed and evaluated by the

> community as well as the parties. Judges must be conscious of this constant weighing and make every effort to achieve *neutrality* and fairness in carrying out their duties. *This must be a cardinal rule of judicial conduct* [emphasis added].

Although he once again reinforces the idea that judges are not required to discount their life experiences, he nonetheless reiterates the requirement for *neutrality.* In contrast, as noted above, Justice L'Heureux-Dubé and the three other justices who concur encourage "contextualized" judging. The "reasonable person" Justice L'Heureux-Dubé envisions expects judges to undertake an open-minded, carefully considered and dispassionately deliberate investigation of the realities of each case, but judges must be aware of the context in which the alleged crime occurred. She asserts that this contextual inquiry has become an accepted step towards judicial impartiality.

In spite of the differences of opinion expressed by the Supreme Court Justices in the *R.D.S.* case about the issue of reference to social context in the judicial decision-making process, this case can be seen as making a substantial contribution to the expansion of the "reasonable person" standard. It of course remains to be seen how the decision will affect future pronouncements on race issues before the courts, but one thing is certain, *R.D.S.* v. *The Queen* will be a useful precedent in the Critical Race litigator's arsenal.

Jury Selection Cases

Although "race" and racism are significant factors in Canadian society, these issues have not become a part of the litigation instinct of lawyers in Canada as they have in the United States. Canadian Black lawyers and others are gradually beginning to seriously consider the role of race in litigation, however, and to develop effective Critical Race Litigation strategies to address issues of race. These strategies will increasingly place these issues before Canadian courts, where, it is hoped, as with gender-based litigation, a body of useful precedents can be developed. In Canada we are also beginning to develop a body of Critical Race Theory and to move beyond theory to practical application, which involves the use of Critical Race Litigation on behalf of Black clients and the Black community as a whole.

Some Critical Race Litigation cases have made their way to the courts such as *R.* v. *Parks* (1993, 84 C.C.C [3d] 353 [Ont. C.A.]), *R.* v. *McPartlin* ([1994] B.C.J. No. 3101 [B.C.S.C.]), *R.* v. *Williams* (1996, 106 C.C.C. [3d] 215 [B.C.C.S.]) and *R.* v. *Cole (D)* (1996, 152 N.S.R. [2d] 321 [N.S.C.A.]). Some have been successful, others have not, but all are important Canadian Critical Race cases. This chapter focuses on these four cases. The *Parks, McPartlin* and *Williams* cases demonstrate a Critical Race Litigation strategy designed to uncover the juror who may be biased against a Black accused through the use of the challenge-for-cause provisions of the Criminal Code. They also demonstrate the deconstruction of rules which have evolved through judicial interpretation of these Code provisions and prevented a Black accused from asking the "race" question in the context of jury selection. The chapter ends with the *Cole* case, which should have taken (but did not take) a Critical Race Theory and Litigation approach to the issue of nondisclosure of evidence by Crown prosecutors to a Black accused in Nova Scotia.

As we have seen in the Rodney King case, in the United States, one of the pressing issues for Critical Race theorists is the use of predominately or all-White juries to try Black people accused of crime and the exoneration by these all-White or predominately White juries of those accused of crimes of violence against Black victims. The problem posed by predominately White juries is not, however, confined to the United States. It is a problem in Canada and of growing concern for Canadian Critical Race theorists and others. The accused's right to a trial by jury is a central element of criminal law. It is of such importance that trial by jury has been entrenched in the Canadian Constitution. Section 11(f) of the *Canadian Charter of Rights and Freedoms* states that any person charged with an offence has the right to the benefit of trial by jury where the maximum punishment for the offence is imprisonment for five years or a more severe punishment.

In 1991 the Supreme Court of Canada in *R. v. Sherratt* (63 C.C.C. [3d] 193 at 204 [S.C.C.]) outlined the fundamental characteristics which a jury must possess to properly exercise its functions and they include "impartiality" and "representativeness."

One of the rationales for the jury system is that it is a means of maintaining public trust in the criminal justice system. It acts as the "conscience of the community" and is the "bulwark" against oppressive laws or their enforcement (NSLRC 1993a). As Cynthia Petersen (1993: 155) points out, however, the exoneration by all-White juries of White police officers accused of racist violence against Blacks has led to "increasing cynicism" toward the Canadian criminal justice system.

The selection of criminal trial juries in Canada is both a federal and provincial responsibility. The lists from which potential jurors are selected are governed by the various provincial and territorial Juries Acts.[27] The provincial statutes are supposed to guarantee representativeness in the initial array of potential jurors through a combination of various "lists" and random selection. The selection of jurors from the jury panel, which occurs "in-court" is governed by the Criminal Code of Canada and is supposed to ensure the "impartiality" of the jury.[28]

The exclusion of Black Canadians from juries happens at both the early stage of the process (the lists from which potential jury panels are selected and the "random" selection process, governed by provincial statutes) and at the "in-court" stage of the process (governed by the federal Criminal Code). The Commission on Systemic Racism in the Ontario Criminal Justice System (1996) found that Black Canadians were under-represented on Ontario juries, and the Law Reform Commission of Nova Scotia (1993a) discovered that concern was expressed by judges and others that people from Black and Aboriginal communities were rarely seen on jury panels. This, the Law Reform Commission concluded, suggested that the provincial areas of responsibility, the jury source lists and the random selection procedures were not working to ensure that jury panels were representative of the community. In addition, the commission also determined that federal government representatives and others involved in the criminal justice system were also apprehensive about other aspects of the jury process (such as peremptory challenges and challenges for cause under the Criminal Code) that have allowed prosecutors or defence lawyers to eliminate Blacks and other people of colour from jury service based on discriminatory factors such as race, ethnic origin or gender.

Under Canadian law, the Crown and the accused may seek to exclude a prospective juror through the vehicle of a peremptory challenge or a challenge for cause. The peremptory challenge permits the exclusion of a prospective juror by either side without that side having to provide a justification or reason why they want the person excused from the jury. Peremptory challenges are regulated by section 634 of the Criminal Code of Canada.[29] A challenge for cause, in contrast, allows either side in a jury trial to seek exclusion of a prospective juror, but a reason must be given for the sought-after exclusion. Challenges for cause are regulated by section 638 of the Canadian Criminal Code.[30]

Historically, Canadian laws *explicitly* prohibited the participation of Aboriginals and women on juries and also precluded the participation of racial minorities (Petersen 1993: 152). In the contemporary Canadian criminal justice system, systemic exclusion of Blacks, other people of colour and women from juries involves the use of antiquated procedures that have discriminatory effects. For example, the Manitoba Aboriginal Justice Inquiry (1991; also see Marshall Commission 1989) concluded that it was a common practice for some Crown attorneys and defence counsel to exclude Aboriginal jurors through the use of stand-asides and peremptory challenges and recommended that the Criminal Code of Canada be amended so that the only challenges which could be made to exclude prospective jurors would be challenges for cause.

As the following cases demonstrate, however, the elimination of discriminatory exclusion is only one of the problems in the jury selection process. The problem of non-representative juries must be challenged by Critical Race litigators at the initial stage of the array, that is by attacking those procedures controlled by provincial statutes, jury lists and random selection which result in the exclusion of Blacks from jury panels. And at the federal level, challenges must be made to Criminal Code procedures which allow prospective White jurors who may be influenced on the basis of race to sit on juries and contribute to non-representative juries by permitting Black jurors to be struck by the discriminatory use of peremptory challenges. (Challenges to the array and the discriminatory use of peremptory challenges will be explored further in Chapter 4 of this book.)

R. v. Parks

The case of *R.* v. *Parks* demonstrates how a Critical Race Litigation strategy was employed to confront the courts with the issue of race in the context of jury selection under sections 7 and 11(d) of the *Charter*. The case was heard by the Ontario Court of Appeal in 1993 (84 C.C.C. [3d] 353 [Ont. C.A.]). Mr. Parks, a Black accused, was charged with the second-degree murder of a White victim. The Crown alleged that the murder occurred in the course of a fight between the victim and the accused over a drug transaction. Prior to the selection of a jury in his murder trial, Parks applied to the court for the right to challenge prospective jurors for cause by asking them whether their ability to judge evidence without bias would be affected by the fact that the accused was Black and the victim was White. The trial judge refused to permit the question, relying on the legal presumption[31] that jurors can be relied on to do their duty and to decide the case without considering their personal biases and prejudices.

Parks was acquitted of murder but convicted of manslaughter. He appealed his conviction for manslaughter on the basis that the trial judge had erred in not allowing him to question prospective jurors on racial bias. The Ontario Court of Appeal in *Parks* agreed and held that the accused Black man should have been allowed to challenge the jurors for racial prejudice because of the overwhelming evidence of anti-Black racism in Metropolitan Toronto and Canada. Justice Doherty (in the absence of evidence presented by counsel) relied on his own research into the existence of racism in Canadian society. Taking judicial notice of the existence of racism and in particular anti-Black racism in Toronto and Canada, Justice Doherty found "an ever-growing body of studies and reports documenting the extent and intensity of racist beliefs in contemporary Canadian society, many deal[ing] with racism in general, others with racism directed at black persons" (at 366). Justice Doherty noted that there was relatively little Canadian data relating to the impact of racial bias on jury verdicts but found that "despite the lack of empirical data,

Canadian commentators have no doubt that racist attitudes do impact on jury verdicts where the accused is a member of a racial minority" (at 378). The Court of Appeal rejected the Crown's submission that allowing the question could "inject racial ... overtones into a case where none existed previously" (Doherty J.A. at 361). Instead, the Court took the position that this argument would only be valid if one were to assume that none of the prospective jurors is racially biased. If one or more of the prospective jurors were racially biased, their presence would "inject" racial overtones into the proceedings: "A question directed at revealing those whose bias renders them partial does not 'inject' racism into the trial, but seeks to prevent that bias from destroying the impartiality of the jury's deliberations" (Doherty J.A. at 362).

Justice Doherty held that the presumption that jurors will perform their duty according to their oath must be balanced against the threat of a verdict tainted by racial bias.

As set out in 1991 in *R.* v. *Sherratt* (63 C.C.C. [3d] 193 at 204 [S.C.C.]), an impartial jury is a crucial first step in the conduct of a fair trial. In *Parks*, Justice Doherty held that the accused's statutory right under section 638(1)(b) of the Criminal Code of Canada to challenge potential jurors for cause based on partiality is the only direct means an accused has to secure an impartial jury. He noted (at 363) that it is not enough, however, for the party seeking to challenge for cause to demonstrate that the question they wish to ask is relevant; "they must go further and show that there is an 'air of reality' to the application—there must be a realistic potential for the existence of partiality."

The Ontario Court of Appeal upheld the right of an accused to a fair trial with an impartial jury and noted that the trial judge must be satisfied that questions asked of potential jurors are relevant to assess the jurors' "partiality." Justice Doherty held that partiality was both attitudinal and behavioural, but biases of themselves are not sufficient to establish partiality. It was purely the impact on the juror's ability to be impartial which was to be the determining factor. This test, which was set out initially by the Supreme Court of Canada in the *Sherratt* case, was held in *Parks* to be both a recognition of the validity of the "presumption" that jurors will do their duty in accordance with their oath, and a recognition that there are limits on the presumption. Where the test is met, as it was held to have been in *Parks*, "continued reliance on the 'presumption' to the exclusion of the challenge process would negate the accused's right to a fair trial by an impartial jury" (Doherty J.A. at 363).

Some commentators have argued that the *Parks* decision was a departure from established principles guiding the use of challenges for cause because it replaced a discretion [held by trial judges] to allow a challenge based on racial prejudice with the right of a black accused to challenge for cause on the issue of racial prejudice and an obligation on the trial judge to allow the question [to be raised] in all cases.... *Parks* established that there is a realistic possibility that a juror will be influenced in the performance of his or her judicial duty on the basis of racial bias.... Some trial counsel estimate that somewhere in the range of 15 to 20 percent of jurors are being successfully challenged on the basis of racial prejudice under the *Parks* scheme (Tanovich 1993: 311).

Tanovich (1993: 310) forcefully argues that the Ontario Court of Appeal in *Parks* stands for the proposition that Black accused are entitled to question jurors about racial prejudice as of right. In other words, the discretion once held by judges to allow or disallow this kind of questioning has been eliminated by the decision in *Parks*. This appears to be supported by Justice Doherty's statement there that:

In my view, a trial judge, in the proper exercise of his or her discretion, could permit counsel to put the question posed in this case in any trial held in Metropolitan Toronto involving a black accused. *I would go further and hold that it would be the better course to permit that question in all such cases where the accused requests the inquiry* (at 379, emphasis added).

The Ontario Court of Appeal decision in the *Parks* case was appealed by the Crown to the Supreme Court of Canada. One of the grounds of appeal was that the Ontario Court of Appeal erred in law "when it collected the evidence on the need to challenge without giving the Applicant an opportunity to respond to that evidence or adduce further evidence" (Henry and Henry 1996: 345). The Supreme Court of Canada denied leave to appeal in the *Parks* case, thereby foreclosing the opportunity to address the issue of race in the context of jury selection. The Supreme Court of Canada also avoided answering the question of whether the existence of racism and in particular anti-Black racism was the proper subject for taking judicial notice at a national level. This is a significant question for Critical Race Litigation, since arguments have increasingly been made that evidence of the existence of racism is still required because "*Parks* did not provide any documentation or expert witness testimony" (Henry and Henry 1996: 347).

The *Parks* decision stands for the proposition that a defendant's right to challenge for cause based on racial partiality is essential to the accused's constitutional right to a fair trial by an impartial jury enshrined in sections 7 and 11 of the *Charter.* The *Parks* decision, while generally considered by Critical Race theorists to be groundbreaking for the recognition by a Canadian Court of Appeal of the existence of racism and in particular anti-Black racism in Canadian society, and for its new approach to the issue of the questioning of potential jurors on racial bias, still left some fundamental questions unanswered regarding the role of "race" in the criminal jury selection process. In particular, with regard to the challenge for cause procedures under the Criminal Code, from a Critical Race Theory perspective, *Parks* did not go far enough in advancing the right of a Black accused to question potential jurors on racial bias.

For example, the question allowed in *Parks* is of limited usefulness in ferreting out unconscious racism. Dr. Francis Henry, a professor of anthropology at York University and a consultant in race relations, testified in a subsequent case with respect to a challenge for cause on the basis of racial bias. In the July 1993 case of *R. v. Griffis (no. 1)* (16 C.R.R. [2d] 322 [Ont. Ct. Gen. Div.])[32] (a case where the accused was an African-American charged with importing heroin into Canada and possession of heroin for the purpose of trafficking), the accused brought a motion to permit a challenge for cause on the basis of the possibility of racial prejudice affecting jury deliberations. Dr. Henry testified that the question allowed in *Parks* was inadequate because it would not get at "attitudinal prejudice" and more than one question would be required to determine whether a prospective juror harboured this type of prejudice. In the *Griffis* case the defence put forth six questions it wanted to ask on the challenge for cause, including:

1. What does the term "racist" mean to you?
2. Do you think racism is a problem in Canadian society?
3. How many Black people do you think live in Canada?
4. Some people think Black people commit more crimes than people of other races. Do you have an opinion on this subject? If so, what is it?
5. Do you hold any opinions about people of the accused's race, particularly with respect to criminal behaviour involving drugs? If so, what are those opinions? and
6. Would those opinions interfere with your ability to try this case fairly?

The Court in *Griffis* allowed all six questions with a slight modification to question 5 to reflect the fact that prospective jurors were not social scientists and required a simplified form of the question.

The *Parks* decision was too narrow in its focus. It permits a very limited inquiry on a challenge for cause. For example, it does not permit the accused to undertake the broad-based inquiry into the prospective juror's lifestyle and personal experiences permitted in the United States in order to facilitate the exposure of racial prejudice. This issue was specifically raised in *Parks* and addressed by Justice Doherty in his judgement. Canadian courts, Justice Doherty explains (at 361), have resisted this approach to jury selection, and he cites cases such as *R. v. Hubbert* (1975, 29 C.C.C. [2d] 279 [S.C.C.]), a pre-*Charter* case, in support of this observation. Justice Doherty did not rule out this argument in the context of challenges for cause based on racial prejudice, however. He merely noted that there were "very difficult problems" in this context which did not need to be addressed in the determination of the *Parks* case because in that case there was only one very specific question. Critical Race litigators may also wish to push the envelope in seeking to delve further into the racial prejudices of prospective jurors than the defence did in *Parks*.

Moreover, the Court in *Parks* only allowed the question that was posed because it was colour-blind, or "race-neutral," as Justice Doherty described it. In other words, the accused in *Parks* did not attempt to argue that only prospective jurors who were White should be subject to the challenge for cause. An approach that was not colour-blind (i.e., a colour-conscious approach) would have attempted to do so, since the Critical Race Theory argument would be that since Blacks and not Whites have been the historically disadvantaged group in society, a colour-blind approach ignores this reality and would treat White jurors, most of whom have not been subject to discrimination or systemic exclusion from jury service, in the same way that it would treat Blacks, most of whom need protection from discrimination.

Justice Doherty appears to indicate (at 360) that if a race-conscious approach had been taken in posing the question, the outcome in *Parks* would conceivably have been different.[33] The decision in *Parks* did not foreclose the opportunity of the trial judge, based on his or her discretion, to disallow any challenge for cause based on racial prejudice. No *Charter* section 15(1) equality rights analysis was offered in *Parks* to challenge the constitutionality of maintaining this discretion.

The obvious interpretation of the *Parks* decision is that an accused making a challenge for cause based on racial bias need not introduce evidence to justify this request because the court can take judicial notice of the existence of racism and in particular anti-Black racism in Canadian society. Indeed, in the Ontario case of *R. v. Wilson* decided in 1996 (47 C.R. (4th) 61), the Ontario Court of Appeal held that the question permitted in *R. v. Parks* is to be allowed in any jury trial in Ontario where the accused is Black. However, because the highest court in the land refused to allow an appeal in the *Parks* case, no pronouncement on this critical race issue had yet been made that was binding on all jurisdictions. As a result, the law with respect to the ability of a Black accused to challenge prospective jurors for cause based on racial bias varied from jurisdiction to jurisdiction. For example, the law was different in British Columbia than it was in Ontario where the *Parks* case was decided. The British Columbian courts were very reluctant to accept the principles set out in *Parks* and insisted that the decision was limited to Ontario. In the British Columbia cases of *R. v. McPartlin* and *R. v. Williams,* the idea of challenge for cause on the basis of racial bias on the part of potential jurors was rejected, even though societal prejudice was not denied outright by the court.

R. v. McPartlin, R. v. Williams and R. v. Drakes
In the British Columbia cases of *R. v. McPartlin* ([1994] B.C.J. No. 3101 [B.C.S.C.]) and *R. v. Williams* (1996, 106 C.C.C. [3d] 215 [B.C.C.A.], rev'g 1994, 90 C.C.C. [3d] 194 [B.C.S.C.]), the idea of challenge for cause on the basis of racial bias on the part of potential jurors was rejected. In the *McPartlin* case, a 1994 case involving a charge of sexual assault where the accused was a Black man and the victim a White woman, a distinction was drawn between partiality and bias. A juror could only be challenged for partiality and not for bias. Hence, even if a juror was shown to be biased against racial minorities in general, the Court held that this is not indicative of the juror's inability to be impartial with respect to the particular racial-minority accused person. Also in *McPartlin,* the Court suggested (at 199) that the existence of widespread bias and prejudice against racial minorities does not in itself establish a realistic potential for partiality on the part of prospective jurors against a particular racial minority defendant that would displace the presumption that jurors can be relied on to do their duty and decide the case without regard to their personal biases and prejudices. The *McPartlin* decision differed from the decision of the Ontario Court of Appeal in *Parks* because, although the Ontario Court of Appeal did not ignore the presumption that jurors can be relied upon to do their duty and decide the case without regard to their personal biases and prejudices, the Ontario Court of Appeal held that this presumption "must be balanced against the threat of a verdict tainted by racial bias" (Roach 1995: 410).

A similar analysis was articulated in 1996 by the British Columbia Court of Appeal in the *Williams* case, which also considered the *Parks* decision. In *Williams,* an Aboriginal man was accused of the robbery of a White victim. Although the Crown in the *Williams* case did not challenge the existence of racism, the British Columbia Court of Appeal still did not accept that there was partiality which could prevent the jurors from making a rational decision. As Roach noted:

Parks also differs from *Williams* in its perceptions about how racial bias among jurors might affect their decision-making. The Ontario Court of Appeal in *Parks* recognized the sub-conscious and institutional nature of anti-black racism, whereas the court in *Williams* seemed only concerned about the likelihood of conscious and intentional racism against an Aboriginal accused.... An implicit model of intentional racism also may explain why [Chief Justice] Esson ... stressed that there was no "racial element" in the robbery that Williams was charged with (1995: 420–21).

The result of these two cases, *McPartlin* and *Williams,* was that a juror could not be challenged on grounds of racial bias in British Columbia. Up to that point, there had been no case in Canada in which a challenge for cause based on racial partiality had been raised where the existence of societal racism had been accepted as a matter of the judge's background knowledge of social reality, common sense and experience. This fact was of particular significance for Critical Race theorists, because denial of the existence of racism in Canadian society is at the heart of the continuing role that race and racism play in law. In 1979, in the case of *R. v. Crosby* (49 C.C.C. [2d] 255 [Ont. H.C.]), a Black man sought to question prospective jurors about racial bias (Petersen 1993). In denying the accused's request, the judge stated:

> Fortunately, in our land we have been spared most of the major manifestations of this phenomenon [racism].... [I]t seems to me that, in the absence of any notorious episode in a community of the type I have mentioned, to permit challenges of this kind to go forward simply on the ground that man [sic] is prejudiced and that black and white may frequently be prejudiced against each other is to admit to a weakness in our nation and in our community which I do not propose to acknowledge (Petersen 1993: 147).

It appears that the courts in British Columbia were not then prepared to acknowledge this "weakness" in our nation. Later, in 1998, in the case of *R. v. Drakes* (122 C.C.C. [3d] 498 [B.C.C.A.]), the British Columbia Court of Appeal dismissed the application to challenge for cause based on racial bias of a Black accused charged with the sexual assault of a White woman. In denying the appeal, Justice Lambert said the following:

> There are those who may think that such an assumption (that if any juror holds the belief that it is possible to draw conclusions about an individual's behavioral characteristics or tendencies based

on race, ... that juror will nonetheless adhere to the juror's oath) is unrealistic, but the jury system depends on it. And in my opinion there is more reason rather than less reason to trust in that assumption in a culturally, racially, and ethnically diverse society of persons accustomed to living together, such as ours, than in a culturally, racially and ethnically homogeneous society, with little or no experience of diversity (at 498).

Based on this reasoning and because of the Court's decision in *R.* v. *Williams*, Justice Lambert refused to apply the *Parks* decision or any other cases which have followed it to any challenge for cause based on race in British Columbia unless

there were reliable evidence that, on a realistic assessment, a significant percentage of potential jurors might be unable to free themselves from any preconceptions relating to the race of the accused and the relationship of an accused of that race to an offence of the type charged. The evidence would have to show that the jurors might be unable to abide by their oath and reach a verdict on the basis of the trial evidence alone, free from any bias either in favour of or against the accused (at 498).

This decision set an impossibly high burden on the Black accused, making it virtually impossible to challenge a prospective juror on the basis of racial bias in British Columbia. Tanovich (1993) argues that the overwhelming evidence of racism leading to the Court's decision in *Parks* involved studies and statistics from across Ontario and the whole of Canada. *Parks*, he asserts,

supplies the evidential foundation for the required "air of reality" in all cases in Canada, thereby entitling all black accused in Canada the right to challenge for cause on the basis of racial prejudice. Any other conclusion would be contrary to the purposive approach which must be applied, given that the right to an impartial jury, a right to be found in ss.7, 11(d) and (f) [of the *Charter*], is critical in safeguarding an accused's right to a fair trial (1993: 310).

Leave to appeal the Critical Race case of *R.* v. *Williams* to the Supreme Court of Canada was granted. The Supreme Court of Canada showed a willingness to address the "race" question in the *Williams* case. The Court held that judicial notice may be taken of the existence of racism in Canadian society.

The fact that both the *R.D.S.* and *Williams* cases have reached the Supreme Court of Canada indicates that, unlike some lower courts, the Supreme Court of Canada now recognizes that the issues of race require judicial consideration. The Supreme Court of Canada heard arguments in the *Williams* case on February 14, 1998, and rendered its decision on June 4, 1998. The Court allowed the defence appeal and ordered a new trial. Justice McLachlin, speaking for a unanimous Court, upheld the principle relating to challenges for cause set down in *R. v. Sherratt*, which is that judges should permit challenges for cause where there is a "realistic potential" of the existence of partiality. Applying the *Sherratt* principle to the *Williams* case, the issue was whether the evidence of widespread bias against Aboriginal people in the community raised a "realistic potential" of partiality. In deciding the issue, Justice McLachlin stated that:

> To suggest that all persons who possess racial prejudices will erase those prejudices from the mind when serving as jurors is to underestimate the insidious nature of racial prejudice and the stereotyping that underlies it. As Vidmar, supra, points out, racial prejudice interfering with jurors' impartiality is a form of discrimination. It involves making distinctions on the basis of class or category without regard to individual merit. It rests on preconceptions and unchallenged assumptions that unconsciously shape the daily behaviour of individuals. Buried deep in the human psyche, these preconceptions cannot be easily and effectively identified and set aside, even if one wishes to do so. For this reason, it cannot be assumed that judicial directions to act impartially will always effectively counter racial prejudice (at para. 21).

Justice McLachlin held that a judge exercising the discretion to permit or refuse challenges for cause must act on the evidence in a way that fulfills the purpose of Criminal Code section 638(1)(b), which is to prevent people who are not indifferent as between the Crown and the accused from serving on the jury, and that section 638, as with all laws, should be interpreted in a way that conforms to the *Canadian Charter of Rights and Freedoms*:

> The challenge for cause is an essential safeguard of the accused's s.11(d) Charter right to a fair and impartial jury.... The right to challenge for cause, in cases where it is shown that a realistic potential exists for impartiality, remains an essential filament in the web of protections the law has woven to protect the constitutional right to have one's guilt or innocence determined by an

impartial jury. If the Charter right is undercut by an interpretation of s.638(1)(b) that sets too high a threshold for challenges for cause, it will be jeopardized (McLachlin J. at para. 47).

Additionally, the Court noted that while the accused's right to be tried by an impartial jury under section 11(d) of the *Charter* is a fair trial right, it was also an anti-discrimination right:

> The application, intentional or unintentional, of racial stereotypes to the detriment of an accused person ranks among the most destructive forms of discrimination. The result of the discrimination may not be the loss of a benefit or a job or housing in the area of choice, but the loss of the accused's very liberty. The right must fall at the core of the guarantee in s.15 of the Charter that "every individual is equal before and under the law and has the right to the equal protection and equal benefit of the law without discrimination" (McLachlin J. at para. 48).

Based on this analysis, the Court rejected the Crown argument and the decision of the British Columbia Court of Appeal that the accused must present evidence that jurors in the case will be unable to set aside their prejudices before the accused can bring a challenge for cause. This, the Court held, was too high a standard and would present the accused with an "impossible" task. Consequently, the Court held that the only way in Canada for an accused to test whether racially prejudiced jurors will be able to set aside their prejudices and judge impartially is by questioning prospective jurors on challenge for cause:

> In many cases, we can infer from the nature of widespread racial prejudice that some jurors at least may be influenced by those prejudices in their deliberations. Whether or not this risk will materialize must be left to the triers of impartiality on the challenge for cause. To make it a condition of the right to challenge for cause is to require the defence to prove the impossible and to accept that some jurors may be partial (McLachlin J. at para 36).

The Supreme Court canvassed the ways that racial prejudice against the accused may be detrimental, such as the fact that the link between prejudice and the verdict is clearest where there was an "interracial" element to the case or a perceived link between those of the accused's race and the particular crime. The Court, however, also pointed out the fact that racial prejudice may play a role in less obvious ways, such as the fact that racial stereotypes may affect how jurors assess the credibility of the accused. Bias, they say, can shape the information received during the course of the trial to "conform" with the bias, and jurors harbouring racial prejudices may consider those of the accused's race less worthy or perceive a link between those of the accused's race and crime in general:

> In this manner, subconscious racism may make it easier to conclude that a black or aboriginal accused engaged in the crime regardless of the race of the complainant.... A prejudiced juror might see the Crown as non-aboriginal or non-black and hence to be favoured over an aboriginal or black accused.... A prejudiced juror might be inclined to favour non-aboriginal Crown witnesses against the aboriginal accused. Or a racially prejudiced juror might simply tend to side with the Crown because, consciously or unconsciously, the juror sees the Crown as a defender of majoritarian interests against the minority he or she fears or disfavours. Such feelings might incline the juror to resolve any doubts against the accused (McLachlin J. at para. 28–29).

In reaching its decision, the Court referred to and relied on various reports on Aboriginal people and the criminal justice system, including the Royal Commission on the Donald Marshall Jr. Prosecution, and on the works of various Critical Race theorists and others in the area of jury racism. The Supreme Court of Canada in the *Williams* decision also, for the first time, *assertively* stated that judicial notice (acceptance of a fact without the requirement of proof) may be taken of the existence of racial prejudice in the community under the rules of evidence:

> The law of evidence recognizes two ways in which facts can be established in the trial process. The first is by evidence. The second is by judicial notice ... [which] applies to two kinds of facts: (1) facts which are so notorious as not to be the subject of dispute among reasonable persons; and (2) facts that are capable of immediate and accurate demonstration by resorting to readily accessible sources of indisputable accuracy.... The existence of racial prejudice in the community may be a notorious fact within the first branch of the rule (McLachlin J. at para. 54).

The Court was also careful to note that once a finding of fact of widespread racial prejudice in the community is made on the evidence—as it was in the *Williams* case because the accused did present evidence of widespread prejudice against Aboriginal people—judges in subsequent cases may be able to take judicial notice of the fact. The Court held that it may also be possible that judicial notice may be taken under the second branch of the evidentiary rule. The taking of judicial notice, Justice McLachlin asserts, will make it unlikely that long and expensive inquiries into the existence of widespread racial prejudice will be required.

Moreover, the Court held that where there was no evidence to the contrary, where widespread prejudice against people of the accused's race is demonstrated at the national level or provincial level, it will be reasonable to infer that this prejudice is reproduced at the "community" level. From a Critical Race Theory perspective, the Supreme Court of Canada decision in the *Williams* case is a long-awaited victory. It affirms that the right to challenge for cause on the basis of racial prejudice is essential to the *Charter* right to a fair trial as held in the *Parks* decision; it affirms that laws (such as provisions of the Criminal Code) must be interpreted in accordance with *Charter* values and that other *Charter* rights must be interpreted in light of the equality guarantees contained in section 15 of the *Charter*. The Supreme Court of Canada assertively states in *Williams* that the existence of racism in Canadian society may be the subject of judicial notice, and that the existence of widespread racial prejudice at the national or provincial level is cause to infer that it exists at the "community" level and that evidence of extreme prejudice is not required because "a threshold met only in exceptional cases would catch only the grossest forms of racial prejudice. Less extreme situations may raise a real risk of partiality"(McLachlin J. at 510).

The Supreme Court of Canada decision in the *Williams* case is also problematic from a Critical Race Theory perspective, however, because it continues to limit the questions to be asked, thereby restricting the usefulness of the challenge for cause based on racial prejudice. And the Supreme Court also draws a distinction between the Canadian position on challenge for cause and the American position. In Canada there is no "automatic" right to challenge for cause in any case involving a Black accused. The right is more restrictive than the American model; Justice McLachlin states that a "realistic potential" that some members of the jury pool may be biased in a way that may impact negatively on the accused is a requirement. But the "realistic potential" may be demonstrated by establishing widespread prejudice in the community against people of the accused's race. The "restriction" referred to by Justice McLachlin may be more illusory than real given the widespread racial prejudice in Canadian society.

However, the Supreme Court of Canada's refusal to treat the existence of racial prejudice in the same way that it has treated gender discrimination is disturbing. These days the taking of judicial notice of the existence of gender discrimination in Canadian society is not left to the discretion of individual judges, because Canadian jurisprudence now accepts without question the existence of gender discrimination in Canadian society.

The "Erasure" of Race: *R. v. Cole (D)*

The case of *R.* v. *Cole (D)* provides an opportunity to examine issues of race in a different context, namely, with respect to the requirements for a fair trial and nondisclosure of witness statements in the Crown's possession. The *Cole* case involved six Black men accused of aggravated assault. It raises disturbing but recurring questions about the ability of the justice system to protect Black accused.

In 1996, six young Black men in Halifax received sentences of up to ten years for an aggravated assault on a White university student, Darren Watts. These charges stemmed from a fight which occurred outside a fraternity house. The White student received serious injuries as a result. The one Black lawyer involved in this case, Evangeline Cain-Grant, was censored by the Crown when she attempted to put the race issues squarely before the Court at the preliminary inquiry. The Crown, interrupting this Black lawyer's cross-examination of a witness, indicated that attempting to introduce racial issues into the proceedings was "setting the stage and trying to suggest there were perhaps racial overtones to whatever went on inside the party.... This isn't a political forum."[34]

Many in the Black community argued that race played a role in the "excessive" sentences received by the Black youth in comparison to sentences received by Whites convicted of the same or more serious offences. A Black group called Brothers Reaching Out Society argued that the sentences were "the highest sentences ever given out in Nova Scotia's history for that type of unpremeditated incident" (Kimber 1996: 18). Stephen Kimber, a White journalist, defined the issue thus:

> Did the young men convicted of beating Darren Watts get unusually harsh prison sentences simply because they are black? Put more generally: is the Nova Scotia justice system racist? (1996: 18).

Kimber concluded that, in contrast to the 1990 case of a White male, Timothy James Connell, who was convicted in the racially motivated beating of Jeremy Paris, a Black student at the Stellarton campus of the Nova Scotia Community College, where the White youth received only a fine for the attack, the six Black youth in the Watts case received excessive sentences. Further, Kimber noted that,

> unlike the highly publicized Watts case, it appeared that the police spent little time or effort attempting to identify and charge any others who might have been involved in the Paris beating.... The Paris case is far from the only obvious incident of what the Marshall commission once delicately referred to as "differential

treatment of racial minorities" in the criminal justice system.... It wasn't that long ago, for example, that a Digby judge—after acquitting a white man of murdering a black—allowed that we know what happens when those black guys get to drinking (1996: 18).

Kimber concluded by saying that:

> The treatment of those involved in the Watts case—four of the men convicted were first offenders—raises a serious question about whether anything has really changed since those findings and the report of the Marshall inquiry. And the issue is serious. "If the courts condone differential treatment of racial minorities," the inquiry judges pointed out, "the integrity of the entire system will suffer." It has. It does. And it will continue to do so until we finally begin to acknowledge and deal with reality (1996: 18).

Subsequently, Damon Cole, one of the six Black men convicted in the Watts case, had his conviction overturned and a new trial was ordered when the Nova Scotia Court of Appeal (1996, 152 N.S.R.[2d] 321) ruled that he might not have received a fair trial because of the nondisclosure by the Crown of witness statements in the Crown's possession. These witnesses placed Damon Cole on the opposite side of the street at the time the assault on Darren Watts occurred. The Court of Appeal held (Pugsley J.A. at 321) that the nondisclosure by the Crown resulted in an infringement of the principles of fundamental justice enshrined in section 7 of the *Charter* because the right of an accused to full and timely disclosure is incident to the right of an accused to make full answer and defence.

The five other Black accused also appealed their convictions and sentences to the Nova Scotia Court of Appeal, and the Court denied their appeals.[35] The issue at the appeal was the effect of the Crown's nondisclosure of four witness statements on the rights of these five Black accused to a fair trial and their rights to make full answer and defence. The majority in the Nova Scotia Court of Appeal adopted the following test to determine the prejudicial effect on the accused's right to a fair trial and to make full answer and defence:

> To show prejudice as a consequence of the non-disclosure, the appellant must satisfy the court that there is a reasonable probability that, had there been proper disclosure, the result might have been different. A reasonable probability is a probability sufficient to undermine confidence in the outcome (Chipman J.A. at para. 98).

Pursuant to this test, the Court held (Chipman J.A. at para. 98) that the accused received a fair trial and that there was no reasonable probability that had the nondisclosed evidence been made available to the accused at or prior to the trial that the result might have been different. The focus of the majority of the Nova Scotia Court of Appeal in determining whether prejudice resulted was on the issue of the reliability of the result.

Justice Bateman (in dissent from the denial of the appeal of the five Black youths) argued that the majority did not adequately take into account the effect of the nondisclosure on the fairness of the trial. She argued that the standard of proof of prejudice which is required in cases involving ineffective defence counsel is an inappropriate one where, as here, responsibility lies with the government. Justice Bateman pointed out that, in ineffective counsel cases, no responsibility lies with the government because the government does not select the accused's lawyer, but in cases involving nondisclosure (a withholding of information) by the Crown,

> responsibility for the withholding of relevant information from the defence lies squarely with the government through its agents. It is the government that has undertaken action impacting upon the trial process (here, the non-disclosure). While I would not go so far as to invoke a presumption of prejudice in favour of the appellant in such cases, where government action (or inaction) is the source of the complaint, a court must carefully scrutinize the fairness of the process (Bateman J.A. at 73).

She also disagreed with the majority that the defence counsel in this case failed to exercise due diligence (that is to actively seek full disclosure from the Crown) to a sufficient degree to override the prejudice resulting from the failure to disclose.

Notably, the issue of race was never raised in these appeals by the White lawyers representing the accused appellants, either with regard to the disparate sentences handed down to these Black men or in reference to the failure to disclose by the Crown prosecutors. For example, it was not argued that the Crown failure to disclose was motivated by race and consequently, due to this improper motivation, a stay of proceedings should be granted. Instead, the defence conceded that improper motivation was not in issue and that the Crown had "inadvertently" failed to disclose. As a result, a new trial was sought, and not a stay of proceedings based on improper (racial) motivation on the part of the Crown. Consequently, the issue of racial motivation could not be raised on appeal to the Supreme Court of Canada because the argument had not been made in the Court of Appeal and the point had been conceded by the defence lawyers.

The book was closed on this case when the Supreme Court of Canada rendered its decision on February 19, 1998 (*R. v. McQuaid et al.* [1998] 1 S.C.R. 298 [S.C.C.]). The court upheld the convictions of three of the Black men convicted in the assault on Darren Watts and ordered a new trial for two of the accused, one with respect to the beating of Watts, the other with respect to the assault of a Mr. Gillis. The Supreme Court of Canada's analysis is based purely on the accuseds' constitutional rights to disclosure and focuses on the effect of defence counsel's lack of diligence in seeking or not seeking out disclosure from the Crown. There is no contextualized, race-related analysis provided by the Court since the issue of "race" had disappeared from the litigation agenda.

In ordering a new trial for Stacey Skinner (one of the two accused entitled to a new trial), the Supreme Court made the following comments about the nondisclosure issue (*R. v. McQuaid et al.* (Skinner Appeal) at 302–3):

> It was accepted that counsel [for Mr. Skinner] here exercised due diligence.... The fairness of the trial process, given that the Court of Appeal found trial counsel [Ms. Cain-Grant] to be duly diligent in pursuing full disclosure, could have been affected by the Crown's failure to disclose that statement because the defence could have garnered additional evidence flowing from this statement that could have affected its strategy (Cory J. at 302–3).

After the Supreme Court of Canada decision, the case against one of the five Black accused, Damon Cole—who won the right to a new trial at the Nova Scotia Court of Appeal because of the failure of the Crown to disclose witness statements to the defence—was dismissed because the Crown had waited too long in making its determination to retry Cole, thus denying him the right to be tried within a reasonable time pursuant to section 11 of the *Charter*. The other Black defendants are either serving their sentences or are awaiting a new trial as ordered by the Supreme Court of Canada.

The "erasure" of race in this case is troubling in light of the fact that race and nondisclosure were the main factors contributing to the wrongful conviction of Donald Marshall Jr., a Mi'kmaq Nova Scotian wrongfully convicted of murder in the stabbing death of Sandy Seale, a Black Nova Scotian, in 1971. In the Marshall case, the Crown failed to disclose earlier inconsistent statements made to police by two of the teenage eyewitnesses who testified they had seen Donald Marshall Jr. stabbing Sandy Seale. In the Watts case, involving six Black youth, the Crown failed to disclose at or prior to the trial the existence of statements of eyewitnesses which might have assisted the accused in raising a reasonable doubt in the case.

The finding by the Royal Commission on the Donald Marshall Jr.

Prosecution (1989) that the nondisclosure by the Crown, as well as racial prejudice, contributed to the wrongful conviction of Donald Marshall Jr. resulted in the Commission making wide-ranging recommendations concerning prosecutions in Nova Scotia. Specifically, based on its findings about lack of disclosure, the Royal Commission recommended that the Attorney General urge the federal government to amend the Criminal Code to provide for full and timely disclosure of the evidence in possession of the Crown, including information that might mitigate or negate guilt. In the Marshall case, the Royal Commission found that the Crown prosecutors of the time generally disclosed the contents of statements of various witnesses to defence counsel *if they asked for such information*. If defence counsel did not ask, however, the Crown would not make any disclosure. The Marshall Commission (1989: Vol. 1, 243) argued that "without request, the accused is entitled ... to receive any other material or information known to the Crown which tends to mitigate or negate the defendant's guilt ... notwithstanding that the Crown does not intend to introduce such material or information as evidence."[36] The Commission also recommended that judges should not proceed with a case until they were satisfied such disclosure had taken place.

Yet, in spite of these recommendations and the adoption of the disclosure directive, seven years after the Marshall Inquiry, the Crown prosecutors in the Darren Watts case failed to make full disclosure to the accused Black men. Despite this failure, the Nova Scotia Court of Appeal upheld the Crown's argument that the defence had an obligation to seek out full disclosure and failure to do so amounted in this case to a trial tactic on the part of the defence and not a failure to disclose on the part of the Crown.

It has been twenty-five years since Donald Marshall Jr. was wrongfully convicted of murder in the province of Nova Scotia because of his race.[37] The Royal Commission on the wrongful conviction of Donald Marshall Jr. completed its task and tabled its report in 1989. The chairman of the Marshall Commission, Chief Justice Alexander Hickman, said at the beginning of the inquiry process in 1987 that:

> We intend to give consideration to the allegations that minorities of this province [Nova Scotia] are not treated equitably by the justice system. It is our ultimate aim to make recommendations which will ensure that the unfortunate events surrounding Mr. Marshall will not be repeated (1989: Vol. 1, xii).

The race and nondisclosure issues arising from the Watts case and the continuing failure of many aspects of the justice system in Nova Scotia, including police, prosecutors and defence, to heed the recommendations of the Marshall Inquiry arguably illustrate that not much has changed in

Nova Scotia in the seven years since the release of the recommendations. When one of Nova Scotia's few Black lawyers attempted to raise the issue of racism at the preliminary inquiry, she was condemned by the Crown. The Supreme Court of Canada was prevented from hearing the "race" question arising in the *Cole* case because the White appellate lawyers for the defendants had "conceded" that the nondisclosure was "inadvertent" and therefore not racially motivated, and because of the appellate rule that an issue that has not been argued in the court below cannot be argued on appeal. The complete "erasure" of race from the case perpetuated the wrong done to these young Black men by the criminal justice system. Critical Race Litigation strategies must be developed to ensure that the race question is addressed by the courts.

As difficult as Critical Race Litigation and activism may sometimes be, an advocate has a duty and a responsibility under rules of professional ethics to "ask every question, raise every issue and advance every argument, however distasteful [or difficult], that the advocate reasonably thinks will help the client's case; and endeavour to obtain for the client the benefit of any and every right, remedy and defence that is authorized by law" (NSBS 1990: Rule 10). A failure to take a Critical Race position in a case that warrants it should be viewed as a breach of this professional obligation, especially in light of the fact that such failures help to perpetuate the racial inequities that are pervasive in Canadian society and embedded in the Canadian legal system.

Summary

While the prevailing myth in the United States is that Americans have overcome their racist past and are no longer racist, the prevailing myth in Canada is that we are a country without a history of racism. Both myths have led to a failure by the courts to confront the issue of "race" and the role it plays in law. In Canada today, discrimination and racism exist in both subtle and sophisticated forms. Discrimination exists usually in systemic form and is concealed in systems, practices, policies and laws that appear "neutral" and "objective" on their face but have serious detrimental and adverse effects on people of colour.

Historically, Canada did not have the constitutional or statutory mechanisms in place to enable Black Canadians and other people of colour to litigate to seek civil rights and freedom from racial oppression. Human rights legislation is problematic because the vast majority of race-based human rights complaints never reach the board of inquiry stage and there is no recourse to the civil courts for redress. Although the adoption of the *Charter* provides a basis in theory for challenging racist legislation or practices by governments, the *Charter* has to date not been effectively used to combat racism. In Canada, there is no body of jurisprudence recognizing racial equality that can compare to the extensive jurisprudence developed in the United States. Critical Race Litigation is beginning to occur in Canada, however.

Critical Race methodology requires a deconstruction of legal rules and principles and challenges the so-called neutrality and objectivity of laws that oppress Black people and other people of colour. Deconstruction is designed to confront subtle forms of discrimination perpetuated by law.

The case of *R.D.S.* v. *The Queen* can be seen as making a substantial contribution to challenges to racism in Canada. Through Critical Race Litigation, the appellants persuaded the Supreme Court of Canada to expand the "reasonable person" standard. The Court held that the "reasonable person" is aware of the social context of a case, such as the prevalence of racism in Canadian society and in a particular community.

The case of *R.* v. *Parks* demonstrates that a Critical Race Litigation strategy can be employed to confront the courts with the issue of race (in this case, in the context of jury selection). *Parks* stands for the proposition that a defendant's right to challenge prospective jurors for cause based on racial partiality is essential to the accused's constitutional right to a fair trial by an impartial jury. The Ontario Court of Appeal in *Parks* also took judicial notice of the existence of racism in Canadian society and, in particular, anti-Black racism.

In the cases of *R.* v. *McPartlin, R.* v. *Williams* and *R.* v. *Drakes,* we witness a continuing refusal by the British Columbia courts to recognize the right of a Black accused to challenge a prospective juror based on racial bias. The British Columbia Court of Appeal denied the existence of racism and the role it may play in jury selection, and attempted to limit the decision in the *Parks* case to Ontario.

Despite occasional setbacks, Critical Race Theory and Critical Race Litigation in Canada is advancing the interests of Black Canadians through substantive legal outcomes. The Supreme Court was willing to hear an appeal in the *Williams* case and, in doing so, showed a willingness to address the "race" question. The Court held that individual judges may take judicial notice of the existence of racism in a community. However, the Supreme Court of Canada did not itself take judicial notice of the existence of racial prejudice in Canadian society. Instead the Court left it to the discretion of individual judges. Having the Supreme Court of Canada take judicial notice of the existence of racial prejudice at the national level, instead of leaving it to the discretion of individual judges in Canada, would have been the preferred outcome from a Critical Race perspective and would have been in accordance with the Canadian jurisprudence which now accepts the existence of gender discrimination in Canadian society. The Supreme Court of Canada decision in the *Williams* case apparently will not resolve the problem that has arisen in the courts of British Columbia and other jurisdictions where denial of the existence of racism is still prevalent. If a finding of the existence of gender discrimination in a community were left to the discretion of individual male judges, it is unlikely that the feminist agenda would have advanced to the degree that it has in Canadian jurisprudence. The Supreme Court of Canada in *Williams* did, however, reaffirm that Canadian laws and *Charter* rights must be interpreted in light of the equality provisions of section 15(1) of the *Charter*.

From a Critical Race Theory perspective, there are other difficulties with the Supreme Court of Canada's decision in the *Williams* case. For example, the restrictions the Supreme Court imposed in the *Williams* case on the right to challenge for cause are problematic. The right to challenge should be granted in any case involving a Black accused. As well, a cost-benefit analysis (the Supreme Court in *Williams* held that permitting the asking of multiple questions would add to the cost of the trial) which limits the questioning to the one question permitted in the *Parks* decision is unwarranted in light of the important rights of a Black accused to be protected.

Finally, the *Cole* case demonstrates how "erasure of race" from a case where it is an issue and the failure to take a Critical Race Litigation strategy in a case that warrants it are detrimental to the rights of a Black accused and may perpetuate racial inequalities.

Chapter 4

How to Engage
in Critical Race Litigation

Raising Issues of "Race"

Social Context

> "[Critical Race Theory] seeks to achieve racial equality
> through the instrumentalities of law"
> —Roy L. Brooks (1994)

American civil rights activist litigation and (American and Canadian) feminist litigation have evolved through the efforts of people who found themselves excluded from the mainstream of society and the legal profession and consequently were propelled to conceive of new strategies and challenges to the status quo. In this chapter, we move forward from the question of whether racial bias has influenced law, and how Critical Race Litigation worked in selected cases like *R.D.S.* and *Parks,* to a discussion of how to actually implement Critical Race Theory (CRT) in practice. As lawyers, social activists, laypersons and students interested in improving the legal and social status of Black Canadians and other disadvantaged groups in society, our goal is to alter existing institutional arrangements by enhancing the rights of Blacks and others through substantive outcomes. "This approach requires an integration of substantive goals with the actual process of representation," as observed by Cahn (1991: 1) in the context of feminist analysis.[1]

The first step in a Critical Race Litigation strategy is to be aware of the history of racism in Canadian society and the role the myth that Canadian society does not have a racist past plays in the perpetuation of racial oppression. To obtain this understanding, one needs to undertake a consciousness-raising approach. For lawyers, it requires a different approach to legal analysis. Roy L. Brooks describes the process this way:

CRT seeks to raise the consciousness of people of colour and whites alike. It attempts to accomplish this by grounding its analysis on the real everyday experiences of people of colour. Implicit in this approach is the belief that legal analysis can proceed from any number of starting points.... Because the existing legal order, including traditional legal analysis, has a built-in bias in favour of whites, CRT consciously looks at the law from the perspective of non-whites, thus legal analyses presented by race crits are informed by the shared values of people of colour (1994: 94–96).

Brooks says such an approach "does not require the total abandonment of traditional legal analysis or abstract reasoning"; it does, however, require an understanding of the "limits of traditional legal analysis" and its role in the perpetuation of racial inequality (1994: 97).

The *R.D.S.* case is an example of consciousness-raising and the grounding of legal analysis in the everyday lives of Black people. The experience of the Black youth in this case was reflective of the experience of Black people as a group, and particularly Black males, with racism, the police arm of the state and the criminal justice system. This experience is different from that of White members of society. The "social context" argument put forward in the *R.D.S.* case is characteristic of a legal analysis that rejects abstraction and ahistoricism and seeks to contextualize the case in terms of its racial meaning.

In order to contextualize from a Critical Race Theory perspective, the advocate must be aware of or inform herself or himself of the experiences of people of colour with subordination and racism. One does not have to necessarily belong to a racially disadvantaged group to gain this "racial perspective." Brooks, Matsuda and other Critical Race theorists argue that because "race" is not fixed but "a matter of social, historical and cultural construction, racial perspectives can be intellectually accessed transracially" (Matsuda 1996: 22). To this I would add, however, that in order to access the racial perspectives of others one must be willing to accept that Blacks and other people of colour possess a unique voice to articulate these experiences that must be listened and deferred to.[2]

The second step in a Critical Race Litigation strategy comprises the ability to identify when race is an issue in a given circumstance and the ability to identify those oppressions that can be overcome or limited through law. The next step is to deconstruct the discriminatory legal rule, principle, doctrine, policy or practice in order to challenge it. Deconstruction, as noted in previous chapters, is designed to confront both overt and subtle forms of discrimination perpetuated by law. The question to be asked by the lawyer, social activist or others engaged in Critical Race

Litigation is: Does the doctrine, legal rule, principle, policy or practice at issue in the particular case subordinate people of colour? If the answer is yes, the next step involves an in-depth analysis of the rule (etc.) to flush out what may often be hidden forms of discrimination. The final step in a Critical Race approach is reconstruction. What are the alternatives, if any, to the existing doctrine, legal rule, principle or practice that will not subordinate people of colour or will lessen the subordination of people of colour? What harm or benefit to the Black client and/or the Black community might result from the adoption or nonadoption by the courts of the change sought? What are the risks in pursuing a Critical Race Litigation strategy?

Issue Spotting: When Is "Race" An Issue?

Lawyers are traditionally trained in law school to "spot issues" involved in particular areas of law. For example, based on an analysis of facts presented in a particular situation, lawyers are trained to identify areas of law that may be relevant to specific facts, that is, whether the problem is a criminal-law, contract-law, tort-law (disputes between individuals governed by the civil courts) or some other kind of problem. From this broad determination, the lawyer is then able to determine what specific legal issues are raised by the facts within the general area of law.

In criminal law, for example, the facts may be that X shot and killed Y and has been charged with murder (the broad issue is identified as a criminal law problem). More specific issues raised by this scenario which must be identified by the advocate in the context of criminal law may be: Can the Crown prove that X committed the *actus reus* of the crime of murder (the physical act of causing someone's death)? Can the Crown prove that X had the requisite criminal intent, or *mens rea,* to cause the death of Y to support a conviction for first- or second-degree murder? Is this a case of accidental death or manslaughter? Does X have any defences to the crime, such as self-defence, provocation, insanity, etc.? Many other issues may arise on the facts as presented by the client, which the lawyer will have to identify and analyse in order to effectively represent her or his client in court.

Law students have not, however, traditionally been taught how to "spot issues" relating to race.[3] For example, what happens when we change the basic facts of X shoots and kills Y, by adding that X (the accused) was Black and Y (the victim) was White? Traditional, noncontextualized and ahistorical legal analysis would dictate no change in the advocate's approach to the legal problem. It would still be a criminal law problem requiring a "neutral" and "objective" analysis which would not take the race of the parties or the social reality of racism into consideration.

A Critical Race Theory analysis, however, would require the advocate to ask the "race" question and to contextualize the problem by putting it in the social context of the history of racism. A Critical Race advocate faced with an interracial crime must ask: What role did race play in the crime itself, and what role will race play in the trial of this Black accused? From that analysis, the advocate can determine what defences may apply to the circumstances (for example, self-defence or provocation) and whether the rules relating to these defences require deconstruction to determine if they subordinate and/or have an adverse impact on people of colour. Additionally, the advocate will analyse the jury selection process to determine whether it impacts adversely on people of colour and will define a legal strategy designed to challenge the constitutionality of these statutory provisions based on the equality provisions of the *Canadian Charter of Rights and Freedoms*. Other Critical Race Litigation strategies may also be required, such as focusing media attention on the racial implications of the case, securing funding support for *Charter* challenges or seeking out Black and other organizations to intervene on appeal.

In interracial sexual assault cases, the issue of race will be a subtext if the victim is White and the accused is Black. The issue of race will also be a subtext if the accused is White and the victim is a person of colour, because it may impact on the outcome of the trial of the White accused, by reducing the likelihood of a guilty verdict, or on the sentence imposed upon him or her to the detriment of the victim's rights. Even if the facts presented do not involve an "interracial" crime of violence but instead some other nonviolent crime, such as drug charges, the issue of race will often be significant, affecting the police officer's decision to lay or not lay charges, pretrial release, conviction and the sentence imposed. The issues of race and racism relevant to these different contexts must also be evaluated, and suitable litigation strategies must be identified.

Nor is "issue spotting" with respect to race confined to the criminal law area of practice. These issues also arise in the context of family law, for example, in access and custody issues involving interracial couples and what is in the best interests of their mixed heritage offspring, or in the context of interracial adoptions.

As well, it is becoming increasingly obvious that the system which confines Blacks and other disadvantaged groups to seeking redress for discrimination through human rights complaints is woefully inadequate (this issue is discussed in depth below) and that a reconsideration of the law that denies victims of discrimination the right to sue in the civil courts should be undertaken. The human rights system has been severely criticized by academics, practitioners, and targets of discrimination, especially with respect to its inability to deal with "new theories of equality and discrimination" (Mendes 1995: 2-36). A *Charter* challenge to the human rights system itself may be the appropriate Critical Race Litigation strategy to pursue.

The guiding rule for determining when "race" is an issue in a given case is to take as a starting point Supreme Court Justice L'Heureux Dubé's holding in the *R.D.S.* case (at para. 47–48) that the reasonable and right-minded person (including lawyers) in Canadian society would be knowledgeable and aware of the existence of racism in the local community and in Canadian society and would also be knowledgeable of *Charter* values and supportive of the principles of equality set out in section 15 of the *Charter*. Armed with this knowledge and awareness, advocates and others involved in Critical Race strategies should ask the "race question" whenever they have a Black client and undertake a contextualized and non-ahistorical analysis of the situation to determine if Critical Race Litigation is required in the best interests of her or his client and/or the Black community as a whole. The issue of race should only be ruled out *after* an analysis that is grounded in the everyday lived experiences of Black people has been made. If "race" and racism are live issues in the case, the advocate should fearlessly raise them, just as she or he would fearlessly raise any other issue that would benefit the client. Critical Race Theory should be methodically applied to all areas of law, and especially to those rules, principles, practices and doctrines which appear "race-neutral," precisely because what appears to be "race-neutral" may in fact be discriminatory in its effects (Brooks 1994: 85).

Some readers may ask whether raising the issue of race merely injects race into the proceeding when it is unwarranted. When a similar question is asked in the context of gender analysis and equality arguments under section 15 of the *Charter,* one commentator responds by asking a question of her own: "Why should equality arguments not be seen as routine?"(Boyle et al. 1994: 203).[4] Raising a live and relevant issue such as race is not only an advocate's duty; disregarding that duty may perpetuate the role that race plays in law. Questioning whether you are "injecting" race into a "race-neutral" process weakens your resolve to perform the advocate's duty to ask every question, raise every issue and advance every argument that will help the client's case and obtain for the client the benefit of any and every right, remedy and defence that is authorized by law. Persons who are tempted to question themselves should reflect on Justice Doherty's observations in the *Parks* case: "A question directed at revealing those whose bias renders them partial does not 'inject' racism into the trial, but seeks to prevent that bias from destroying the impartiality of the jury deliberations" (at 361–62).

Summary

The first step in a Critical Race Litigation strategy is to be aware of the social reality of racism in Canadian society. This awareness comes about by undertaking a consciousness-raising approach. A race-conscious approach requires a different methodology of legal analysis. Critical Race Theory requires that we look at the law from the perspective of people of colour and allow our analysis to be informed by this perspective. Although this approach may not require a total abandonment of traditional legal analysis, it does require an understanding of the limits of that analysis.

The second step in a Critical Race Litigation strategy is to identify when "race" is an issue. Something happens to the analysis when we contextualize the problem. A Critical Race Theory analysis requires the advocate to ask the "race" question and to locate the problem within the social reality of racism. This knowledge and awareness should prompt advocates and others involved in Critical Race strategies to ask the "race" question whenever they have a Black client and to do a contextualized and non-ahistorical analysis of the situation to determine if a Critical Race Litigation strategy is required in the circumstances of the case. The issue of race should only be ruled out after an analysis that is grounded in the everyday lived experiences of people of colour has been made. Critical Race Theory should be applied to all areas of law, including those rules, principles, practices and doctrines which appear "neutral" on their face because they may be discriminatory in effect. The final steps in a Critical Race Litigation strategy include identifying those oppressions that can be overcome or limited through law and deconstructing the discriminatory legal rule, principle, doctrine or practice and challenging it through law. The final step is rendering a reconstruction of the discriminatory law that benefits as much as possible the Black community, people of colour in general or other disadvantaged groups in society.

Deconstruction/Reconstruction:
Framing the Issue in the Canadian Context

Jury Selection Cases

An important step in Critical Race Litigation is to identify those oppressions that can be overcome through law. A significant point of oppression for Black people and other people of colour is in the area of jury selection. All too often, Black people are excluded from jury service in Canada. Extensive social science research in the United States shows that racially prejudiced attitudes translate into discriminatory verdicts within the jury room, and empirical studies using mock juries suggest that juries are more inclined to convict defendants who are not of the same race as themselves. However, this is not just an American phenomenon. Justice Doherty, in the *Parks* decision, noted that "these studies go at least as far as to indicate that there is a realistic possibility that jurors' verdicts are affected by the race of the accused where that accused is of a different race than the juror" (at 369). The Royal Commission on the Donald Marshall Jr. Prosecution and the Manitoba Justice Inquiry both documented that the perception of Black Canadians is that they are not treated fairly by the criminal justice system. Based on consultations with Black and Aboriginal Nova Scotians, the solicitor representing the Attorney General at the Royal Commission inquiry recommended that a study of proportional representation of visible minorities on juries in Nova Scotia should be undertaken, and the Royal Commission endorsed this recommendation. As of the time of writing, the recommended study had still not been conducted (NSLRC 1993a).

Through Critical Race Theory we can work at the individual level of representation or collectively to effect precedent-setting cases in the area of jury selection, not just with respect to the challenge for cause procedures under section 638 of the Criminal Code addressed in the *Parks* and *Williams* cases discussed above, but also with respect to challenges to the array and the discriminatory use of peremptory challenges. This requires us to raise the race-consciousness of judges and officials who administer the jury selection process and to develop jury discrimination case law. We must begin to formulate deconstruction strategies on three fronts: (1) *Charter* challenges to the composition of the jury (challenges to the array), (2) elimination of the peremptory challenge to prevent its discriminatory use by prosecutors, or alternatively, a move away from the notion of "formal equality" in the context of its use and (3) expansion of the *Parks* decision to allow for properly constructed questions (not just the one question permitted in *Parks*) with respect to challenge for cause designed to eliminate racial prejudice on the part of jurors. The deconstruction process necessitates the asking of two important questions. The first is: "Does this legal rule, principle, doctrine, policy or practice subordinate people of colour?"[5] In order to provide an answer to this question, Critical Race Theory methodology requires that people of colour be placed at the centre of the analysis. Remember that a Critical Race Theory analysis requires a contextualized approach which rejects legal abstraction and ahistoricism and seeks to contextualize the problem within its racial meaning. For example, the experience of Black people and other people of colour with the jury selection process is different than that of White people. To be able to intellectually access this racial perspective interracially, a non-Black person has to listen to and defer to the experiences of Black people with the jury selection process and be aware of or make themselves aware of the impact of racism on this process.

If the answer to the first question is yes, the next question to be asked in the deconstruction process is: What aspect(s) of the legal rule, principle, doctrine, policy or practice contribute to the subordination? This facet of the deconstruction process requires an in-depth analysis of the rule from a Critical Race Theory perspective, that is, it requires the advocate to reject the traditional legal analysis that adheres to the concept of "neutrality'" and "objectivity" in law and to invoke an analysis that goes behind laws that may appear to be "race-neutral" on their face to determine whether they may have a discriminatory effect on people of colour.

When we deconstruct the jury selection process by asking the first question required of a deconstruction analysis—Does this process subordinate people of colour?"—what answer do we get? By placing Black people at the centre of the analysis as a Critical Race Theory approach requires us to do, we discern that the Royal Commission on the Donald Marshall Jr. Prosecution and the Manitoba Justice Inquiry both documented that the perception of Black Canadians is that they are not treated fairly by the criminal justice system. We discern also, based on consultations with Black and Aboriginal Nova Scotians, that the solicitor representing the Attorney General at the Royal Commission inquiry recommended that a study of proportional representation of visible minorities on juries in Nova Scotia should be undertaken, and the Royal Commission endorsed this recommendation. In addition to these inquiries which documented the experiences of people of colour, there are numerous other commission and task force reports, including the report of the Commission on Systemic Racism in the Ontario Criminal Justice System, which documented that:

> Many black and other racialized persons perceive members of their communities as under-represented on juries. General concerns about their exclusion were raised repeatedly during public consultations. Specifically, participants stressed that under-representation on juries trying racialized accused persons or "high-profile" white accused—such as police officers—who have killed or injured a racialized victim tend to promote distrust in the system.... Black Ontarians are especially likely to be under-represented on juries.... Findings from the Commission's general population survey ... though by no means conclusive, support the perception that black people are under-represented on Ontario juries. No black residents reported having served on a jury (1995: 250).

Anti-racism advocacy groups such as the Urban Alliance on Race Relations (1993: 41) founded in 1975, Black academics and especially those in disciplines such as the social sciences and the human services sector have also documented the exclusion of Blacks and other people of colour from the jury selection process in Canada (James 1996).[6] And in 1994 and 1993, Justice Canada and the Nova Scotia Law Reform Commission (NSLRC), respectively, undertook studies into the jury selection process in Canada and Nova Scotia. The Justice Canada–commissioned study, conducted by David Pomerant in April 1994, concluded that "clear criteria for representativeness that include representation for racial, ethnic and cultural minorities, should be implemented across the country" (Pomerant 1994: 79), and the Law Reform Commission of Nova Scotia concluded that "there are concerns that people from Black and Aboriginal communities are rarely seen on Jury Panels" (1993: 2).

Based on this contextualized analysis, the advocate can conclude that the answer to the first question required of a deconstruction analysis— Does the jury selection process in Canada subordinate people of colour?"—is yes. From this question we move to the second question required of a deconstruction analysis: What aspect(s) of the legal rule, principle, doctrine, policy or practice (in this case the jury selection process) contribute to the subordination? As previously noted, this facet of the deconstruction process requires an in-depth analysis from a Critical Race Theory perspective, that is, it requires the advocate to reject traditional legal analysis that adheres to the concepts of "neutrality" and "objectivity" in law and to invoke an analysis that goes behind law that may appear to be "race-neutral" on its face to determine whether or not it has a discriminatory effect on Black Canadians.

The Provincial Jury Selection Process and Challenges to the Array

As noted, the jury selection process in a criminal proceeding is governed by both federal statute (the Criminal Code of Canada) and provincial statutes (provincial juries Acts). The Criminal Code governs the "in-court" portion of the jury selection process, that is, challenges for cause, peremptory challenges and challenges to the array. Peremptory challenges and challenges for cause (discussed more fully below) are governed by sections 634 and 638 of the Criminal Code. Challenges to the array (an in-court challenge by either the crown prosecutor or the defence lawyer to the jury panel) are governed by sections 629 and 630 of the Criminal Code. The basis for challenging the jury panel, or the *array,* as it is most commonly referred to, is severely restricted by the Criminal Code sections. The only grounds for challenge under section 629 are intentional wilful misconduct, or partiality or fraud by the sheriff in returning the panel.[7] The provincial statutes govern the first stage of the jury selection (the out-of-court, or pretrial) process, which includes the eligibility criteria (who can serve as a juror) and the creation of the jury source lists (rolls) and random selection procedures which ultimately create the jury panels.

Taking Nova Scotia as an example of the provincial responsibility for jury selection in criminal jury trials only, the Nova Scotia *Juries Act*[8] governs the rules for the pretrial selection of prospective jurors. The procedures for jury selection in Nova Scotia were outlined by the Nova Scotia Law Reform Commission in its *Discussion Paper on Juries* in 1993.[9] Under the Act, the province is divided into jury districts and each district is responsible for drawing up the jury list for criminal trials in that district for the year. Each district has a jury committee made up of a jury officer, a representative of each municipal unit in the district and a representative of the Department of Justice which is responsible for drawing up the jury list and presenting it to a judge for approval. Under section 7(5) of the *Juries Act,* the names of prospective jurors for the year are taken from the election or voting lists or other available information and, under section 7(1) of the Act, the jury committee is to select the names of qualified prospective jurors "randomly" from the jury list.[10] The jury committee reviews each name randomly selected from the voter's list to determine whether the person is qualified. Section 5 exempts certain people from jury duty (such as lawyers, doctors and so on) and the prospective juror must be eighteen years of age, a Canadian citizen and have resided in the jury district for one year. The *Juries Act* does not describe the method of random selection and the jury list review undertaken by the jury committee is confidential. The Law Reform Commission of Nova Scotia notes that, in some small communities, personal knowledge may also be used to disqualify people. Once the jury list has been drawn up, a judge approves it or sends it back for another if he or she is not satisfied.

Once this process is completed, the approved jury list will be used in the district for one year to provide jury panels. Jury panels are selected from this jury list at the start of each Supreme Court criminal term or session. Juror notices will be sent out to a random selection of names on the jury list. The persons randomly chosen must appear in court and make themselves available to be chosen for the final jury panel unless they are excused or exempt in advance. "Once the Panel is in Court and a roll call has taken place to ensure that all people summoned and not excused in advance are in attendance, then the 'in-court' selection procedures begin.... the procedure from this point forward is governed by the Criminal Code" (NSLRC 1993: 8).

In 1991 the Supreme Court of Canada in the *Sherratt* case (63 C.C.C. [3d] 193 [S.C.C.]) analysed the importance of trial by jury and concluded that:

> The Law Reform Commission of Canada ... sets out numerous
> rationales for the past and continued existence of the jury. The
> jury, through its collective decision making, is an excellent fact-
> finder; due to its representative character, it acts as the con-
> science of the community; the jury can act as the final bulwark
> against oppressive laws or their enforcement; it provides a means
> whereby the public increases its knowledge of the criminal jus-
> tice system and it increases, through the involvement of the
> public, societal trust in the system as a whole.... The modern jury
> ... was envisioned as a representative cross-section of society,
> honestly and fairly chosen at 203.

The provincial responsibility in the jury selection process (through
provincial juries acts) is to guarantee representativeness in the initial
array, while the federal responsibility (through the Criminal Code provisions) is to guarantee impartiality. From a Critical Race perspective there
are problems with both the provincial and Criminal Code jury selection
procedures. The provincial jury selection process is problematic in that
the initial array, that is, the jury lists prepared by the sheriff or other
official under the provincial Acts, systemically excludes or causes under-
representation of Blacks and other people of colour. Additionally, the
random selection procedures (a process by which the person making the
selection for the final jury panel from the jury lists does not have the
ability to choose a particular individual based on race or personal preference) do not ensure the representation of Blacks on a jury panel. Simultaneously, the Criminal Code provisions limit the ability of Blacks to
challenge the array by imposing a proof-of-intent requirement, while
ignoring the adverse-effects form of discrimination imbedded in the process. As Cynthia Petersen notes:

> The jury selection procedure in criminal trials is deeply flawed....
> Exclusion results from the combination of numerous factors which
> arise at different stages in the jury selection process.... In most
> provinces, sheriffs are authorized to exercise their discretion in
> selecting the lists from which the jury rolls are compiled. In some
> areas, provincial and municipal electoral lists continue to be used
> in the preparation of jury rolls, notwithstanding that their enu-
> meration processes often result in the under-representation of
> certain segments of the population. Municipal assessment rolls
> are also used and they similarly under-represent particular populations.
> They include only the names of property owners and thereby
> exclude lower income groups. This exclusion has a dispropor-
> tionate impact on people of colour who are over-represented

among the poor and working class and are therefore under-represented in municipal assessment rolls (1993: 147–48).

In Nova Scotia, for example, under section 7(5) of the *Juries Act,* the names of prospective jurors are primarily taken from the election or voting lists (although they may be taken from other available information). David Pomerant, after canvassing the various provincial juries acts in his study of the jury selection process for Justice Canada, concluded that:

> An analysis of all of the Provincial approaches must cause one to question seriously the assertions of the Supreme Court of Canada, in *Sherratt*, that provincial selection procedures, particularly governing the assembly of source lists and the requirement of random selection, guarantee representativeness in the sources of jury selection, and that little objection can be made regarding this characteristic of Canadian juries (1994: 48).

Jury panels have been challenged in the past on the basis that they were not properly representative of the community. As noted by Cynthia Petersen, who canvassed the existing Canadian jurisprudence on challenges to the array based on racial exclusion, the first Canadian jury case involving an allegation of racial discrimination was *R. v. Bradley and Martin*, decided in 1973 (23 C.R.N.S. 33 [Ont. H.C.]). In this case, two Black men challenged the array because there were no Black jurors. Petersen notes that the Ontario High Court in its decision in this case applied a formal equality approach (a similarly situated test requiring that all accused persons be treated the same) to the challenge under the *Canadian Bill of Rights*. The trial judge concluded that the Bill did not guarantee or require that there be persons of a particular race, national origin, colour, religion or sex present on a jury, and that under the Criminal Code the mere fact that no Black people were on the jury panel did not prove partiality on the part of the sheriff. Peterson also observes that it is not surprising that reliance on the *Bill of Rights* in subsequent cases proved to be unsuccessful (Petersen 1993: 168).

A number of cases involving challenges to the array have been brought by Aboriginal persons. In 1984, in the case of *R. v. Bird* ([1984] 1 C.N.L.R. 122 [Sask. C.A.]), an Aboriginal man who was convicted by a jury containing no Aboriginal persons challenged the array[11] on appeal on the ground that the jury selection process systematically excluded Aboriginal people. As noted by Petersen (1993), this case was promising because, "for the first time, an appellate court had departed from the traditional requirement that a challenge to the array had to be based on partiality, fraud or wilful misconduct on the part of the sheriff." Even though in the *Bird* case itself the court held that the Aboriginal accused had not established that the jury selection process in his case had resulted in systemic exclusion of an identifiable group, the court stated as *obiter dictum* (remarks in a court opinion entirely unnecessary for the resolution of the particular case) that a jury selection process that systemically excluded an identifiable group may be a sufficient ground to overturn a conviction even if the exclusion was unintentional.

This analysis in the *Bird* case "went virtually unnoticed by courts in future cases involving a challenge to the array, and cases like *Bradley and Martin* served as precedent to support the principle that proof of intentional exclusion was required to found a violation of the Bill of Rights" (Petersen 1993: 150). Petersen argues that the Supreme Court's suggestion in the *Sherratt* case that the existing provincial legislation governing the jury selection process guarantees representativeness, at least in the initial array, is wrong. She points to the fact that the Court does not mention the jurisprudence or literature which contradicted these findings and suggests that these comments in the *Sherratt* case "were unrelated to the issue before the Court as the case at bar did not involve a challenge to the array" (1993: 164). Other commentators have made similar observations. For example, David Pomerant, in his study on the jury selection process funded by Justice Canada noted that the Court in *Sherratt* relied on a study prepared for the Law Reform Commission of Canada in determining that the provincial selection procedures "guarantee" representativeness in source lists and jury panels, but a direct examination of the study referred to by the Court, as well as an examination of the existing provincial statutes and the administration of these statutes "suggests that this conclusion [that provincial procedures guarantee representativeness] should be viewed with caution" (1994: 20).

In examining the case law on challenges to the array made under the *Canadian Charter of Rights and Freedoms*, Petersen (1993: 163) concludes that, for the most part, challenges to the array under the *Charter* have been unsuccessful and she attributes this to a number of factors. First, the earlier cases such as *R. v. Nepoose (no. 1)* of 1991 (85 Alta. L.R. [2d] 8 [Alta. Q.B.], a case alleging an under-representation of women, including Aboriginal women, on a jury panel) relied on the *Charter* section 11 right to trial by jury. This reliance, Petersen contends, effectively removed the ability to discuss equality under section 15(1) of the *Charter,* thereby making it "impossible" to discuss the importance of representative juries. Second, challenges to the array based on a violation of section 11 of the *Charter* would only assist some defendants and would, as Petersen notes, "be of no assistance to a man like Rodney King [because] it fails to address equality considerations.... It is intended merely to protect legal rights of individuals who come into conflict with the law" (1993: 164). Third, section 11 of the *Charter* is a limited solution because it only applies to persons charged with an offence (accused persons), which Petersen contends would not protect the right of a Black victim of racist violence to have proportional representation of Black people on the jury panel. In other words, section 11 of the *Charter* is only helpful to defendants, it is of no benefit to the Crown or victims in criminal cases or to any party in civil jury trials (Petersen 1993: 166).

Petersen argues that the issue of representativeness on jury panels is really a question of equality and should be addressed as such. She points out, however, that when the relevance of section 15(1) of the *Charter* was argued in the 1986 case of *R. v. Kent, Sinclair and Gode* (40 Man. R. [2d] 160 [Man. C.A.], a case where an Aboriginal accused alleged that his equality rights had been violated because members of his race were under-represented on his jury panel), it was unsuccessful. The Manitoba Court of Appeal followed prior cases under the federal statutory *Bill of Rights* and concluded that there had to be evidence of intentional exclusion for a challenge to the array to succeed under the *Charter*; it was not enough that there was under-representation of members of a particular race on the array (Petersen 1993: 166). Petersen notes, however, that *Kent* was decided before the Supreme Court of Canada rendered its decision in the *Andrews* v. *The Law Society of British Columbia* case ([1989] 1 S.C.R. 143 [S.C.C.]), which abandoned the doctrine of formal equality followed under the *Bill of Rights*. Instead, the Supreme Court of Canada in the *Andrews* case held that proof of intent was not required to show discrimination, instead, proof of discriminatory effects of a particular law, policy, principle or practice was sufficient to establish a violation of *Charter* rights. As a result of the *Andrews* decision, Petersen and others argue that provincial statutes governing out-of-court jury selection procedures may be unconstitutional despite the good intentions of the people who administer these statutes because they result in under-representation of people of colour and have a discriminatory effect on them. Petersen also argues that section 629(1) of the Criminal Code, which restricts challenges for cause to those cases where "willful misconduct" or intent is required, may also be unconstitutional (1993: 167).

Petersen (1993: 167) notes, however, that legal arguments incorporating the doctrine enunciated in *Andrews* have not been made in subsequent cases involving challenges to the array. In one such case before the British Columbia Supreme Court, no allegations of an infringement of section 15(1) of the *Charter* was made. In the absence of such arguments, the Court indicated that the *Bill of Rights* cases determined the issue under the *Charter*, so that proof of intentional discrimination or "willful misconduct" must still be established. The issue has not yet made its way to the

Supreme Court of Canada.

A Critical Race Litigation strategy should be used in an appropriate case to challenge unrepresentative arrays both with respect to the source lists and the jury panel itself as a violation of an accused's section 15(1) equality rights under the *Charter*. A challenge could be brought with respect to the provincial statutes, alleging that jury selection procedures governed by these statutes have an adverse effect on Black Canadians, even though the statutes may appear "race neutral" on their face, and thereby infringe the right of the Black accused (or victim) to equality before and under the law. In an appropriate case, a challenge could also be brought with respect to the federal legislation governing jury selection, with respect to the section 629 restriction of challenges to the array to cases involving intentional misconduct on the part of officials. Such a section 15(1) challenge would be based on the argument that the restriction is not in keeping with the principles set out in *Andrews,* which recognized that neutral rules may have an unintended discriminatory impact that can support *Charter* relief. The Supreme Court of Canada decision in the *Williams* case discussed above also supports the notion that laws must be read in light of equality before and under the law enshrined in section 15 of the *Charter*.

There is ample evidence in the form of academic literature, department of justice studies, law reform commission studies and other sources to support the argument that there is an under-representation and exclusion of people of colour and, in particular, Black people from Canadian juries. This literature also documents the harmful effects of this exclusion on the affected groups and on the legitimacy of the administration of justice in our society. Ensuring representativeness on the jury panel will also enhance the appearance of fairness in the eyes of the accused and other members of minority groups facing discrimination.

The Reconstruction Question in the Provincial Jury Selection Process
The final step in a Critical Race Theory and Litigation approach is reconstruction. What are the alternatives, if any, to the existing doctrine, legal rule, principle, policy or practice that will not subordinate people of colour or lessen the subordination of people of colour? In the reconstruction analysis of the jury selection process, a number of alternatives can be canvassed. Critical Race theorists contend that merely requiring representative jury lists does not ensure that the final jury panel will be representative. This is true because Blacks constitute a minority and are outnumbered by Whites. The discrepancy is sufficiently great that merely putting Black names in a box with the majority and selecting randomly will not guarantee that Black names will be drawn.

With respect to the jury selection procedures governed by section

629 of the Criminal Code, the appropriate approach would be to seek to have the section declared unconstitutional by the court because it violates section 15(1) of the *Charter* and declared to be of no force or effect under section 52(1) of the *Charter*. Section 52(1) states that the Constitution of Canada is the supreme law of Canada, and any law that is inconsistent with the provisions of the Constitution is, to the extent of the inconsistency, of no force or effect. Parliament would then have to amend the section to reflect *Charter* values.

Lobbying the political arm of government to amend the section prior to litigation may also prove effective. Any amendment effective in eradicating the subordination of Blacks and other people of colour would have to recognize that a challenge to the array should be permitted where the effect of the existing jury selection process is to exclude or cause an under-representation of the disadvantaged group with respect to jury service.

The provincial statutes governing the jury selection process would have to be dealt with on a case-by-case basis. To again take the Nova Scotia *Juries Act* as an example, after acknowledging that this legislation does not fulfil its function of ensuring representativeness, the Law Reform Commission of Nova Scotia undertook a review of the existing procedures. The Commission made recommendations designed to improve the Act's effectiveness with respect to the goals of representativeness, impartiality and administrative efficiency. The Commission recommended that the random selection process should be maintained while expanding the sources from which the jury lists are chosen by including such sources as medical service insurance lists, so the voters' list would not be the only source. This proposal is woefully inadequate, however, and will not ensure that Blacks and Aboriginal Nova Scotians will be represented on juries in that province. In fact, two members of the Nova Scotia Law Reform Commission (1993b) voiced this concern in a separate, dissenting report which stated the following:

> We advocate that a jury selection process which will ensure representations of visible minorities on Jury Panels is necessary to achieve the goal of an accused person being judged by one's peers. We disagree with a majority of the Commissioners who propose that pure random selection is the goal.... Because the majority of the Commission and the advisory group have made random selection their goal, we have not explored the necessary research and possible options available to determine how to ensure that a Black or Aboriginal person, if seeking trial by jury, will have persons from their same cultural/racial background on the jury.

The recommendation made by the dissenting Nova Scotia law reform commissioners was that instead of having one box of jurors' names from which all potential jurors are chosen, as advocated by the majority of the law reform commissioners, there should be three boxes from which the judge picks the names of the jury panel: one box containing the names of Black Nova Scotians, one for Aboriginal Nova Scotians and one for all other residents. They advocate that proportional representation should be determined on the basis of race or cultural group rather than on municipal residency.

The majority of the Nova Scotia law reform commissioners do not provide an analysis of why the random jury selection procedure should be maintained. They say only that, "The principles of representativeness, impartiality and administrative efficiency in the context of the jury system should be achieved through random selection and removal of systemic and other discriminatory exclusions and exemptions rather than through selective representation" (1993a: 23).

As is so often the case, the failure to provide a disciplined analysis of the reasons behind the recommendation prevents a critique of the values or assumptions underlying the preference for maintaining a discriminatory status quo. At the time of writing, recommendations made by the Law Reform Commission of Nova Scotia which would allow people such as doctors, dentists, clergy and Armed Forces personnel to serve on a jury have been implemented, but the issue of under-representative juries for Blacks and Aboriginal people is still left unaddressed.

The debate over proportional representation, or affirmative action, in relation to jury selection has been raging in the United States for some time. Many Critical Race theorists argue that the only way to end all-White juries is to take a colour-conscious approach in jury selection procedures (Alschuler 1995: 707). There are some affirmative-action jury selection measures in place in the United States. For example, Alschuler notes that in Arizona the state bar has proposed dividing jury lists into subsets by race and drawing jurors from each subset. He notes, however, that there seems to be less controversy over seeking to provide "racial balance" in the jury pools than there is over seeking racial balance in the final juries themselves. He argues that the reason for attempting to create racially balanced jury pools (as the majority of the Nova Scotia law reform commissioners were prepared to do) is to make racially balanced juries more likely. Why, he asks, is it different in principle to reject a "colour-blind" policy when actually selecting the jury panel based on race? (1995: 711–12).

In the United States the principle of colour-blindness may give rise to successful constitutional challenges to affirmative action in the jury selection process. In Canada, however, an affirmative action approach to jury selection may actually be protected by the *Charter*.

One of the arguments put forward by opponents of affirmative jury selection procedures is that they constitute "reverse discrimination." Such a challenge under section 15(1) is unlikely to be successful, however. Affirmative action jury selection procedures will likely be saved under section 15(2) of the *Charter*, which states that:

> (2) Subsection (1) does not preclude any law, program or activity that has as its object the amelioration of conditions of disadvantaged individuals or groups including those that are disadvantaged because of race, national or ethnic origin, colour, religion, sex, age or mental or physical disability.

Affirmative jury selection procedures are arguably a reasonable limit on the right of White persons to serve on a jury and could be justified under section 15(2) of the *Charter* because the goal, or object, of such measures would be to ameliorate the condition of a disadvantaged group. In this case, the condition of disadvantage is the under-representation of Blacks and other people of colour on juries in Canada. Affirmative jury selection procedures probably would not be found "void" because they "promote, rather than impede, the public policy of equality" (*Canada Trust Co.* v. *Ontario [Human Rights Commission]*, 1990, 74 O.R. [2d] 481 [Ont. C.A.]). This analysis is also in keeping with the position taken (but not generally followed) by the Supreme Court of Canada in the *Andrews* case that a court should be cognizant of the "social" and "historical" context of the particular disadvantaged group under consideration.

Another argument put forward by opponents to an affirmative jury selection process is that:

> Engineering jury composition to reflect only the interests or characteristics of the accused, or of the accused and victim ... would be incompatible with the purpose of jury trials stated by the Supreme Court of Canada ... which has clearly stated that the jury is a vehicle for *public* involvement in the administration of justice and a vehicle for the expression of a *community* conscience (Pomerant 1994).

Critical Race theorists are puzzled by this argument and refute it by arguing that all-White juries do not act as a vehicle for public involvement since they exclude by their very nature a significant portion of the population, namely people of colour. Nor can they be seen as expressing a "community conscience," unless you take this term to mean a "majoritarian conscience," or "the conscience of the dominant group." In fact, there is no single "community" or "public" perspective, but rather a variety of community perspectives reflecting different experiences. To reflect the community accurately, measures should be taken to ensure that all relevant perspectives are present on juries.

Other arguments against affirmative action in jury selection often include the "slippery slope" argument addressed by Justice McLachlin in the context of the challenge for cause procedure under consideration in the *Williams* case. In the present context, this argument goes something like this: To participate in an affirmative-action jury selection process would mean extra costs, entail complex procedures and where do you draw the line? Must a jury panel be composed of all racial, ethnic and other groups that make up a community? Justice McLachlin's response in the context of the section 11 right to a fair trial was that practical concerns cannot outweigh or negate the right to a fair trial and a cost-benefit analysis cannot ultimately be determinative. Nor should such concerns negate the right to equality before and under the law contained in section 15 of the *Charter* in the context of affirmative action in jury selection.

Given the widespread racial prejudice in Canada experienced by Blacks and Aboriginals, as amply documented by various task forces, royal commissions and law reform commissions, and recognized by the Supreme Court of Canada in *Williams* and *R.D.S.,* and by the Ontario Court of Appeal in *Parks,* any jury panel selected by a "random" process that has the effect of excluding or under-representing Black and Aboriginals is suspect. Line drawing is something that occurs in law on a regular basis and difficulties inherent in identifying the outer limits of policies or procedures have not prevented useful new initiatives in other contexts. To the extent that any segment of Canadian society is systematically excluded from the jury selection process, corrective measures should be undertaken once the fact of exclusion has been established by appropriate evidence.

What harm or benefit to the Black client/or the Black community might result from the adoption or nonadoption by the courts of the argued-for change? The benefits, if this Critical Race Litigation strategy is successful, might include some or all of the following changes:

1. the elimination of the use of restrictive and discriminatory jury selection source lists like the voters' or enumeration lists and the inclusion of broader based source lists to ensure representation of Black Canadians in the jury selection process,
2. a finding that the Criminal Code provision (section 629) is unconstitutional because it violates the equality provisions of the *Charter*,

3. amendments to the Criminal Code to reflect the adverse-effects principle outlined in the *Andrews* decision, thereby eliminating the impossible requirement of proof of wilful or intentional conduct on the part of officials in the exclusion of Blacks from the jury panel before a challenge to an array can be successful and

4. the elimination of the colour-blind approach of random selection and the implementation of a race-conscious approach to jury selection designed to ensure that not only the jury lists will be representative but also that the actual jury panel will be.

What harm to the Black client and/or the Black community might result from the adoption or nonadoption by the courts of the proposed change? The harm resultant from the adoption of the above-noted changes is minimal compared to the harm caused by the continual exclusion or under-representation of Blacks on Canadian juries.

Backlash may take place in the form of accusations that a Black juror is biased in favour of the Black accused or other Black party to the proceedings. These accusations have proven to be unfounded, however, in studies conducted in the United States which found that jury decisions involving Black accused were not more likely to be more favourable to the accused (where the jury contained Black jurors).

What are the risks in pursuing a Critical Race Litigation strategy? The risks must be carefully weighed before this strategy is undertaken, given that this kind of litigation is likely to have an impact on the entire group as well as on the individual client involved. Losing the case is always a risk, as are having a partially favourable decision or a favourable one that is misinterpreted by the public or in subsequent decisions. With respect to the jury selection process, any change is unlikely to have as negative an effect as the existing system, however, so these risks seem acceptable.

The Federal Jury Selection Process and Peremptory Challenges

Peremptory challenges are permitted pursuant to section 634 of the Criminal Code. They are one of two types of challenges permitted by the in-court jury selection procedures under the Criminal Code. Unlike the challenges for cause under consideration in the *Parks* and *Williams* cases, which require the party making the challenge to give reasons for it, peremptory challenges allow the Crown and the defence to challenge jurors without having to provide any reasons. This results in the automatic exclusion of a juror. Under section 634 of the Code, both the Crown and the defence are entitled to twenty peremptory challenges if the crime charged is high treason or first-degree murder, twelve peremptory challenges if the crime charged carries a prison sentence of longer than five years, and four peremptory challenges in all other cases. Except for the first juror, whom the defence is required to challenge first, the Crown and the defence will alternate in declaring first if the juror will be challenged.

The peremptory challenge, the Law Reform Commission of Canada's working paper on juries (1980) states,

> has been attacked and praised. Its importance lies in the fact that justice must be seen to be done. The peremptory challenge is one tool by which the accused can feel that he or she has some minimal control over the makeup of the jury and can eliminate persons, for whatever reason, no matter how illogical or irrational, he or she does not wish to try the case.

What answers do we get when we deconstruct the federal jury selection procedure of peremptory challenges contained in section 638 of the Criminal Code by asking the first question of a deconstruction analysis, Does this process subordinate people of colour? By placing Black people at the centre of the analysis, for example, we can determine that, although the section is couched in terms that would lead one to conclude that the peremptory challenge would be a tool favourable to a Black accused (she or he may exclude any juror without explanation), the opposite is in fact true. The peremptory challenge has been highly criticized because the Crown has used it to exclude Blacks and other racial minorities from jury service.

In the United States, the use of peremptory challenges to exclude jurors based on race has led the United States Supreme Court to limit both prosecution and defence discretion in their use. The leading American case is *Batson* v. *Kentucky* (1986, 476 U.S. 79), in which the prosecutor secured an all-White jury by using his peremptory challenges to strike the only four Blacks on the jury panel (see Frashier 1995). The Black accused was convicted by the all-White jury and subsequently appealed his conviction on the basis that discriminatory use of the peremptory challenge had violated his constitutional rights under the Fourteenth Amendment. However, the United States Supreme Court did not abolish the peremptory challenge but merely attempted to restrict its use to prevent racially based challenges.

In the United States, Critical Race theorists have called for an outright abolition of the peremptory challenge. The basis for this critique is that the federal rules governing peremptory challenges, in spite of the ruling in *Batson* (and some would argue because of it), allow the prosecution to continue to discriminate based on race and then simply explain away their challenges in "neutral" or nonracial terms. The Supreme Court also expanded the scope of *Batson* to apply to not just the prosecutor's use of race-based peremptory challenges but also to that of an accused. This meant that a Black accused could not use her or his peremptory challenges in an attempt to ensure that Black persons were on the jury. The objection of Critical Race theorists to this approach is that it treats Whites, who have not been historically discriminated against and excluded from jury service, in the same way (with "formal equality") as it treats Blacks, who have been historically subject to discrimination as a group in American society.

When we move to the next question in the deconstruction analysis— What aspects of the peremptory challenge procedures contribute to the subordination of Black people?—we must analyze these procedures from a Critical Race Theory perspective. The law itself is "race-neutral." In Canada, however, the peremptory challenge currently may be used in a discriminatory fashion. Pomerant (1994: 64) notes that although the procedure seems fair, in that it allows the same number of peremptory challenges to both the prosecutor and the defence, in fact it can be effectively used to exclude members of minorities because, statistically, fewer minorities are likely to be listed on each jury panel. He quotes from an American article by T.L. Altman, which suggests that:

> The peremptory challenge can work far more effectively to exclude minorities than to assure their presence.... For example, given the generally small percentage of blacks in the jury pool, the peremptory challenge system makes it simple for a prosecutor or defence attorney to eliminate them from any jury. Conversely, it is very difficult for a black defendant to reduce significantly the representation of whites on the jury or to prevent the elimination of black potential jurors (1986: 801).

There have been calls for the abolition of peremptory challenges in Canada. David Pomerant (1994) in his study for Justice Canada, argued that abolition would eliminate the ability of lawyers to remove jurors based on discrimination and racial stereotypes. Abolition, he asserts, would protect the interests of minorities, improve the public perception of the jury selection process and eliminate the advantage that lawyers who wish to exclude minorities have over those who wish to include them. Pomerant (1994: 80) recommends that the peremptory challenge be abolished or at least reformed to ensure that it is not used for improper purposes. At the time of writing, the study paper prepared by Pomerant and its recommendations had not been implemented, and a call to Justice Canada confirmed that the study was being sent on to the newly constituted Law Reform Commission of Canada with instructions to conduct its own study on the jury selection process.[12]

Commentators have noted that the Canadian courts have yet to be "confronted" with constitutional challenges to the discriminatory use of peremptories. However, Cynthia Petersen (1993) draws attention to Justice Gonthier's dissenting opinion in *R.* v. *Bain* ([1992] 1 S.C.R. 91 [S.C.C.]) which implied that the *Charter* provided protection against the prosecution abuse of peremptory challenge procedures by discriminating against jurors based on race. Moreover, in the 1993 case of *R.* v. *Biddle* (24 C.R. [4th] 65; 84 C.C.C. [3d] 430 at 435), Justice Doherty for the Ontario Court of Appeal (in *obiter dictum*) indicated that the Crown's abuse of its peremptory challenge power might give rise to remedies at trial and that the exclusion of potential jurors based on their sex might also implicate an accused's rights under section 15 of the *Charter*. But as Petersen emphasizes, in the *Sherratt* case, L'Heureux-Dubé "upheld the legitimacy of peremptory challenges even though they may be used to alter the degree to which the jury represents the community" (Petersen 1993: 147).

Arguably, however, based on the recent Supreme Court of Canada decision in the *Williams* case, which acknowledged the impact that racial prejudice has on the trial process, in a proper case a challenge to the peremptory challenge procedure under sections 11 and 15 of the *Charter* may now prove successful. David Tanovich (1994), writing prior to the Supreme Court of Canada decision in *Williams,* notes that the issue of whether a prosecutor can use peremptory challenges in a discriminatory way or whether this is unconstitutional is an "uncharted" area in Canada. After asking the question, "Does the *Charter* prohibit the discriminatory use of peremptory challenges?" he concludes:

> It seems a trite principle that the prosecution's use of its allotted peremptories in a discriminatory fashion violates s.15's guarantee of equal protection. This conduct implicates an accused's right to have a jury selected in a non-discriminatory fashion and the juror's right not to be discriminated against on the basis of one of the enumerated grounds in s.15.... It is submitted that *Bain, Biddle* and *Batson* pave the way for the defence to challenge the prosecutor's use of their peremptory challenges under s.15 of the Charter (1994: 325).

The Supreme Court of Canada's decision in *Williams* may pave the way for a defence challenge to a prosecutor's discriminatory use of peremptory challenges under section 15 of the *Charter* (see Tanovich 1994: 310).

The Reconstruction Question in the Federal Jury Selection Process
Applying the final step in a Critical Race Theory and Litigation approach—reconstruction—what are the alternatives, if any, to the existing peremptory challenge procedure that will eliminate or lessen the subordination of Black people?

The abolition of peremptory challenges would certainly prevent their abuse. However, abolition may not be the answer, because it would also prevent a Black accused from using peremptory challenges in an attempt to ensure that there are Black people or other people of colour on the jury panel.

Some commentators have suggested that reform of the jury selection process should include a *Batson*-like approach to the problem. The United States Supreme Court decision in *Batson* requires the accused to introduce facts supporting an inference of discrimination, and then the burden shifts to the prosecution to provide a "race-neutral" explanation for the exclusion of the juror by peremptory challenge (Gordon 1993). This ruling in *Batson* has come under considerable criticism from Critical Race theorists and others in the United States. Gordon notes that the main problem with the *Batson* approach is that prosecutors simply have become very adept at offering "pretextual" nonracial explanations for the exclusion of Black jurors by way of the peremptory challenge, and courts have "been unable to distinguish legitimate reasons for a peremptory strike from those that serve as 'mere' excuses for discrimination." As a result, Gordon explains, *Batson's* goal of eliminating the racial discriminatory use of the peremptory challenge in the jury selection process "remains unfulfilled" (1993: 694).

In the Canadian context, with the added advantage of extensive American jurisprudence on the *Batson*-like approach, we should be very cautious about adopting an approach that is in reality an "illusory" response to the racially discriminatory abuse of the peremptory challenge. Outright abolition would be preferable to the *Batson* approach because it would at least guarantee that prosecutors will not use such challenges to discriminate against Blacks and other people of colour. The issue of negative impact on the Black accused of outright abolition of the use of peremptory challenges can and should be addressed by implementing a strengthened and expanded challenge-for-cause procedure, coupled with representative source lists and affirmative-action jury selection.

Another alternative suggested by Critical Race theorists is a race-conscious approach to the use of peremptory challenges. A race-conscious approach recognizes that Blacks have been and are excluded from jury service based on their race and takes an "asymmetrical" approach to balancing the inequities. This would permit Black accused to peremptorily strike White jurors to ensure that at least some Black persons will be present on the jury (a representativeness approach) but would prevent prosecutors from striking Black jurors on the basis of race or a pretextual excuse that masks a racial exclusion. This race-conscious approach calling for affirmative action in the jury selection process will no doubt be criticized, but as Paul Butler notes, "it is unfortunate that race-conscious solutions sometimes engender more controversy than race-conscious problems" (1997: 889).

What harm or benefit to the Black client/or the Black community might result from the adoption or nonadoption by the courts of the changes to the federal jury selection procedure of peremptory challenges discussed above? The obvious benefit of outright abolition would be that prosecutors would no longer be able to exclude Black people from Canadian juries through their discriminatory use. The benefit would increase tenfold if, in conjunction with the abolition of the peremptory challenge, the challenge for cause procedure was strengthened and expanded to allow for more in-depth questioning of prospective jurors in order to determine racial prejudice. The benefit would again increase if, in conjunction with the above reform, the jury source lists were expanded to ensure true representativeness and the random selection process was replaced with affirmative-action jury selection to ensure that Blacks and other people of colour are truly represented on Canadian juries. A benefit would also accrue to a Black accused and the Black community if a race-conscious approach to the use of peremptory challenges was adopted in lieu of outright abolition.

The potential risk of adopting a Critical Race Litigation approach to the problems inherent in the jury selection process is that the court will not find the existing provincial statutes or the Criminal Code provisions governing the jury selection process to be unconstitutional. Arguably, this result would merely maintain the status quo and would have no effect on the existing condition of Black people, so the risk seems worth taking.

A Critical Race Theory Expansion of Parks and Williams: Challenges for Cause

As noted in Chapter 3, with regard to challenge-for-cause procedures under the Criminal Code, the *Parks* decision did not go far enough from a Critical Race Theory perspective in advancing the right of Black accused to question potential jurors on racial bias. A Critical Race Theory approach would attempt to push the envelope with respect to the type and number of questions a Black accused should be permitted to ask potential jurors in order to adequately detect racial prejudice. The question allowed in *Parks* is of limited usefulness in ferreting out unconscious racism. As noted earlier, Dr. Henry in the *Griffis* (no. 1) case testified that the question allowed in *Parks* was inadequate because the question allowed would not get at "attitudinal prejudice" and more than one question would be required to determine whether a prospective juror harboured this type of prejudice. The six questions proposed in the *Griffis* case are repeated here: (1) What does the term "racist" mean to you? (2) Do you think racism is a problem in Canadian society? (3) How many Black people do you think live in Canada? (4) Some people think Black people commit more crimes than people of other races. Do you have an opinion on this subject? If so, what is it? (5) Do you hold any opinions about people of the accused's race, particularly with respect to criminal behaviour involving drugs? If so, what are those opinions? and (6) Would those opinions interfere with your ability to try this case fairly? The Court in *Griffis* allowed all six questions, with a slight modification to question 5 to reflect the fact that prospective jurors were not social scientists and required a simplified form of the question.

Another critique of the *Parks* decision is that it is too narrow in its focus. It permits a very limited inquiry on a challenge for cause. For example, it does not allow the accused the broad-based inquiry into the prospective juror's lifestyles and personal experiences permitted in the United States in order to facilitate the exposure of racial prejudice. Canadian courts, Justice Doherty explains in *Parks*, have resisted this approach to jury selection, and he cites cases such as *R.* v. *Hubbert* (1975, 29 C.C.C. [2d] 279 [Ont. H.C.]), a pre-*Charter* case, in support of this observation. However, Justice Doherty did not rule out this approach in the context of challenges for cause based on racial prejudice; he merely noted that there were "very difficult problems" in this context which did not need to be addressed in the determination of the *Parks* case because in that case only one very specific type of question was proposed. Another problem with the *Parks* decision is that the Court in *Parks* only allowed the question that was posed because it was colour-blind or "race-neutral," as Justice Doherty described it. In other words, the accused in *Parks* did not attempt to argue that only prospective jurors who were White should be subject to challenge for cause. An approach that was not colour-blind but race-conscious would have attempted to do so. The Critical Race Theory argument would be that, because Blacks and not Whites have been the historically disadvantaged group in society, a colour-blind approach ignores this reality and treats White jurors who have not been subject to discrimination or systemic exclusion from jury service in the same way that it treats Blacks, who need protection from discrimination if a purposeful interpretation of section 15 is adopted.

Can Critical Race litigators push the envelope by persuading the Court to take a race-conscious approach to the challenge-for-cause procedures? A Critical Race Theory approach was taken by the African Canadian Legal Clinic (ACLC), an intervener in the *Williams* case before the

Supreme Court of Canada. The ACLC argued that:

> The most persistent and pervasive form of racism in Canadian society is unconscious racism.... Discrimination may be introduced into the criminal justice system through a variety of means. Racially neutral norms or practices within the system may disparately impact on a group defined by an enumerated or analogous ground [under section 15 of the *Charter*]. The criminal justice system also provides numerous opportunities for the exercise of unregulated discretion, through which the conscious or unconscious prejudices of individual decision-makers may be transmitted.[13]

Within a deconstruction analysis of the Supreme Court decision in the *Williams* case discussed above, it would seem that Justice McLachlin may have effectively closed off these potential Critical Race Theory arguments. In her argument for the majority, she points out the different approaches taken to the challenge-for-cause procedure in the United States and Canada. In the United States, every prospective juror may be subject to a challenge and questioned about preconceptions and prejudices at any trial. Justice McLachlin notes that the result is that lengthy questioning of jurors is routine. She asserts that in Canada, however, the prospective juror is presumed to be impartial. Before a challenge for cause can be made, this presumption must be displaced. She observes that some lower courts in Canada have taken a "conservative" approach to a challenge for cause based on racial prejudice because of a fear that allowing this kind of challenge will result in more lengthy, complex and costly trials, and because there are concerns for the privacy of jurors and that the Canadian approach could "evolve" into an exact version of the American approach. In response to these concerns, in *Williams,* Justice McLachlin takes the position that:

> In my view, the rule enunciated by this Court in *Sherratt* suffices to maintain the right to a fair and impartial trial, without adopting the United States model or a variant on it. There is no automatic right to challenge for cause, and in order to establish such a right, the accused must show that there is a realistic potential that some members of the jury pool may be biased in a way that may impact negatively on the accused. A realistic potential of racial prejudice can often be demonstrated by establishing widespread prejudice in the community against people of the accused's race. *As long as this requirement is in place, the Canadian rule will be much more restrictive than the rule in the United States* [emphasis added] (at 515).

With respect to the issue of more detailed questioning to determine racial prejudice, Justice McLachlin supported the trial judge's decision in *Williams* to allow only two main questions to be asked "subject to a few tightly controlled subsidiary questions.... This is a practice to be emulated" (at 515).

Justice McLachlin (at 515) also apparently rejected the approach put forward by the intervener, the ACLC, in its factum[14] to the Supreme Court of Canada in the *Williams* case, that:

> The *Charter* requires [that] any African Canadian accused have the right to challenge for cause for potential anti-Black partiality. By virtue of historic disadvantage, continuing social, economic, and political marginalization, and systemic discrimination in the context of the criminal justice system, the right to challenge for cause for anti-Black bias is minimally required to safeguard the right of an African Canadian accused to a fair trial before an impartial jury (para. 44 at 15).

The Supreme Court of Canada in the *Williams* case has moved considerably from its traditionally conservative approach to issues of race. However, the restrictive approach to the questions to be asked, and the Court's failure to accept the position that a challenge for cause should be permitted in all cases involving a Black or Aboriginal accused, is disappointing from a Critical Race Theory perspective and indicative of the continuing "conservatism" with respect to issues of race on the Supreme Court of Canada bench. As a result, one challenge for the Critical Race litigator will be to influence how the decision in the *Williams* case will be interpreted and modified in future cases by lower courts.

One shining and perfect example of the power of Critical Race Litigation to shape the interpretation by the court of the Supreme Court of Canada's decision in the *Williams* case occurred on December 30, 1998, with the Ontario Court of Appeal decision in *R. v. Siew Thiam Koh, Eng Chuan Lu, and Buan Haut Lim* (unreported).

The accused Chinese men were convicted on September 26, 1996, by the Ontario Court (General Division) of conspiracy to import a narcotic into Canada, conspiracy to traffic in a narcotic and having possession of a narcotic for the purpose of trafficking contrary to the *Narcotic Control Act*. They each received life sentences for one or more of the charges. They appealed their convictions and sentences to the Ontario Court of Appeal. The issue before the Ontario Court of Appeal was the refusal of the trial judge to allow the accused Chinese men to question prospective jurors on a challenge for cause based on racial and national origin. The question the accused wanted to ask the jurors was: "Would the fact that the accused are persons of Chinese origin and visitors from Singapore affect your ability to judge the evidence fairly and without prejudice?" (Finlayson J. at para. 8).

In denying the challenge for cause, the trial judge made a distinction between what he termed "racial prejudice in the social sense" and "racial prejudice in the judicial sense." Racial prejudice in the "social sense" was related, the trial judge asserted, to prejudice in obtaining jobs or renting an apartment. And racial prejudice in the "judicial sense" was a "racial bias in the setting of a jury trial" (Finlayson J. at para. 11). The trial judge concluded that, based on cases such as *R. v. Parks,* there must be evidence showing not only racial prejudice in the "social sense" but also evidence demonstrating that a prospective juror who harbours this racial prejudice would be prepared to act on those prejudices to the detriment of other races. "[T]he trial judge concluded that the evidence in this case did not establish a social level of prejudice against 'Asians' or 'Chinese' so great as to raise an apprehension of bias in the judicial setting" (Finlayson J. at para. 12).

Justice Finlayson, writing for a unanimous Ontario Court of Appeal, held that the trial judge applied the wrong test by drawing a distinction between "social prejudice" and "prejudice in a judicial setting" and that this proposition was supported by the subsequent ruling of the Supreme Court of Canada in *R. v. Williams,* where the Court rejected a similar distinction based on "general prejudice" and "prejudice that can be equated with partiality" (at para. 13). Justice Finlayson noted that the Supreme Court of Canada rejected this distinction and stressed Justice McLachlin's point in the *Williams* case that "The question is whether there is reason to suppose that the jury pool may contain people who are prejudiced and whose prejudice might not be capable of being set aside on directions from the judge" (at para. 495).

The trial judge in the present case also took judicial notice of the fact that "Chinese people are judged individually and are not classed as a race"(Finlayson J. at para. 16). Justice Finlayson notes that this "fact" was not one of which the trial judge was entitled to take judicial notice under the established categories of facts as reaffirmed by the Supreme Court of Canada in the *Williams* case. Accordingly, the Ontario Court of Appeal determined that "It is apparent from the conflicts between the trial judge's ruling and the subsequent judgment of the Supreme Court of Canada in *Williams* ... that the ruling cannot stand (Finlayson J. at para. 19). The Court of Appeal did not accept the Crown's submission that the appeal should be dismissed because the accused did not establish an evidential foundation for the challenge for cause based on race and allowed the accused appeal, set aside the convictions and ordered a new trial (Finlayson J. at para. 20).

The Ontario Court of Appeal, in response to the arguments put forward by the accused and the intervener (the Chinese Canadian National Council) that the court find that the accused had satisfied the onus of establishing an apprehension of racial bias against persons of Chinese origin, held that:

> having regard to the amorphous nature of what is termed *evidence* on the issue of racism generally, we might now ask the question as to whether the issues of prejudice against visible minorities has been the subject of sufficient judicial concern that consideration can be given to accepting similar challenges without formal proof of community prejudice in the case of *all* visible minorities (Finlayson J. at para. 28, emphasis added).

The Ontario Court of Appeal held that in that jurisdiction (Ontario), they had arrived at the stage in the development of the law relating to challenges for cause for racial prejudice that,

> absent sustainable objection from the Crown, the trial judge should allow a challenge for cause by a member of a visible racial minority without strict compliance with *Sherratt*.... The prejudice, where it occurs, is triggered by skin colour. The same would apply to all visible non-Caucasian minorities (Finlayson J. at para. 30).

In coming to this decision, Justice Finlayson, speaking for the Court, opined that this result was consistent with a natural extension of the principles established in *Sherratt, Williams* and other "race" jurisprudence of the Ontario Court of Appeal. The Court held that the "rule" against an "automatic" right to challenge for cause has no application in the context of racial prejudice:

> The fact of racism may well be amenable to judicial notice under the branch of the judicial notice rule which permits the acceptance without proof of facts that are so notorious as to be the subject of dispute amongst reasonable persons. Alternatively, the accused member of a visible minority can be taken as having established a prima facie [on its face] case by merely requesting the right to make the challenge in view of the successive holdings in *Parks, Wilson, Ho,* and now *Williams,* which all speak of the existence of the evil of racism (Finlayson J. at para. 38).

The decision of the Ontario Court of Appeal in *R.* v. *Siew Thiam Koh,*

Eng Chuan Lu, and Buan Haut Lim shows the powerful and accumulative effect of sustained application of Critical Race Theory in litigation strategies. The Court drew on the amassed efforts of racial minority appellants, community organizations and interveners in cases such as *R. v. Parks, R. v. Williams, R. v. R.D.S.* and others under consideration in this book. From *R.D.S.* the Court in this case drew from the decision of Justices McLachlin and L'Heureux-Dubé with respect to the "reasonable person" and the fact that the reasonable person must

> "be taken to be aware of the history of discrimination faced by disadvantaged groups in Canadian society protected by the Charter's equality provisions.... The reasonable person is not only a member of the Canadian community, but also, more specifically, is a member of the local communities in which the case at issue arose (in this case, the Nova Scotia and Halifax communities). Such a person must be taken to possess knowledge of the local dynamics, including the existence in the community of a history of widespread and systemic discrimination against black and aboriginal people, and high profile clashes between the police and the visible minority population over policing issues.... The reasonable person must thus be deemed to be cognizant of the existence of racism in Halifax, Nova Scotia" (Finlayson J. at para. 39).

The Ontario Court of Appeal in this case also provided a definitive statement with respect to the existence of racism in Canadian society against all "racialized" groups and provided what the African Canadian Legal Clinic had been pushing the Supreme Court of Canada for in its intervener factum in the *Williams* case, that is, a decision that would recognize that

> the *Charter* requires that any African Canadian accused have the right to challenge for cause for potential anti-Black partiality. By virtue of historic disadvantage, continuing social, economic, and political marginalization, and systemic discrimination in the context of the criminal justice system, the right to challenge for cause for anti-Black bias is minimally required to safeguard the right of an African Canadian accused to a fair trial before an impartial jury (ACLC factum at para. 44).

The decision in this case takes us a long way on our journey towards racial justice. However, it is "jurisdictional," in the sense that it is not a decision of the Supreme Court of Canada. How jurisdictions other than

Ontario will interpret the holding in this case remains to be seen. Will they attempt to "confine" it to Ontario or will judges in other jurisdictions require racial minority accused to re-argue the issue in every case? Such a position is unsustainable. However, lawyers and others involved in Critical Race Litigation may be required to push the "jurisdictional" envelope in subsequent cases.

There are many areas of the criminal law (procedural and substantive) to which a Critical Race analysis can and should be applied. In this volume, I have focused mainly on the procedural area of jury selection under provincial and federal jurisdiction, the substantive area of defences, such as self-defence and provocation, the role of "race" and the "reasonable person" and the interpretation of the *Charter* in the context of "race." However, as previously indicated, criminal law is not the only area of law to which a Critical Race Theory and Litigation strategy may be applied. Critical Race Theory should be methodically applied to all areas of law. One of the most significant areas of law requiring the immediate attention of Critical Race theorists, litigators and social activists is the administrative law field of human rights.

The Human Rights System

It is widely recognized by victims of discrimination, by social activists and by organizations, law reform commissions, various surveys, reports and studies, as well as academics and those involved in the administration of Canada's human rights codes, that the present human rights system, which was designed in the 1960s before the implementation of the *Canadian Charter of Rights and Freedoms*, is significantly lacking. Many Black Canadians are deterred from filing human rights complaints, given the knowledge within the Black community that the human rights system is designed to benefit majoritarian interests by functioning as a "balm" for White guilt and not as a meaningful remedy for Black people who experience discrimination.

Human rights protection in Canada is the exclusive domain of provincial and federal human rights commissions. "These commissions, and the Statutes under which they operate, have developed over time in response to a change in public opinion and in particular growing international public opposition to overt discrimination" (Mendes 1995: 1-20).[15] These reactions were in part a direct response to Nazi atrocities inflicted upon European Jews, Gypsies and others based on ideologies of "racial" superiority prior to and during World War II. The United Nations was also formed at this time and a *Universal Declaration of Human Rights* was adopted by the General Assembly of the United Nations in 1948, thereby making otherwise sovereign states accountable to the world for human rights violations (Mendes 1995: 1-20). Although the *Canadian Bill of*

Rights was implemented in 1960, it was limited in scope and did not apply to provincial governments or to private actors. By the end of the 1970s all provinces in Canada had implemented human rights legislation intended to "protect" minorities from discrimination and to provide "redress" for the discriminatory acts of private actors and government. In addition to the provincial human rights statutes (which prohibit discrimination by private individuals, businesses and government entities) in provincial areas of jurisdiction such as school boards, public accommodation and services, the Parliament of Canada adopted the *Canadian Human Rights Act* in 1977, which prohibits discrimination in activities under federal jurisdiction such as federal government departments and crown corporations.[16]

Human rights legislation prohibits discrimination on the basis of race and other grounds such as, but not limited to, gender, sexual orientation, religion, national or ethnic origin, colour, marital and family status and disability.

Human rights legislation reflects modern public policy with respect to discrimination and is "compensatory" in nature, in that it is designed not to "punish" discriminators but to compensate monetarily those discriminated against. Provincial and federal human rights laws are administered by specialized commissions (human rights commissions) which have "exclusive" jurisdiction in matters of human rights. These statutes and their administration must, however, comply with *Charter* values.

Discrimination in Canadian society on the basis of race has generally become covert and systemic,

> leaving one to conclude that through our institutions and laws, society condones racist behaviour.... The vast majority of human rights complaints dealing with race are rejected at the [Human Rights] Commission's investigatory stage and never make it to a hearing" (Mendes 1994: 3-83).

By deconstructing the human rights system in Canada and placing people of colour at the centre of the analysis, it is readily apparent, with respect to the Canadian human rights system, that the answer to the question, "Does this legal rule, principle, doctrine, policy or practice subordinate people of colour?" is yes. Under this system, cases based on race are dismissed more often than cases on any other ground such as gender, disability or family status, and the delays inherent in the system, while detrimental to all disadvantaged groups, are more severe in cases based on race. The purpose of the human rights process as expressed by the Supreme Court of Canada is "remedial—to eradicate anti-social conditions without regard to the motives or intention of those who cause them."[17]

However, the current human rights system in Canada has been widely disparaged as being not only ineffective but also discriminatory in its own right. Mendes and others have concluded that:

> Canadian courts and human rights tribunal systems are not serving the needs of visible minority Canadians. While incidents of racism flourish, the vast majority of formal complaints are being rejected at the investigatory stage and court cases are being dismissed, often on procedural grounds. Impediments to justice include time lags [delays], evidentiary burdens, procedural hurdles such as standing for minority groups, and ineffective remedies .... The present backlog attests to the fact that the present system is not designed for real change (Mendes 1994: 3-83).

The human rights system in Canada depends on a complaint system. The person discriminated against files a complaint with the human rights commission, either federal or provincial, depending on the jurisdiction and nature of the complaint, and the commission both investigates and adjudicates the case ("adjudicates" in the sense that it determines whether or not the case should go on for judgement by a board of inquiry). The human rights commission has as its mandate the "conciliation," or informal resolution, of the problem. Human rights commissions also have educational functions. If the case cannot be resolved informally, the commission may appoint a board of inquiry to judge the complaint. The major criticisms levelled against the human rights system in Canada at both the provincial and federal levels are that:

- race cases are dismissed more often than cases based on other grounds, especially in the federal jurisdiction and the Nova Scotia jurisdiction,
- complaints can be dismissed even when the complainant wants to proceed to a board of inquiry and, once dismissed, there is no recourse to the courts for a remedy,
- delays are extensive (especially in race-based complaints) and obstruct complainants from utilizing the system
- the system is "victim"-driven and depends mainly on individual complaints,
- there is an assumption underlying the human rights system that equality already exists in Canadian society and that a complaint is merely a "deviation" which, once corrected, will restore racial equality,
- the human rights commissions have no expertise in group or systemic complaints and are only able to detect and rectify

obvious and overt forms of discrimination,
- the commissions have "incompatible" functions such as their "investigation," "conciliation" and "adjudicative" functions,
- monetary awards are inadequate, do not eliminate discrimination and are not punitive in nature, and
- human rights commissions are not politically independent and free from political interference (for an in-depth discussion, see Mendes 1995: Chapter 2, and Berlin 1996: 224).

Condemnation of the human rights system in Canada comes from those who use the system (victims of discrimination) and those who administer it. For example, in its 1997 annual report, the Chief Commissioner of the Canadian Human Rights Commission, Michelle Falardeau-Ramsay, made the following observations:

> Our current model of human rights protection in Canada has not really changed since the Ontario Human Rights Code was adopted in 1962. When looking to improve the existing system, three key challenges must be addressed: whether the definition of human rights in Canadian legislation is too restrictive; whether existing enforcement mechanisms exclude certain types of human rights problems from being dealt with because they do not fit into the specific categories of current human rights laws; and whether a better process can be found to reduce the often negative impact of delays on individual complainants and their families. *Because of these and other problems, we need to fundamentally re-examine the human rights system* (Falardeau-Ramsay 1997, emphasis added).

In response to some of the criticisms levelled at the existing human rights system in Canada at the federal level, Parliament passed Bill S-5 amending the *Canadian Human Rights Act*.[18] The amendments received royal assent on May 12, 1998, and were effective in the fall of 1998. These amendments impose an express duty, short of undue hardship, on employers and service providers to accommodate the special needs of religious minorities and people with disabilities. The legislation creates a permanent, fifteen-member human rights tribunal which will be staffed with people with human rights expertise and legal training. It provides greater protection for complainants against retaliation. It also strengthens the provisions of the federal Act which deal with the distribution of hate messages to provide for monetary penalties against the perpetrator.

Under the new legislation it is possible for a complaint of discrimination to be filed on multiple grounds (allowing, for example, a Black women to file a complaint based on race as well as gender or disability) so the commission and tribunals can take account of the effect of a combination of these prohibited grounds on the complainant. In the past the complainant was forced to choose between the grounds of discrimination. The legislation also makes it possible for policy complaints (complaints pursued by the commission itself and not by an individual complainant) to be filed in discrimination cases relating to services as well as employment. The Canadian Human Rights Commission will now report directly to Parliament. In addition, the new amendments increase monetary awards for pain and suffering caused by discrimination.

These amendments seem to have been undertaken in a piecemeal fashion, however, and do nothing to address the more serious and systemic problems with the existing human rights system in Canada. The legislation does not address, for example, the very serious concern that race cases are being dismissed more frequently than cases on any other ground, or the fact that delays in race cases are longer than in any other cases. It also does not address the issue of exclusive jurisdiction and the denial of the right of access to the courts, or the problems inherent in an individual complaint-driven process, rather than a group-complaint process designed to address systemic forms of discrimination. Finally, amendments to the federal legislation, by definition, will have no direct impact on provincial human rights complaints.

The second question required of a deconstruction analysis—"What aspects of the human rights system contribute to the subordination of people of colour?"—ideally requires a full analysis of all aspects of the human rights system. An in-depth analysis of only two aspects of the human rights system is undertaken here, however.

One significant point of oppression inherent in the existing system is the doctrine of exclusivity of jurisdiction in human rights commissions laid down in the *Bhadauria* case. The fact that disadvantaged groups do not have the ability to pursue a civil remedy for discrimination (especially when they have no control over whether or not their complaint is dismissed by the human rights commission) is arguably contrary to the equality provisions of the *Canadian Charter of Rights and Freedoms*.

The Supreme Court of Canada's decision in *Bhadauria,* which denied victims of discrimination the right to sue in the civil courts and granted exclusive jurisdiction over cases of discrimination to human rights commissions, was decided before the *Charter* came into being. Mendes (1995: 5-16) argues that the question is open as to whether the exclusive jurisdiction accorded human rights agencies, as well as their operations, could be the subject of challenges under the *Charter*. It has been argued that the right to choose whether or not to pursue a discrimination complaint through the human rights process or through the civil courts should lie with the victim and that legislative amendments should be adopted to explicitly contain such a right. The Cornish Report (Ontario 1992) recommended that victims of discrimination be given access to the civil courts, and the Nielson Report (Study Team 1985) also recommended that further study be undertaken into the issue of access to the courts (Mendes 1995: 2-31). One provincial jurisdiction, Quebec, already provides for this alternative route in the existing legislation.

Mendes explores possible *Charter* challenges to the existing human rights system in terms of section 11 and section 7 rights (the right to an impartial and independent tribunal and the right to be tried within a reasonable time under section 11, and the right under section 7 to fundamental justice). These *Charter* sections are mainly "respondent"-based (they provide protection for defendants, that is, the alleged discriminators) and are not founded on a breach of the equality rights of the complainant under section 15 of the *Charter*. Mendes does argue, however, that section 7 of the *Charter* may guarantee the victim of an injury the right to address a "court" to obtain compensation on the basis that his or her life, liberty or security of the person has been compromised and points out that the Ontario High Court, in the case of *Streng* v. *Winchester (Township)* (25 C.R.R. 357 at 363 [Ont. C.A.]), held that the right of access to the courts, although not specifically mentioned in the *Charter*, exists by implication (Mendes 1995: 5-17). Mendes points out that the ability of human rights commissions to dismiss complaints without ever sending them to a board of inquiry may deny the victims of discrimination access to the human rights tribunal, but once a complaint has been sent on to a board of inquiry, an argument that a denial of access to the courts has occurred may be more difficult to sustain (Mendes 1995: 5-17).

A challenge to the exclusivity doctrine set out in the *Bhadauria* case, however, may be more successful if it is taken under section 15 of the *Charter* on behalf of the victim of discrimination on the basis that the denial of the right to access the courts has an adverse impact on the groups protected by section 15. The fact that there is no recourse to these disadvantaged groups is discriminatory on the basis of race, gender, disability and the other enumerated grounds set out in section 15 of the *Charter,* in that it denies access to the courts only to victims of discrimination. Victims of most other kinds of wrongful conduct are not denied access to the courts. The Supreme Court of Canada should reconsider its decision in the *Bhadauria* case in light of *Charter* impact principles and overrule it. Another possible *Charter* challenge to the existing human rights system under section 15 is to the differential application of the system itself. Because "race" cases are dismissed by human rights commissions more often than other types of cases, the administration of the human rights system discriminates against people of colour contrary to section 15 of the *Charter*.

Mendes points out that, on a technical point, it would seem impossible to argue any of this before a court because the *Bhadauria* rule's prohibition on courts addressing cases on human rights issues due to the exclusivity of the statutory agency's jurisdiction could be interpreted to prohibit *Charter* challenges to the human rights system (1995: 5-20). He notes, however, that even though the Court would, based on the *Bhadauria* decision, have to deny jurisdiction to hear the merits of the human rights complaint, the constitutional issues could be raised at this preliminary stage. Notwithstanding this technical argument, provincial and federal human rights commissions and statutes are actions of either the Parliament and government of Canada or the legislature and government of the provinces and are therefore (pursuant to section 32 of the *Charter*)[19] subject to *Charter* scrutiny. A human rights system which discriminates based on race by dismissing race cases in greater and more alarming percentages than other discrimination cases is a form of governmental action and is subject to a challenge based on an infringement of the equality provisions of the *Charter*.

The Reconstruction Question and the Human Rights System

If the current human rights system in Canada fails *Charter* scrutiny and is found to be of no force and effect because it discriminates against people of colour, it follows that the exclusivity doctrine falls with it. Access to the civil courts would likely result. In addition to recourse to the civil courts what, if any, other system would be a desirable replacement? What are the alternatives, if any, to the existing human rights system that will not subordinate people of colour or lessen the subordination of people of colour? One obvious alternative would be a revamped human rights system that provides complainants with the option to pursue a civil action (including an action in tort for discrimination such as was proposed but rejected in *Bhadauria*) if they prefer, rather than limiting their options to the human rights system. A revamped human rights system (as noted by Mendes [1994], Berlin [1996] and others) should also:

- be free from the threat of political interference,
- permit stiffer monetary and punitive damages, and in the case of employment discrimination, a remedy that includes reinstatement in the work place,
- define some forms of discrimination such as racial harassment as a criminal offence,
- provide protection against delays,
- ensure that cases based on race receive the same treatment as those based on other grounds,
- eliminate onerous standards of proof in race-based discrimina-

tion cases,
- ensure that "conciliation" is no longer perceived as the main function of the system, substituting instead a "deterrence" model designed to discourage discrimination by making examples of those who do discriminate and
- supplement the individual complaint-driven process with group complaints and class actions designed to attack systemic forms of discrimination.

Reconstruction of the human rights system in Canada requires reform at both the federal and provincial levels. Piecemeal reform should stop and an overall review of the entire Canadian human rights systems should be undertaken. In a study funded by the Research Section of Justice Canada, which conducted a survey of complaint and redress mechanisms relating to racial discrimination in Canada and other places such as the United States and New South Wales, it was noted that "any system that intends to address a problem as multifaceted as racial and ethnic discrimination must continually explore new techniques of enforcement and make use of a variety of mechanisms, applying each to the aspect of the problem it is best suited to remedy" (Mendes 1994: 16e). The authors concluded that the right to sue under the American model allowed complainants to seek a wide range of remedies in the courts and that there was a "deterrent" element to such civil lawsuits. They assert, however, that these remedies are not enough on their own. Other measures, such as the right to bring class actions and ensuring that court proceedings are public, are also required to bolster deterrent mechanisms. Redistributive measures are also necessary (Mendes 1994).[20]

In the final step of Critical Race analysis—"What harm or benefit to the Black client and/or the Black community might result from the adoption or nonadoption of the proposed changes to the human rights system?"—Critical Race Litigation strategies can and should be formulated with a view to challenging and improving the existing human rights system. The changes discussed above, if implemented, would have the benefit of providing legitimacy to the human rights system. The Court Challenges Program could be extended to include civil cases of discrimination in its funding program in appropriate cases involving the public interest. This would ensure that a broad range of challenges to discriminatory practices could be undertaken. With adequate funding, effective Critical Race Litigation would be encouraged whenever it is needed.

Summary

The goal of lawyers, social activists, laypersons and students interested in improving the legal and social status of Black Canadians and other disadvantaged groups in society is to alter existing institutional arrangements by enhancing the rights of Blacks and others "through substantive outcomes," and as Naomi Cahn notes in the context of feminist theory, this approach requires the integration of substantive goals with the actual process of representation (1991: 1). This approach requires an integration of substantive goals with the actual process of representation.

The first step in a Critical Race Litigation strategy is to be aware of the history of racism in Canadian society and the role it plays in law. One is required to undertake a consciousness-raising approach. For lawyers it requires a different approach to legal analysis, one that is grounded in the everyday lives of Black people. But one does not have to belong to the racially disadvantaged group in order to gain a "racial perspective"; it can be accessed transracially. However, Blacks and other people of colour possess a unique voice to articulate these experiences that must be listened and deferred to by White allies. The second step in a Critical Race Litigation strategy is identifying when "race" is an issue in a given circumstance and identifying those oppressions that can be overcome or limited through law.

A deconstructive analysis designed to confront both overt and subtle forms of discrimination perpetuated by law requires that two important questions be asked. First, Does the legal rule, principle, doctrine, policy or practice subordinate people of colour? Second, What aspect(s) of the legal rule, principle, doctrine, policy or practice contribute to the subordination? The first question requires a contextualized approach to the problem which places people of colour at the centre of the analysis; the second question requires an in-depth analysis of the rule etc. from a Critical Race Theory perspective, rejecting a traditional legal analysis that adheres to the concept of "neutrality" and "objectivity" in law and invoking an analysis that goes behind what appears to be a "race-neutral" law to determine whether or not it has a discriminatory effect on people of colour.

The final step in a Critical Race Theory and Litigation approach is reconstruction. What are the alternatives, if any, to the existing doctrine, legal rule, principle, practice or doctrine that will not subordinate or will lessen the subordination of people of colour? What harm or benefit to the Black client and/or Black community might result from the adoption or nonadoption by the courts of the argued-for change? If "race" and racism are live issues in the case, the advocate should fearlessly raise them as she or he would fearlessly raise any other issue that would benefit the client.

Chapter 5

Ethical and Other Considerations

Tough Choices: When to Raise the Issue of "Race"

*"The pervasive and systemic role of racism in the legal
system belies the assumption that the world can be
neatly divided into 'race cases' and 'non-race' cases"*
—Margaret M. Russell (1997: 787)

Not only those lawyers who are interested in public interest litigation and
pursue this kind of practice will be involved in Critical Race Litigation.
Lawyers involved in practices involving corporate law, administrative
law, family law, labour law, environmental law, tort law, constitutional
law etc. can and should ask the "race" question and analyse how it impacts
on the given area of law. For example, Black business owners and entre-
preneurs are continually denied business loans by White banking institutions. Human rights systems have a discriminatory impact on people of
colour. Environmental racism (the dumping of toxic wastes near communities of colour) occurs on a regular basis. Trade unions fail to represent
their members of colour equally. Existing categories of tort law do not
provide adequate protection against discrimination and racial harassment.
Black children caught in custody disputes between interracial parents (or
adopted by White parents) are denied access to a parent of colour who
may provide a connection to their shared racial heritage. Most generally,
section 15 (the equality provision) of the *Charter* is not being fully
utilized to advance the equality rights of Blacks and other people of
colour. The foregoing list of areas of law amenable to a deconstruction
and reconstruction analysis is certainly not exhaustive. A Critical Race
Theory approach to lawyering should therefore be undertaken in all areas
of law in order to identify those oppressions that can be overcome through
law.

In the previous chapter we looked at *how* to execute Critical Race
Theory in practice. Here we shall look at *when* to execute it. For example,
should a Critical Race Litigation strategy be taken in every case involving
a Black person or other person of colour, or only in those cases involving

"interracial" fact patterns arising in the context of criminal law? Is it ethical to raise the issue in any legal context? What limits, if any, are placed on the legal advocate by professional codes of conduct? In whose interest is the lawyer acting, that of the individual client or that of the Black community or society as a whole? Does raising the issue amount to playing the "race card" for strategic advantage and will it simply reinforce existing stereotypes?

Not surprisingly, given the paucity of Black and other legal scholars of colour, there is an absence of scholarly writing on the topic of race-conscious lawyering in Canada. In the United States, where Critical Race Theory was born, one of the major criticisms of the movement has been its failure to incorporate an advocacy component into its analysis.[1] One recent American attempt to address this deficiency was a symposium entitled "Representing Race," which appeared in the *Michigan Law Review* in the winter of 1997. Margaret Russell noted that, for attorneys of colour, "representing race" was a "fundamental" and "inescapable" part of their professional identity and political function; Black lawyers involved in race advocacy, according to Russell (1997: 771), often face a heavy burden of "justifying either that race really exists as an issue at all, or that they are competent to address the topic of race in a fair and reasoned manner." Non-minority lawyers engaged in Critical Race Litigation will no doubt face obstacles as well. Arguably, they will meet with less hostility, however, than Black lawyers, who will often be challenged on the stereotypical basis of competency and "self-interest."

Codes of Professional Conduct

In Canada, as in the United States, lawyers are governed by law society codes of legal ethics and responsibility which set out standards of professional conduct. The Canadian Bar Association (CBA) first adopted rules of conduct in 1974 that were accepted and in some cases varied by all of the individual provincial law societies. The CBA and provincial codes of professional responsibility consist of rules, guiding principles and commentaries that Gavin MacKenzie (1993) says are designed in some cases to prohibit unethical conduct and in others to establish examples of high ethical standards to which members of the profession should aspire. The Supreme Court of Canada describes the rules of professional conduct as "important statements of public policy that express the collective views of the legal profession regarding the appropriate standards to which lawyers should adhere even though they are not binding on the courts."[2]

The existing codes of professional responsibility in Canada do not specifically address or guide lawyers with respect to the issue of race in the conduct of litigation in criminal, civil or administrative law. It has only been very recently that some provincial law societies have addressed ethical issues regarding discrimination with respect to access to the profession (admission of people of colour to law schools and to the practice of law) and in the delivery of legal services (equal legal representation for everyone in society regardless of race, colour, ethnicity, gender, sexual orientation, or disability). Not all provincial law societies have established specific anti-discrimination rules in their codes of professional responsibility, however.

The Nova Scotia Barristers' Society is one of the few provincial legal societies to adopt explicit anti-discrimination policies. For example, chapter 24 of its *Legal Ethics and Professional Conduct* handbook (NSBS 1990) states that "a lawyer has a duty to respect the human dignity and worth of all persons and to treat all persons with equality and without discrimination." The commentary that follows this rule states that "a lawyer has a duty to ensure that no one is denied services or receives inferior service because of any irrelevant characteristic or beliefs," and that the lawyer has "a duty to ensure that her or his employment practices do not offend the Rule or the Guiding Principles." The anti-discrimination rule is reinforced by rule 1, which states that "a lawyer has a duty to act with integrity," and rule 23, which states that the "lawyer has a duty to carry out all of the duties in the handbook in spirit as well as to the letter." The anti-discrimination rule is further reinforced by commentary 18.9, which tells the lawyer that she or he has a duty to foster human rights and the freedoms set forth in the *Canadian Charter of Rights and Freedoms*. The note following these commentaries states that a lawyer has a duty to become familiar with and understand the equality section of the *Charter* (section 15), as well as provincial and federal human rights legislation. The note also exhorts lawyers to "cultivate a knowledge and understanding of Canadian case law of the meaning of equality and discrimination and on adverse impact analysis, i.e. that proof of intention is not a prerequisite for proof of discrimination and that evidence of discriminatory effect or impact is sufficient to establish discrimination under Canadian Human Rights Codes and the Charter" (NSBS 1990).

Although Canadian codes of professional responsibility do not specifically address the issue of race in the conduct of litigation, the foregoing anti-discrimination rules (in provinces where they exist) coupled with the *Charter* and human rights codes would arguably preclude the use of insidious, racialized strategies in litigation such as the discriminatory use of peremptory challenges by Crown prosecutors or racial stereotyping of Black accused, victims or witnesses.

Most significantly, codes of professional responsibility in Canada do not prohibit a Critical Race Theory and Litigation approach but in fact offer (though not explicitly) some guidance to lawyers in this regard. For example, chapter 21 of the Nova Scotia Barristers' Society code of professional responsibility says that "a lawyer has a duty to encourage public respect for justice and to uphold and try to improve the administration of justice"; lawyers, according to the guiding principles, are, "by training, opportunity and experience, in a position to discover the strengths and weaknesses of laws, legal institutions and public authority, and hence have a duty to provide leadership in seeking improvements to the legal system." Further, the Nova Scotia rules[3] say that a lawyer may speak to the media on behalf of organizations which represent various racial, religious or other special interest groups, and the lawyer may also be involved as an advocate for special interest groups whose objective is "to bring about changes in legislation, government policy or even heightened public awareness about certain issues. The lawyer may properly comment about such matters" (NSBS 1990).

Chapter 3 of the Canadian Bar Association (CBA) *Code of Professional Conduct* (1987) states that the lawyer must be honest and candid when advising clients, and commentary 8 states that:

> A *bona fide* test case is not ... precluded.... So long as no injury to the person or violence is involved, the lawyer may properly advise and represent a client who, in good faith and on reasonable grounds, desires to challenge or test a law and this can most effectively be done by means of a technical breach giving rise to a test case. In all such situations the lawyer should ensure that the client appreciates the consequences of bringing a test case.

A "test case" is described in note 7 of the CBA code (1987) as challenging, for example, "the jurisdiction for or the applicability of a shop-closing by-law or a licensing measure, or to determine the rights of a class or group having some common interest."

In addition to the above-mentioned rules, guiding principles and commentaries, all provincial codes of professional conduct and the Canadian Bar Association *Code* emphasize that "the lawyer has a duty to represent the client resolutely and to ask every question, raise every issue and advance every argument" that she or he thinks will help the client's case.[4] Therefore, it appears that Critical Race Litigation strategies would meet the current ethical standards of representation set out in the Canadian Bar Association and the various provinces' codes of professional conduct. That is not to say, however, that lawyers employing race-conscious litigation strategies will not meet pressures and constraints when addressing issues of race in legal proceedings.

Applying a Critical Race Theory analysis to the existing rules of professional conduct, it can be argued that in Canada, as Margaret Russell has argued with respect to the American rules of professional conduct, what is required is a canon of legal ethics that adopts a race-conscious rather than a colour-blind stance to lawyering in order to guide the conduct of lawyers and judges when confronting matters of race (1997: 786). With respect to allegations of "playing the race card" (a hostile term used to "censure" lawyers who raise issues of race), Russell points out that the intolerance conveyed by this accusation (that a lawyer is somehow introducing the race issue where no issues of race existed) acts as a "policing" device to prevent lawyers from addressing the role of racism in law. Russell notes that: "Race-conscious lawyering will have a chance to develop only if lawyers are given the latitude to theorize about the connections between individual cases and a broader societal framework of racial hierarchy" (1997: 792).

Does this mean that lawyers and other advocates on behalf of Black people should introduce "race" into every case regardless of relevance? As indicated earlier the issue of race should be ruled out in a given case, regardless of the area of practice, only after an analysis that is grounded in the everyday, lived experiences of Black people. A Critical Race Theory analysis requires the advocate to undertake an analysis that goes behind apparently racially neutral situations or laws to determine whether or not existing practices and rules have a discriminatory impact or other racial overtones. Only by applying a Critical Race or "race-conscious" analysis to the problem can unjustified rules, procedures, practices and prejudices based on race be identified or ruled out. Although there is an absence of literature on race and lawyering in Canada and a near absence of analysis on the topic in the United States, one general commentator on legal ethics in Canada has recognized the usefulness of the deconstruction and reconstruction process: "The challenge [for lawyers] is to condemn unfailingly the injustices of the present system, but at the same time, to affirm constantly the possibilities for transformation; to be a deconstructive pessimist and a reconstructive optimist" (Hutchinson 1995: 768).

Client Versus Community Interests

"Lawyers have a duty to represent the public ...
to be social reformers"
—Thurgood Marshall (cited in K.A. Kennedy 1995)

The main duties of the lawyer include the duty to her or his client and the duty to perform her or his duties in the public interest. In a Critical Race Litigation strategy, who is the client?

There are many kinds of advocates who may separately or simultaneously represent the interests of an individual Black community member or the interests of the Black community as a whole. These advocates include not only professional advocates, such as lawyers, but also lay advocates such as community workers, activists and public interest organizations. Lawyers and others may engage in Critical Race Litigation by representing individuals or, at the public interest level, by presenting arguments that address the problems of entire communities. However, the line between the two types of advocacy is very fine and in Critical Race Litigation may often be blurred.

For lawyers, this fine line between individual representation and group/public interest representation may create particular conflicts between the "client" and the lawyer, because the lawyer may be faced with a perceived division of loyalties between the group (and the greater public) interest and the interests of the individual client, thereby blurring the "traditional" professional distinction of the lawyer's obligations to the client (for an excellent discussion of public interest lawyering, see Kirk A. Kennedy [1995] and Judith Mosoff [1992]). For example, the lawyer may have to make determinations as to whether or not to raise issues of race in a given case in spite of the reluctance of an individual client. On the other hand, lawyers can raise issues of race when they arise on the facts or on the law and thereby assist the individual victim of discrimination. The resulting decisions in individual cases may have far-reaching consequences for Black Canadians as a group, but there is no guarantee that individual lawyers in particular cases will make the effort to consult the larger Black community before they adopt particular litigation strategies. Despite these problems, the adoption of Critical Race Litigation strategies in individual cases can be an effective way of addressing issues of race and obtaining substantive outcomes for the Black community as a whole. The decisions in *Parks* and *Williams,* for example, benefited the individual clients involved in the litigation, because in one case an acquittal was restored and in the other a new trial was ordered. But these decisions also had beneficial consequences for all Black and Aboriginal accused people in future cases involving challenges for cause, as well as on the Black and Aboriginal communities as a whole, because of the findings in those cases that judges could take judicial notice of the existence of racism in a particular community and in Canadian society generally. Similarly, a *Charter* challenge through an individual case to the existing human rights system on the basis that it infringes section 15 of the *Charter* because it has a differential impact on Blacks and other people of colour (cases based on race are dismissed more often than cases based on any other ground) will benefit not only the individual litigant but people of colour generally and all disadvantaged groups enumerated in the human rights legislation.

Although group litigation and class actions might address some of the problems with individual litigation identified above, these actions may be more difficult to sustain in Canada. For example, although under Canadian common law, class actions are generally permitted by rules of civil procedure, judicial interpretation of class-action rules has been restrictive.[5] Class-action suits allow lawyers to bring a civil lawsuit on behalf of many people with the same claim and may or may not have a public interest component. For example, in Canada, the tainted blood lawsuit allowed a class of people (those who had contracted hepatitis or HIV through blood transfusions) to sue the government and the Red Cross together, in a single proceeding, instead of each individual filing a separate lawsuit.

By contrast, litigation with a purely public interest (where the client is a public interest organization, as opposed to a group of litigants filing a class action) may not always benefit an individual litigant and is based on a different idea than class actions. Public interest litigation, which may be brought by Black organizations or other equity-seeking groups rather than by a single individual client is, as Friedlander (1995: 57) describes it, litigation which will have an impact beyond that of a single individual; the impact may be broad because of the importance of the issue(s) raised (as in the *Parks*, *Williams* and *R.D.S.* cases) or because of the extent of its impact. As we have seen in the foregoing chapters, the *R.D.S.* case started out at the level of individual representation of an individual (the Black youth), but because of its potential impact on the Black community, especially Black judges, and on the public generally, it had become a public interest case by the time it reached the Supreme Court of Canada.

Friedlander (1995: 57) identifies two barriers to public interest litigation: (1) historically, only those parties with a personal interest in the outcome had legal standing, that is, the right to challenge a law in court and (2) although the Supreme Court of Canada has somewhat expanded the categories of standing to allow for increased access to the courts in public interest cases,[6] the Supreme Court seems to have been retreating from this liberal stance in recent cases.

Friedlander (1995) notes that the Supreme Court has also not addressed the barrier created by the awarding of costs against the losing party in public interest litigation. In Canada, the financial barriers to initiating public interest litigation are increased by the fact that the group initiating the litigation must obtain funding not only to cover its own legal costs but also to cover the costs of the other side if the group loses the case. There is also the risk that a group wishing to launch public interest litigation may have to provide security for costs (a deposit made to the court to ensure payment of costs if the group/litigant loses the case) before the litigation actually begins (Friedlander 1995: 55).

In spite of these barriers, the lawyer engaging in Critical Race Litigation has a number of strategy options. Historically, there were no rights-based litigation organizations in Canada to conduct Critical Race Litigation at first instance. Few cases of this nature went to the appellate courts either because of the unreceptiveness of Canadian courts to arguments based on race, the paucity of Black lawyers to bring these cases forward or the unwillingness of White lawyers to raise the "race" issue. Black organizations have recently begun to "intervene" in racially significant cases. For example, a government-funded African Canadian Legal Clinic has been created whose mandate is to address systemic racism and racial discrimination in Ontario and the rest of Canada. It is mandated to do this through test-case litigation (cases brought forward by a willing individual client to "test" a law) and intervener status in cases initiated by others. Lawyers with cases requiring a Critical Race Litigation strategy can either work with this clinic on potentially precedent-setting cases or, alternatively, seek out potential test-case litigants and Black or other organizations to become plaintiffs or to intervene in the Critical Race case they are conducting.

Options for obtaining funding for Critical Race Litigation may also be available, including the Court Challenges Program, which funds section 15 *Charter* challenges in appropriate cases, and labour unions or other public interest organizations. For example, the Ontario Legal Aid Plan has in the past provided legal-aid certificates for test cases and there is also a class-actions fund in Ontario, as well as an intervener funding project which allows some administrative tribunals to award costs to interveners.[7]

It may also be appropriate to engage in an "overall" Critical Race Litigation strategy, working with other lawyers or community organizations in different parts of the country who may have similar cases, to determine whether some jurisdictions are better for test-case strategies or funding options than others. A Critical Race Litigation strategy might also include a Critical Race Theory analysis and deconstruction of civil procedure rules in order to bring a constitutional challenge to the cost-recovery rules which inhibit access to the courts for racial minorities and other historically disadvantaged groups in society.

With respect to the question, "Who is the client in a Critical Race case, where the ultimate decision may have an impact both on an individual and on a group of people in society or on the public generally?" the lawyer has an obligation and a duty under the codes of professional conduct to be both honest and candid when advising clients. Most of the criticism directed at lawyers by Black organizations, and in some cases, by individual clients is that, when a case involves race issues, the community and the individual are not empowered in the process. The (usually White) lawyer makes the decisions without consulting with the lay people who must live with the consequences of the litigation. Specific race issues may be ignored or the litigation goal may not conform to the goals of community activism. Critical Race Litigation requires a departure from the "traditional" paradigm where the lawyer is the sole decision-maker. Most grassroots activists and organizations are informed lay advocates. They argue that community organization is often fundamental to strategic, rather than piecemeal, litigation and seek greater input into litigation strategies (Epstein 1993: 41). Individual clients who voluntarily choose to become "test case" litigants generally will not require as much counselling by the lawyer on race issues as would an individual client who finds herself or himself as an unintended "test case." The individual Black client may not want to pursue a Critical Race Litigation strategy because of a lack of understanding of the broad issues involved or because of a fear of lack of support or reprisal. It is crucial that the lawyer inform the client of the way in which she or he will conduct the case, involving the client in the process on an ongoing basis and encouraging community input and support for the client and the litigation goals. The lawyer should be respectful of the individual client's interests. However, if the client does not (after being fully informed of the broader public interest impact of the case) want to pursue the race question, the lawyer may have to determine whether to continue representing the client (especially if not pursuing the race issue will have detrimental consequences for the Black community as a whole) or to withdraw, keeping in mind that the lawyer has certain duties to the client, the court and the administration of justice which must be balanced in the decision-making process. Louise Trubek (1996: 415) discusses "lawyering for social justice" and talks about a "new theoretical lawyering model for subordinated people." Such a model emphasizes

> community organizing ... and addresses two major concerns: improving lawyer-client relationships in order to more effectively serve subordinated groups, and rethinking the relationship between legal work and political mobilization .... It views client work as transformative in and of itself, lessening the tension between advocating on behalf of individual clients and pursuing transformative goals (Trubek 1996: 416).

In the final analysis, lawyers must resolve difficult ethical issues almost daily. It is not possible to predict with certainty or to address here all of the ethical issues which may arise in race-based cases. It is safe to assume, however, that the ethical issues arising in Critical Race Litigation, while different in many respects from those arising in other types of litigation, will be legitimate and important ones, such as the need to balance the individual client's interests with community and public interests. These ethical issues require a considered and "race-conscious" analysis in order to arrive at a proper balance.

Summary

Existing codes of professional responsibility in Canada do not specifically address or guide lawyers on the issue of race in the conduct of litigation. Only a few of them explicitly prohibit discrimination in access to the profession and in the delivery of legal services. Despite these limitations, the existing professional responsibility codes do not prohibit Critical Race Litigation, and this kind of litigation strategy meets the current ethical standards of representation set out by the Canadian Bar Association and in the various provincial codes of professional conduct. Arguably, these codes, when coupled with the *Canadian Charter of Rights and Freedoms* and human rights legislation, preclude the use of insidious racialized strategies in litigation such as the discriminatory use of peremptory challenges by Crown prosecutors or racial stereotyping of Black accused, victims or witnesses.

The main duties of the lawyer include the duty to her or his client and the duty to perform her or his duties in the public interest. There is a fine line between individual representation and group/public interest representation which may create conflicts for the lawyer engaged in Critical Race Litigation. The lawyer may be faced with a perceived division of loyalties between the group and the greater public interest cause and the interests of an individual client. In resolving this ethical dilemma, the lawyer has a duty under the code of professional conduct to be both honest and candid when advising both kinds of clients.

Lawyers must continually resolve difficult ethical and moral issues. Ethical issues arising in Critical Race Litigation can be legitimate or illegitimate ones. Valid ethical concerns such as possible conflicts between the interests of individual clients and the community and the public interest require considered and race-conscious analysis in order to arrive at a balancing of the interests involved. On the other hand, accusations levelled at lawyers of using the "race card" to inject race into an otherwise "race-neutral" procedure must be distinguished from valid ethical concerns.

Extralegal Strategies

Community Activism and Coalition Building

While some have criticized Critical Race Theory as being removed from the practice of law and not adequately offering practitioners litigation and lawyering strategies, community activists have argued that both theorists and practitioners have not listened to the voice of the community. They argue that CRT has to be made accessible and viable to the activist. Legal practitioners and theorists must develop much stronger connections with Black communities in order to understand what the community issues are and to support those engaging in social activism. Where do Critical Race Theory and Litigation fit into the overall goals of the Black community? What kind of litigation and body of substantive law does the community need to use in a given situation? The *Charter*? Legislative reform? How can Critical Race Litigation strategies be combined with strategies for political organizing?

Community activism may involve both litigation and non-litigation strategies. Lawyers involved in Critical Race Litigation, whether representing individuals or using a broader public interest strategy, can use a wide range of strategic options such as test-case strategies, class actions (where applicable), client education, legislative lobbying, administrative reform, grassroots activism, media attention, sit-ins, demonstrations and coalition building, to name a few.

Recent empirical studies conducted in the United States stress the importance of integrating community activism, lawyering and academic theorizing to effect significant social change (see Yamamoto 1997: 837 and Kessler 1990: 121–26). In the Canadian context, community activists who are "rooted" in the community "continue to organize and facilitate grass-roots action that embodies the hopes and energy of many, fuelling the agenda for organizational change and social justice" (James 1996). Additionally, community activists and lay advocates are involved in the court process, advocating for social justice on behalf of individual community members, as well as raising broad public interest issues such as racist policing, discriminatory educational and employment practices, human rights and so on in the political and other arenas.[8] Their value to the Critical Race litigator cannot be underestimated. Yamamoto emphasizes the critical need for cooperation between theorists, community groups and lawyers:

> Without a strong alliance between political lawyers and community groups articulating coherent, substantive counter-messages and showing political support, court agendas reflect "the prevailing distribution of power in the external environment" in forms less threatening to powerful interests. What scholar-theorists bring to the community-lawyer alliance are critical socio-legal analysis, specific counter-messages, and larger intellectual frameworks for justifying not only legal results but also social structural changes. They [scholar-theorists] connect how we think and talk to how we act—a connection at the core of political mobilization (1997: 838–39).

This kind of cooperation among Critical Race theorists, community organizations and lawyers was highly evident in the *R.D.S., Parks* and *Williams* cases. For example, in the *R.D.S.* case (involving a Black youth) the African Canadian Legal Clinic and community-based organizations such as the Afro-Canadian Caucus of Nova Scotia and the Congress of Black Women of Canada acted as joint interveners at the Supreme Court of Canada, stating in their joint motion that they represented the African Canadian communities throughout Canada and traditionally advocate on their behalf in areas of legal, political and social concern.[9] The community-based Parent Student Association of Preston, Nova Scotia, which was formed in 1989 in response to the racial disturbances at Cole Harbour District High School in Dartmouth also filed an intervener notice stating that they represented the Black community of Nova Scotia, "who have suffered injustice at the hands of the justice system."[10]

In addition to these Black community organizations and the African Canadian Legal Clinic, coalitions were also formed transracially to intervene in the *R.D.S.* case. For example, the feminist Women's Legal Education and Action Fund (LEAF) and the National Organization of Immigrant and Visible Minority Women of Canada (NOIVMWC) filed a joint motion for intervener status. NOIVMWC is itself a coalition of member organizations which include the women's committees of the Canadian Hispanic Congress, the Chinese Canadian National Council and the Canadian Council of Filipino Associations. In the *Williams* case (involving an Aboriginal person), the diverse interveners included the Aboriginal Legal Services of Toronto Inc., the African Canadian Legal Clinic, the Urban Alliance on Race Relations (Justice) and the Criminal Lawyers' Association of Ontario. Coalition-building in this way can greatly increase resources, expertise and transracial understanding. It can also broaden the applicability of the desired litigation outcome and give the litigation higher public and political visibility.

In addition to community groups, minority legal clinics and other practitioners, legal academics were involved in the cases under discussion. They included Black academics with expertise in Critical Race Theory, Aboriginal scholars whose expertise relates to Critical Indigenous Theory, and academics whose specialties reflected other theoretical perspectives, such as feminist, leftist or traditional liberal theory.

A lawyer who is already involved in a Critical Race Litigation case or wishes to develop a Critical Race strategy can benefit immensely from involving community activists and organizations in the process. First, it is a way for White practitioners to gain a "racial perspective" which will better enable them to ground their legal analysis on the real, everyday experiences of Black people and see the law from the perspective of "non-Whites." For the Black lawyer, it provides an opportunity to reacquaint herself or himself with the aspirations of the community and provides

nurturing and support in a non-hostile environment. Further, it can provide much needed political support from the Black community for the
client and the legal strategy and help the practitioner understand the
overall political and legal goals of the community. Additionally, such
consultations may broaden the framing of the issues, provide "expert"
evidence of differential or adverse impact and identify other or similar
cases that non-Black lawyers, in particular, may not be aware of.

Yamamoto (1997) lists the ways in which Critical Race theorists and
academics can get involved with the communities about which they write.
He suggests that they can work with or advise political organizations,
litigate or consult with litigation teams, supervise law students working
on cases challenging institutional authority or actions, lobby legislative
and administrative bodies on behalf of specific organizations, work with
or serve on boards of social service and legal service groups, cultivate
relations with journalists covering community justice issues, develop
advocacy positions on specific issues for organizations, draft legal briefs,
train lay advocates and give issue and strategy presentations to community groups (1997: 900). Many of these suggestions can also be adopted
by the practitioner interested in or involved in Critical Race Litigation.
Getting to know community activists and leaders and subscribing to
community publications may also be useful strategies.

"Controlled" Civil Disobedience

> *"The lawyer for an organization can assist in the*
> *inevitable confrontation by either of two approaches:*
> *shut up and get out of the way and/or help the group*
> *discuss the best options to provoke or defend the*
> *resulting confrontation"*
> —William P. Quigley (1994: 475)

Among the many extralegal strategies which can be employed by disempowered
groups in society, demonstrations, sit-ins and "testing" laws continue to
be those most commonly used. These strategies may be employed in
conjunction with Critical Race Litigation strategies in much the same way
that Martin Luther King Jr., the NAACP and civil rights activists used them
during the struggle for "rights" in the United States. Community organizations may also decide to employ them as alternatives to litigation. What
is the lawyer's role with respect to the use of these strategies? Few
debates have occurred in Canada regarding the limits to which lawyers
may properly go in defying the law or advising or participating in "civil
disobedience."[11] Commentators in the United States also acknowledge
that published literature on the involvement of lawyers in civil disobedi-

ence or what they term "social change lawbreaking," is surprisingly slight (Abrams 1994: 753).[12]

Ethically, there would appear to be no bar against a lawyer advising clients in this regard. The Canadian codes of professional responsibility hold that lawyers are permitted to advise and represent a client in challenging or "testing" a law by breaching it, provided that no injury to the person or violence is involved (Canadian Bar Association 1987: Chapter 3, Commentary 8). However, the lawyer has a duty in these situations to ensure that the client appreciates the possible consequences, such as potential criminal conviction, should the challenge fail. Lawyers have a duty to encourage public respect for justice and to uphold and improve the administration of justice. They have a duty to provide leadership in seeking improvements to the legal system and should not hesitate to speak out against an injustice. However, the codes specify that, in discharging this duty, the lawyer should not become involved in violence or injury to the person and should not subvert the law by counselling or assisting in activities which are in defiance of it.

The Canadian rules of professional responsibility seem to set up a false dichotomy between, on the one hand, the lawyer's ability to advise and represent a client in challenging a law, and his or her duty to provide leadership in improving the legal system and speaking out against injustices and, on the other hand, her or his duty not to subvert the law by counselling or assisting in activities which are in defiance of it. Tangled up in this dichotomy is the exhortation against violence or injury in discharging their duties.

Canadian lawyers, it seems, can advise and represent clients attempting to establish a test case by employing a technical breach of the law in question, but can a lawyer be the subject of the test case? That is, can the lawyer employ civil disobedience, herself or himself, to bring attention to an unjust law or procedure? Again, very little assistance is provided to Canadian lawyers in this regard, either by the present academic literature or the current codes of professional responsibility. The codes seem to implicitly assume that lawyers, in encouraging respect for the administration of justice while at the same time trying to improve it, are obligated to do so within the confines of the law and not by violating it.

However, as Kathryn Abrams points out, a lawyer may in some cases be better situated to demonstrate the unjustness of a law than a layperson (1991: 775). She gives the example of a lawyer who applied civil disobedience techniques himself. This lawyer, a criminal defence attorney in Virginia, applied this strategy in a procedural, rather than substantive, context. The jury impanelled to try the lawyer's Black client was not a representative one. This lawyer informed the judge that he would not proceed with the case because of racial discrimination in the jury panel.

He was cited for contempt of court and jailed but persisted in his refusal to go forward. Abrams notes that this lawyer, in defending his actions, explained that "lawyers have the same responsibility as other citizens for making the dramatic, self-sacrificing statement that can produce a major legal change, a responsibility that too few are willing to accept" (1991: 775).

Whether or not an individual lawyer is willing or even permitted under existing rules of professional conduct to serve as a "test case," it is certain that under Canadian rules they can advise and represent others who wish to test a law by breaching it. I believe it is not desirable for the organized Bar, through rules of professional conduct, to attempt to limit the scope of the lawyer's choices in strategies for social change. (The lack of discussion and academic literature on this issue in Canada, however, is unfortunate and this void should be filled.)

Despite any uncertainties associated with the rules of professional conduct, lawyers in Canada (in cooperation with disadvantaged groups and clients) have still successfully combined litigation with extralegal strategies. These strategies have included political pressure, focusing media attention on the issue, and peaceful demonstrations. Such strategies may have legal risks, however. For example, as a result of a recent Nova Scotia case, two lawyers representing three twelve-year-old Black female school children who were allegedly strip-searched in their school by a White female police officer in the suspected theft of ten dollars are being sued for defamation by the police officer, who is alleging that the lawyers damaged her character and professionalism at a news conference at which she claims they portrayed her as a racist. The lawyers speculated at the news conference about whether or not White children from affluent families would have been subjected to a strip search. Should the police officer win this defamation suit, the ability to use the extralegal strategy of focusing media attention on issues of race may be seriously curtailed despite the ethical rule permitting it. Depending on the outcome of this case, lawyers may not, for example, be able to speak to the media about the way police forces deal with minorities in future cases. There is clearly a need for Critical Race Litigation to resist this lawsuit, in order to avoid an outcome which would have an adverse effect on the Black community. Indeed, success by the police officer in this lawsuit might expose even Black lay people to defamation suits if they attempt to discuss racism in public. (A detailed analysis of the law of defamation and libel is outside the scope of this book, but these race-related issues should be an explicit focus of the defence of the two lawyers in this defamation suit.)

Summary

Community activists have argued that theorists and practitioners have not listened enough to the voices of the Black community. Legal practitioners and theorists alike must develop much stronger connections with Black communities in order to understand what the community issues are and to support those involved in community activism. This connection will provide the non-Black lawyer with the racial perspective required to ground his or her legal analysis on the real, everyday experiences of Black people and to look at the law from the perspective of subordinated people. For the Black lawyer, this connection can provide a reacquaintance with the aspirations of the community and generate mutual nurturing and support.

Community activism may involve both litigation and non-litigation strategies. Lawyers involved in a Critical Race Litigation case or wishing to conduct Critical Race Litigation, whether representing an individual client or the public interest, should access the wide range of strategic options available, including, but not limited to, legislative lobbying, grassroots activism, media attention, client education, class actions, test cases, sit-ins, demonstrations and coalition-building. It is important to integrate community activism, lawyering and academic theory in order to effect significant social change.

There is no ethical bar in Canada against advising clients who wish to challenge a law by engaging in a technical breach of that law. Can or should the lawyer be the subject of a test case, and how far can the lawyer go in engaging in extralegal strategies? There is little guidance in the academic literature or in professional responsibility textbooks in this regard. Attempts should be made to fill this obvious void. Arguably, it is undesirable for the organized Bar to limit the scope of the lawyer's choices of nonviolent strategies for social change through its rules of professional conduct.

Lawyers have often used the extralegal strategy of bringing media attention to an issue. And the codes of professional responsibility generally sanction the use of the media by lawyers to assist public understanding of an issue or a case. For example, in the Nova Scotia rules (NSBS 1990), Chapter 22, Commentary 22.9, states that the lawyer may be involved as an advocate for a special interest group whose objective is to bring about changes in legislation, government policy or public awareness about certain issues, and that the lawyer may properly comment about such matters outside the courtroom.

Conclusion

"A man who stands for nothing will fall for anything"
—Malcolm X

What place do Critical Race Theory and Critical Race Litigation have in Canada's future? I believe we are on a journey of discovery in Canada. The first leg of this journey requires us to travel into our racial past to discover the role that "race" has played in Canadian law. The second leg of this journey requires us to pause in our present, to discover the role that "race" continues to play in law and to deconstruct this role. The final leg requires us to envision law in the future from a reconstructionist standpoint.

This book has outlined the history of Critical Race Theory, which had its beginnings in the United States but is being developed into a uniquely Canadian version by theorists of colour. Theory development is essential for meaningful social change to occur. Two problems have been identified with respect to further Critical Race Theory development in Canada, however. First, there is a paucity of Black and other scholars of colour in the legal academy and in other disciplines to facilitate greater development of this theory. The role of Critical Race Theory in Canada's future therefore depends on the willingness of institutions of higher education to diversify not only their student bodies but their faculties as well. Second, Critical Race Theory has been criticized for being too removed from the practice of law and for not adequately offering practitioners, communities and social activists litigation and social-change strategies. The future challenge for Critical Race theorists will be to develop ideas which are more accessible to legal practitioners, lay advocates, social activists, students and those in other academic disciplines. The future challenge for the legal practitioner engaged in Critical Race Litigation and race-conscious lawyering is to develop stronger connections to the communities of colour and to educate and involve these communities and their clients in the legal strategy. Some ethical issues will be "illegitimate," in the sense that they result from a resistance by courts, other lawyers, Bar societies and some members of society to prevent those interested in social change from asking the "race" question. These invalid ethical issues may include accusations that the lawyer is "playing the race card" in order to inject race into an otherwise "race-neutral" proceeding and thereby obtain some kind of strategic advantage, or that raising issues of race is not in the public interest. Part of the lawyer's challenge, therefore, will be to cultivate an ability to distinguish between valid ethical concerns and those predicated on fear of or resistance to social change.

The future of Critical Race Litigation in Canada really depends on the willingness and ability of lawyers to ask "race" questions in all areas of legal practice (whether they be corporate, labour, environmental, criminal, family, administrative, human rights or tort law) and to identify the oppressions which can be overcome through law. The challenge will be to reconceptualize the basic question. We should not ask why "race" is an issue, but rather why "race" is *not* an issue.

Abbreviations

Acronyms and Initialisms

ACLC	African Canadian Legal Clinic
ACLU	American Civil Liberties Union
CBA	Canadian Bar Association
CLS	Critical Legal Studies
CRL	Critical Race Litigation
CRT	Critical Race Theory
GAO	U.S. General Accounting Office
HIV	human immunodeficiency virus (which can lead to AIDS)
LAPD	Los Angeles Police Department
LEAF	Women's Legal Education and Action Fund
MDTs	mobile digital terminals
NAACP	National Association for the Advancement of Colored People
NACDL	National Association of Criminal Defence Lawyers
NOIVMWC	National Organization of Immigrant and Visible Minority Women of Canada
NSLRC	Law Reform Commission of Nova Scotia
PCP	Phencyclidine (angel dust)
WAARP	Women's Action Against Racist Police

Legal Abbreviations

2d Cir.	Second Circuit
A.B.A.J.	American Bar Association Journal
A.G.	Attorney General
All E.R.	All England Law Reports
Alta. L. Rev.	Alberta Law Review
Alta. Q.B.	Alberta Queen's Bench
Alta. T.D.	Albert Trial Division

B.C.C.A.	British Columbia Court of Appeal
B.C.J.	British Columbia Judgement
B.C.R.	British Columbia Reports
c.	Chapter
C.A.	Court of Appeal
C.A.C.	Canadian Appeal Court
Cal. L. Rev.	California Law Review
C.C.C.	Canadian Criminal Cases
C.J.S.C.	Chief Justice of the Supreme Court
C.J.W.L.	Canadian Journal of Women and the Law
C.N.L.R.	Canadian Native Law Reporter
C.R.	Criminal Reports
Crim. L.Q.	Criminal Law Quarterly
Dkt.	docket
D.L.R.	Dominion Law Reports
F.	Federal Reporter (U.S.)
F. Supp.	Federal Supplement
Harv. C.R.-C.L. L. Rev	Harvard Civil Rights and Civil Liberties Law Review
H.C.	High Court of Justice
H.L.	House of Lords
H.R. Y.B.	Human Rights Year Book
How. L.J.	Howard Law Journal
J.	Justice
JJ.	Justices
J.L. & Pol.	Journal of Law and Policy
Law & Soc. Rev.	Law & Society Review
L.J.	Law Journal
Loy. L. Rev.	Loyola Law Review
L. Rev.	Law Review
Man. C.A.	Manitoba Court of Appeal
Man. R.	Manitoba Reports
Mich. L. Rev.	Michigan Law Review
Minn.	Minnesota
N.S.C.A.	Nova Scotia Court of Appeal
N.S.R.	Nova Scotia Reports
N.W.	North Western Reporter
Ohio N.U. L. Rev.	Ohio Northern University Law Review
O.J. Comm.	O.J. Simpson Commentary
O.L.R.	Ontario Law Reports
Ont. C.A.	Ontario Court of Appeal
Ont. Ct. Gen. Div.	Ontario Court General Division

Ont. H.C.	Ontario High Court of Justice
R.	Regina (The Queen)
R.S.C	Revised Statues of Canada
R.S.M.	Revised Statutes of Manitoba
R.S.N.S.	Revised Statutes of Nova Scotia
R.S.O.	Revised Statutes of Ontario
R.S.P.E.I.	Revised Statutes of Prince Edward Island
s.	Section
Sask. C.A.	Saskatchewan Court of Appeal
S.C.	(provincial) Supreme Court
S.C.C.	Supreme Court of Canada
S.C.J.	Supreme Court Judgement
S.C.N.S.	Supreme Court of Nova Scotia
S.C.R.	Supreme Court Reporter
S.Ct.	Superior Court
S.Ct.	(U.S.) Supreme Court Reporter
S.N.S.	Statues of Nova Scotia
Stat.	Statutes
Sup. Ct.	Superior Court
Tex. L. Rev.	Texas Law Review
U.N.B.L.J.	University of New Brunswick Law Journal
U. Pitt. L. Rev	University of Pittsburg Law Review
U.S.	United States Supreme Court
U.S.C.	United States Code
v.	versus
WL	Westlaw (software)
YO	Youth Court

Notes

Preface

1. Full legal citations for these and other cases are provided in the text where the cases are discussed in detail. Legal citations may also be found in the References.

Introduction

1. The Commission on Systemic Racism in the Ontario Criminal Justice System (1995) noted that a major study of admissions to Ontario prisons indicates that "for the period studied, the majority of prisoners are white, but that black men, women, and male youths are massively over-represented.... The over-representation of black people reflects a dramatic increase in their admissions to prison between 1986/87 and 1992/93. By the end of these six years, black adults were admitted to prison at over five times the rate of white adults, proportionate to their representation in Ontario's population." The Commission also found that although more black men than black women are in jail, black women are more over-represented among prison admissions than black men. And the most dramatic differences in admission rates of white and black adults involve pre-trial imprisonment for highly discretionary charges. The Commission documented that "In 1992/93 the black pre-trial admission rate for drug trafficking/importing charges was 27 times higher than the white rate; for drug possession charges, the black pre-trial admission rate was 15 times higher, and for obstructing justice charges, the black pre-trial admission rate was 13 times higher." The Commission concluded that the data could not be "rationalized" by racial or cultural propensities and that "wherever broad discretion exists, racialization can influence decisions and produce racial inequality and outcomes" (1995: iv).
2. The comments contained here first appeared in my article, "Take The Long Way Home: *R.D.S.* and Critical Race Theory" (1999). These comments relied on A. Altman (1990).
3. Naomi R. Cahn (1994) developed these concepts in the context of feminist litigation, from which I have borrowed in many respects. However, Critical Race Litigation differs significantly from feminist litigation. The main similarity is that both aim to integrate theory and practice.

Chapter 1

1. For a critique of Critical Legal Studies, in addition to Andrew Altman (1990), see Unger (1986). For an example of a Critical Race Theory critique of liberalism and the Critical Legal Studies movement, see Williams (1997); and Bell (1990), reprinted in Delgado (1995: 2). Also see Spann (1971), reprinted in Delgado (1995: 21).

2. These comments regarding the rule of law and the Critical Legal Studies movement's attack on it as being a "myth" first appeared in my article, "Take the Long Way Home" (1999).

3. These views were expressed at the Critical Race Theory Conference, held at Yale University on November 13–15, 1997, by Aboriginal and Indigenous scholars, such as Patricia Monture-Angus, John Burrows, Kekailoa Perry and Estevan Rael Y Galvez, speaking on a panel entitled "CRT and Indigenous Peoples." The wide-ranging topics of discussion for this panel were stated thus: "Indigenous Peoples law/theory by necessity focuses on issues of political and economic identity and survival. Indigenous scholars and advocates concern themselves primarily with territorial sovereignty, responsible governance, economic development, legal structural development, and religious freedom in specific geographic sites. As of yet, few explicit connections exist between CRT and Indigenous law/theory. Why does this gap exist? Does CRT have relevance to the Indigenous law/theory movement? Would the adoption of critical race concepts and methods inadvertently further the assimilative and destructive force of western law on Indigenous ways, theories and values? What can CRT scholars learn from Indigenous studies? Would, for example, such attention deepen CRT's capacity to critique colonialism? Are there barriers (epistemological, attitudinal or political) that keep CRT scholars from opening themselves to Indigenous scholars' concerns, work and visions for change?

4. "Jim Crow" refers to the "separate but equal" doctrine first embraced by the United States Supreme Court in *Plessy* v. *Ferguson*, (1896, 163 U.S. 537), which held that "separate but equal policies such as existed in education, housing, transportation and virtually all aspects of American society, were acceptable as long as the 'races' were treated equally once they were separated." The courts authorized racial segregation and discrimination in public schools, libraries, rest rooms, public accommodations, places of employment and other areas of life. As Brooks and Newborn put it: "In short, under the separate-but-equal policy, African Americans were legally locked out of mainstream society by a system of apartheid that controlled all aspects of life in the South and by a looser but still prominent form of racial segregation in the North" (1994: 789). The name "Jim Crow" originally came from the title of a minstrel song that portrayed Blacks as childlike and inferior beings.

5. This formulation of the tenets of Critical Race Theory emanates from a number of sources. It should be noted, however, that Critical Race theorists are not monolithic and some divisions do exist. However, I have canvassed the existing Critical Race Theory material and collapsed the various opinions into what I consider to be the majority consensus on the ideology and

methodology of the movement, including my own views. Some of these sources include: Calmore (1997), Matsuda (1987), Aylward (1998), Cook (1990), Delgado (1987), Lawrence (1987), Crenshaw (1988), Johnson (1994), Bell (1985 and 1992), Aleinikoff (1991), St. Lewis (1994) and Thornhill (1994).

6. It should be noted that in recent years some mainstream feminist scholars have attempted to address these shortcomings. See, for example, Kline (1989) and Backhouse (1994).

7. For further works on the Canadian experience of slavery, see Cahill (1994) and Holman (1982).

8. These task force and royal commission reports include some of the following: *Report of The Royal Commission on the Donald Marshall Jr. Prosecution* (Nova Scotia, 1989); *The Report on Systemic Racism in the Ontario Criminal Justice System* (1996) and *Law Enforcement and Race Relations in Canada* (1992). For an extensive listing, see Canadian Centre for Police-Race Relations (1993) and Aylward (1998: 249).

9. For further works by scholars of colour and others on the various aspects of racism in Canada, see McKaque (1991).

10. Referred to in the Indigenous Blacks and Mi'kmaq Programme Curriculum Review Project, *Black Perspectives on Criminal Justice: The Individual and the State,* by Natalie Francis, student researcher, supervised by Catherine Cogswell and coordinated and developed by Carol A. Aylward, Halifax, Dalhousie Law School (available from the director of the Indigenous Black and Mi'kmaq (IB&M) program at Dalhousie Law School), 47.

Chapter 2

1. All references to the facts in the Rodney King case and to Rodney King's personal history are taken from Jewelle Taylor Gibbs' well-researched book, *Race and Justice: Rodney King and O.J. Simpson, A House Divided* (1996), as well as highly publicized news accounts at the time of the L.A. riots. Rodney King had been initially stopped for a (less serious) misdemeanour offence of drunk driving, but no charges of any kind were ultimately laid against King, including charges of resisting arrest. See Levenson (1994: 524).

2. 18 U.S.C., s. 242 (1988), deprivation of rights under colour of law. On August 4, 1992, a federal grand jury indicted the four officers. Officers Powell, Briseno and Wind were charged under federal law with wilful use of unreasonable force, and Officer Koon was charged with wilfully permitting the other officers to use unreasonable force during the arrest. After a trial in the United States District Court for the Central District of California, the jury convicted Officers Koon and Powell but acquitted Officers Wind and Briseno.

3. The riots in Los Angeles also triggered violence in San Francisco, Seattle, Miami, Las Vegas, Atlanta and Toronto. See Davis and Graham (1995: 397).

4. For a discussion of the Slave Codes (a mixture of legislation controlling the behaviour of slaves), see Forte (1998: 569).

5. *Emancipation Proclamation, 1863,* 12 Stat. 68: "I, Abraham Lincoln, President of the United States ... do ... order and declare that all persons held as slaves within said designated States and parts of States are, and henceforward shall be, free; and that the Executive Government of the United States, including the military and naval authorities thereof, will recognize and maintain the freedom of said persons."

6. The Black Codes were based on the Slave Codes and as Forte (1998: 579) notes, "The codes placed blacks in a semi-permanent servitude on plantations.... Under the Mississippi Code, for example, sheriffs and justices of the peace were directed to apprentice all black orphans or minors whose parents were without means of support with the former [slave] owners having first preference."

7. See Davis and Graham (1995: 359), in which they discuss cases such as *Missouri* v. *Jenkins* (1990, 495 U.S. 33), *Board of Education of Oklahoma City Public Schools* v. *Dowell* (1991, 498 U.S. 237), *Freeman* v. *Pitts* (1992, 112 S.Ct. 1430), and *United States* v. *Fordice* (1992, 112 S.Ct. 2727), where the current U.S. Supreme Court still had school desegregation cases on its agenda in the 1990s. These major cases before the Court dealt with the issue of whether there were limits to a Federal Court's supervision of school desegregation orders. Davis and Graham conclude that these cases indicate that "truly desegregated schools were, at most, an ideal" (1995: 359).

8. Kimberlé Crenshaw, in her critical piece, *Race, Reform, and Retrenchment: Transformation and Legitimation in Antidiscrimination Law* (1988: 1378), observes that "the civil rights movement achieved material and symbolic gains for blacks, yet left racist ideology and race-baiting politics intact" (referred to by Harris 1994: 743).

9. Derrick Bell, a Critical Race theorist and a founder of the movement, also notes in his article, *Racial Realism* (1992b: 369): "A paradigm example presents itself in *Bakke*. Relying heavily on the formalistic language of the Fourteenth Amendment, and utterly ignoring social questions about which race in fact has power and advantages and which race has been denied entry for centuries into academia ... the Court effectively made a choice to ignore historical patterns, to ignore contemporary statistics, and to ignore flexible reasoning."

10. "In the eighty-one-second video, King can be seen getting upon his hands and knees at least twice, covering his face to ward off the blows, and trying to escape from the brutal assault.... The video records a group of police officers standing around watching but not attempting to intervene to stop it" (Gibbs 1996: 30). Notably, the Grand Jury which indicted the four police officers in the state trial declined to indict any of the other seventeen officers who watched the beating. Gibbs notes that the District Attorney stated at the time that "however morally wrong their failure to intercede in California law there is no criminal statute under which these officers can be indicted. The Black community was incensed by this injustice" (1996: 30).

11. Statement by the NAACP Legal Defence and Education Fund (1992). Four weeks after the beating of Rodney King, LAPD officers fatally shot a twenty-eight-year-old Black man, Henry Peco. This fatal shooting again caused a confrontation between LAPD officers and residents of a Black housing project

in Watts. See Harris (1997: 184).

12. The federal charges in this case alleged a violation of King's Fourteenth Amendment right to be kept free from harm while in official custody and his Fourth Amendment right to be free from the use of unreasonable force. To supplement Fourteenth Amendment constitutional protection, there are federal civil rights statutes in the United States designed to prohibit private conduct that interferes with federal constitutional rights. Sections 241 and 242 of Title 18, U.S.C., are contained in federal criminal statutes that address private violations of federal civil rights under the Fourteenth Amendment. See also Davis and Graham (1995: 156).

13. Title 18, U.S.C. (1991), sections 241 and 242 are the federal criminal statutes that address private interferences with federal civil rights. See Davis and Graham (1995: 155–56). Section 241 states: "If two or more persons conspire to injure, oppress, threaten, or intimidate any inhabitant of any State, Territory, or District in the free exercise or enjoyment of any right or privilege secured to him by the Constitution or laws of the United States, or because of his having so exercised the same; or if two or more persons go in disguise on the highway, or on the premises of another, with intent to prevent or hinder his free exercise or enjoyment of any right or privilege so secured, they shall be fined not more than $10,000 or imprisoned not more than ten years, or both; and if death results, they shall be subject to imprisonment for any term of years or for life." And section 242 states: "Whoever, under colour of any law, statute, ordinance, regulation, or custom, willfully subjects any inhabitant of any State, Territory, or District to the deprivation of any rights, privileges, or immunities secured or protected by the Constitution or laws of the United States, or to different punishments, pains, or penalties, on account of such inhabitant being an alien, or by reason of his colour, or race, than are prescribed for the punishment of citizens, shall be fined not more than $1,000 or imprisoned not more than one year, or both; and if bodily injury results shall be fined under this title or imprisoned not more than ten years, or both; and if death results shall be subject to imprisonment for any term of years or for life." Also see Levenson (1994: 565).

14. In *Screws* v. *United States* (1945, 325 U.S. 91), Clause Screws, the sheriff of Baker County, Georgia, and another policeman arrested a black man for stealing a tire. He was beaten while handcuffed and died without regaining consciousness. The policemen were convicted under what is now section 242 of Title 18, U.S.C., for violating the victim's federal due process rights as officials acting under colour of law. They were charged that, acting under colour of state law, they had "wilfully" deprived the prisoner of the right not to be deprived of life without due process of law, the right to be given a fair trial, and the right to be punished in accordance with the laws of Georgia, and that the denial of these rights violated the Fourteenth Amendment. The Court interpreted the section narrowly by requiring specific intent to deprive a person of a federal right. See Davis and Graham (1995: 73); also see Bell (1992a).

15. See the United States Sentencing Guidelines, 1992 U.S.S.G., s. 2H1.4. The U.S. Sentencing Guidelines establish ranges of criminal sentences for federal offences and offenders. A District Court must impose a sentence within the

applicable guideline range if it finds the case to be a typical one. See *Koon* v. *U.S.* (1996, 116 S.Ct. 2035 at 2040).

16. Statement made by defence lawyer Johnnie Cochran following the conviction of his client, Black Panther Geronimo Pratt.

17. See Dershowitz (1996: 53). Dershowitz relies upon a report by the Mollen Commission, which was established to look into cases of police corruption in the New York Police Department in 1994. The Commission noted (1994: 36) that "officers reported a litany of manufactured tales. For example, when officers unlawfully stop and search a vehicle because they believe it contains drugs or guns, officers will falsely claim in police reports and under oath that the car ran a red light (or committed some other traffic violation) and that they subsequently saw contraband in the car in plain view. To conceal an unlawful search of an individual who officers believe is carrying drugs or a gun, they will falsely assert that they saw a bulge in the person's pocket or saw drugs and money changing hands. To justify unlawfully entering an apartment where officers believe narcotics or cash can be found, they pretend to have information from an unidentified civilian informant." Dershowitz (1996: 56) notes that such corruption has been found to exist in virtually every large city and that almost every city, "from Philadelphia, to Chicago, to Pittsburgh, to Detroit, to New Orleans, to Boston has experienced epidemics of evidence planting, false testimony, police cover-ups, and the like."

18. Davis (1987: 427) discusses the United States Supreme Court's failure to provide a clear and effective remedy for discriminatory pretextual traffic stops. In *Whren* v. *United States* (1996, 116 S.Ct. 1769), the Black motorists claimed that "pretextual stops" of Black motorists (stops in which a police officer pretends to stop a person for one reason to cover up the fact that he or she is investigating the person for an entirely different reason) violate the Fourth Amendment of the Constitution and are racially motivated. The Court rejected this claim and upheld the constitutionality of these stops based on probable cause, noting that claims of racial discrimination should be challenged under the Equal Protection Clause (Fourteenth Amendment). Davis (1977: 426) argues that the Court effectively sidestepped the subtextual issue of race in pretextual traffic stops.

19. Alschuler (1995: 704) notes that in Miami in 1980 four White police officers were tried on charges that they had beaten to death an African-American arrested for a traffic offence. The defendants' attorneys rejected every potential Black juror, and an all-White jury ultimately acquitted the officers. The Miami riots followed. Alschuler (1995) observes that, "Few statements are more likely to evoke disturbing images of American criminal justice than this one: 'the defendant was tried by an all-white jury.'" Many Critical Race theorists argue for colour-conscious jury selection methods to ensure racial proportionality not only in the initial jury pool but in the selection process as well. Bell (1992a: 5.20) argues that "the jury system must be structured to produce a substantial number of blacks on juries trying cases directly affecting the interests of black litigants or the black community."

20. Judicial Council Advisory Committee (1994): "Only 3.8% of all state court judges are African-American and in Los Angeles less that 10% of the prosecutors are Black or Hispanic. Out of 200 criminal and civil Assistant United

States attorneys in Los Angeles, only 19 are Black or Hispanic." The Judicial Council Advisory Committee on Racial and Ethnic Bias in the Courts was one of many task forces and committees designed to investigate racial issues affecting the administration of justice in California and across the United States. The Committee found that Whites constitute more than eighty percent of the judiciary and hold the majority of top-level management positions and Blacks only make up two percent of the active attorney population in California out of 150,000 attorneys, even though the number of Black law school graduates has doubled from 1984 to 1994. Also see Levenson (1994: 564–65).

21. There is a legislative differentiation between penalties for the possession of powdered cocaine and crack cocaine. Five Black Americans challenged a Minnesota statutory scheme which provided forty-eight months imprisonment for the possession of crack cocaine but only twelve months imprisonment for the possession of powdered cocaine. The plaintiffs alleged that because 96.69 percent of those charged with crack possession were Black, and 79.6 percent of those charged with possession of powdered cocaine were White, the statutes had a discriminatory impact had on Blacks. A Black female judge ruled that the state had made an insufficient showing with respect to the pharmacological differences between the two forms of cocaine to justify the disparate impact sanctions on Blacks. See *State* v. *Russell* (1991, 477 N.W. [2d] 866 [Minn.]) referred to by Barnes (1995: 338). See also NACDL (1997), in which the NACDL reports that in February 1995 the U.S. Sentencing Commission released a report confirming that the harsher federal sentences for crack and powder cocaine are being imposed almost exclusively on Blacks and other minorities. See also Butler (1995: 718), where he notes that under United States federal law, if someone possesses fifty grams of crack cocaine, the mandatory minimum sentence is ten years. In order to receive the same sentence for powder cocaine, the defendant must possess five thousand grams. Butler notes that there is an extreme disparity between crack and powder in both the enforcement of the law and actual sentencing because most of the people who are arrested for crack cocaine offences are Black and most arrested for powder cocaine are White.

22. One of the reasons the National Association of Criminal Defence Lawyers in the United States opposes capital punishment is that it is disproportionately sought and carried out against racial minorities, particularly Blacks. In June 1997 the NACDL policy statement declared that numerous studies "have revealed that the race of the defendant, the race of the victim, and the defendant's social and economic status are significant factors in the application of capital punishment." At the state level, a U.S. General Accounting Office (GAO) report concluded that available research "shows a pattern of evidence indicating racial disparities in the charging, sentencing, and imposition of the death penalty" (GAO 1990). At the federal level, a March 1994 report by the House Judiciary Subcommittee on Civil and Constitutional Rights concluded that "Racial minorities are being prosecuted under the federal death penalty law far beyond their proportion in the general population or in the population of criminal offenders" (NACDL 1997).

23. Superior Court of the State of California in and for the County of Los

Angeles, August 1995, Department 103, Case No. BA097211, *People* v. *Orenthal James Simpson*, Judge Ito's First Ruling on the Fuhrman Tapes.

24. "Defendant's Motion That the Defence Be Permitted to Cross-examine Detective Fuhrman About His 1981–1983 Lawsuit in Which He Admitted to an Uncontrollable and Disabling Rage and Bigotry Against Criminal Suspects and African-Americans" (*People of the State of California* v. *Orenthal James Simpson*, No. BA097211 [Cal. S.Ct.], 1994, 1995 WL 516132). See Dershowitz (1996), *Fuhrman* v. *City of Los Angeles*, Findings, at 1; and *Memorandum of Points and Authorities in Support of [Fuhrman's] Petition for Writ of Mandamus*, Sup. Ct., Dkt. No. C465544 (Los Angeles County, August 23, 1983), at 5–6, referred to by Dershowitz (1996), urging that Fuhrman be found "clearly disabled from his position as a police officer on the ground that his return to any police-related activities would present a threat to petitioner himself, the Police department and to the public at large." Judge Ito ruled that the defence could not use the disability claim to impeach the credibility of Detective Fuhrman. See Dershowitz (1996: 60–61) where he quotes from an interview given by F. Lee Bailey to ABC's "Good Morning America" show on March 15, 1995: "These are Fuhrman's own words, and we're not being able to confront him with his own words. And so we get a situation where he says he's not a racist. [Kathleen] Bell [a witness who subsequently testified for the defence] says he is a racist. The jury can't resolve it because they're being denied the tools necessary to resolve these issues."

25. Butler (1995: 700) notes that it is the prerogative of juries to nullify and that, in the United States, the doctrine of jury nullification originally was based on the common law idea that "the function of a jury was, broadly, to decide justice, which included judging the law as well as the facts. If jurors believed that applying a law would lead to an unjust conviction, they were not compelled to convict someone who had broken that law.... Although most American courts now disapprove of a jury's deciding anything other than the 'facts,' the Double Jeopardy Clause of the Fifth Amendment prohibits appellate reversal of a jury's decision to acquit." Butler (1995: 712) describes the distinction between the 'traditionally approved' examples of jury nullification and its contemporary practice (by African-Americans): "Traditionally, jurors refused to apply a particular law, e.g., a fugitive slave law, on the grounds that it was unfair, while in the case of [contemporary practice by African-Americans], jurors are not so much judging discrete statutes as they are refusing to apply those statutes to members of their own race." Butler also argues that if it is right that the presence of Black jurors sends a political message it is right that these jurors use their power to control or negate the meaning of that message" (1995: 712).

26. See Dershowitz (1996: 85) quoting from an interview given by White juror Anise Aschenbach on CBS's TV show "This Morning" on October 12, 1995: "I didn't feel good about the evidence. There was so ... much doubt ... with the possibility of Fuhrman, you know, possibly planting the glove ... plus that same evidence maybe getting into the Bronco ... made me doubt the credibility of [the prosecution's] best evidence, which was blood and trace evidence.... If we made a mistake, I would rather it be a mistake on the side of a person's innocence than the other way."

Chapter 3

1. Portions of Chapter 3 have been adapted from my earlier article, "Take The Long Way Home: R.D.S. and Critical Race Theory" (1998).

2. Also see Mendes (1995: 3-2) where it is emphasized that "the *Charter* has not been used extensively as a litigation tool to combat racism in Canadian society."

3. *R.D.S. v. The Queen*, Appellant's Factum, Supreme Court of Canada, File No. 25063, at 26 (available from the author).

4. The Critical Race Theory method of narrative has been criticized. See, for example, Rosen (1996), in which he denounces the narrative or storytelling strategy employed by Johnny Cochran in the defence of O.J. Simpson. Cochran, he says, through storytelling, set out to "create a narrative that transformed O.J. from coddled celebrity into the civil rights martyr of a racist police force.... He put Mark Fuhrman's racial epithets on trial, suggesting ... that, because reality is owed to language, hate speech can be compared to physical assault." Rosen categorizes narrative or storytelling methodology as "nothing more than a proposal for broadening the narratives available to judges and juries, to help them get (quite literally) to the bottom of things.... Instead of being limited by a legal system that 'disaggregates and atomizes' communal grievances into individual disputes, Critical Race theorists recommend that litigants think about group grievances rather than their own, and tell 'the broad story of dashed hopes and centuries-long mistreatment that afflicts an entire people and forms the historical and cultural background of your complaint'" (1996: 2).

5. Professor Glasbeek was asked to look into the way in which the criminal justice system dealt with eight shootings of Black citizens following encounters with the police in Ontario.

6. Examples of the police excessive-use-of-force cases contained in this book are taken from Glasbeek (1995), unless otherwise indicated.

7. This committee was formed by Black community activists to address the issue of police shootings of Black persons in Ontario and elsewhere in Canada. Other community groups also formed around this issue, for example, the Coalition Against Racist Violence; Women's Action Against Racist Police (WAARP), 1989; Chinese Canadian National Council; Toronto Coalition Against Racism; and the African Canadian Legal Clinic. For publications dealing with this issue, see *Target Magazine*, a publication of the Coalition Against Racist Police Violence; and *Currents, Readings In Race Relations: Race and the Canadian Justice System,* published by the Urban Alliance on Race Relations (founded in 1975), a quarterly magazine supported by the Department of Canadian Heritage, the Municipality of Metropolitan Toronto, the City of Toronto, the Trillium Foundation and the United Way of Greater Toronto.

8. Statistical sources referred to by Nolan (1996) include Geller and Scott, (1992); 1991 Census, Statistics Canada; and the Cole-Gittens Commission. *Data refers to fatal shootings only.* See also *Target Magazine* (April 1997) statistics for Metro Toronto police shootings for 1996 (first six months):

three persons of colour shot, and the shooting death of Hugh George Dawson, a Black teenager, on March 30, 1997, by Metro Toronto police officers Richard Shank and Rajeev Sukurman. This is the second shooting death of a Black youth involving officer Shank. He also shot and killed Ian Coley, a twenty-year-old Black man, in 1993.

9. The Royal Commission on the Donald Marshall Jr. Prosecution (Nova Scotia, 1989); Policing on the Blood Reserve (Alberta, 1990); the Aboriginal Justice Inquiry (Manitoba, 1991); Maloney Report to the Metropolitan Toronto Police (1975); the Royal Commission into Metropolitan Toronto Police Practices (by Hon. Justice Morand, 1976); the Walter Pitman Report: *Now Is Not Too Late* (1977); *Report to the Civic Authorities of Metropolitan Toronto Council and Its Citizens* (by Cardinal Carter, 1979); Dr. Reva Gerstein's *Report of the Task Force on the Racial and Ethnic Implications of Police Hiring, Training, Promotion and Career Development* (1980); the Clare Lewis *Report on Investigations into Relations Between Police Forces, Visible and Other Ethnic Minorities* (Montreal, 1988); the Stephen Lewis Report (Toronto, 1992); the *Commission des droits de la personne/Investigation Committee on relations between police forces, visible and other ethnic minorities* (Quebec, 1988); Follow-up Committee to oversee actions in response to the recommendations made by the Investigation Committee (Quebec, 1995); the Yarosky Report (Montreal, 1992); the Corbo Report (Montreal, 1992); the Malouf Report (Montreal, 1994); the Thomassin Report (Montreal, 1993); the Reid Report, *Law Enforcement and Race Relations in Canada* (July 1992); Cherif and Niemi, *And Justice for All/A Report on the Relations Between Police and Visible Minorities in Montreal* (Montreal, 1984); Task Force on the Relations Between the MUC Police and the Black Community of Montreal, Canada (Ottawa, 1993); see also Canadian Centre for Police-Race Relations, *Federal and Provincial Royal Commissions, Task Forces and Inquiries into Police/Aboriginal and Police/Visible Minority Relations: A Compilation*, (March 1993); and the *Report on Systemic Racism in the Ontario Criminal Justice System* (1996).

10. Also see Cox (1991: A8), who notes: "Halifax police didn't adequately investigate allegations that officers beat a black man and shoved him through a window and called another 'nigger' as they broke up a racial brawl in July, civilians on a panel reviewing the incident say."

11. Saunders (1995) notes that the lawyers were criticized sharply by Halifax Police Chief Vince MacDonald, who "decried the suggestion, saying he considered it 'out of order' and 'unusual.'" The police officer involved filed a lawsuit based on defamation against the two lawyers, and the matter is still pending.

12. *R.D.S.* v. *The Queen*, Appellant's Factum, S.C.C., File No. 25063, March 10, 1997, at 29.

13. Ibid., at 14.

14. Ibid.

15. Ibid., at 35–36.

16. *R.D.S.* v. *The Queen*, Respondent's Factum, S.C.C., File No. 25063, March 10, 1997, at 47.

17. Note that Justices McLachlin, La Forest and Gonthier concur in this analysis,

but Justices Cory and Iacobucci do not. It goes without saying that dissenting Chief Justice Lamer and Justices Major and Sopinka also do not support this position and specifically state that: "Whether racism exists in our society is not the issue. The issue is whether there was evidence before the court upon which to base a finding that *this* particular police officer's actions were motivated by racism. There was no evidence of this presented at the trial" (at para. 6).

18. See Ross, (1989) also found in Delgado (1995), in which Ross theorizes about narratives. In discussing the *City of Richmond* v. *J.A. Croson Co.* case (1998, 448 U.S.), he reads judicial opinions as narratives, as a way of "illuminating the idea of law as composed essentially of choices made for and against people, and imposed through violence.... The *Richmond* case spawned six opinions—six potential narratives. Each narrative is rich. Yet, the most powerful, complex, and important narratives are the concurring opinion by Justice Scalia and the dissenting opinion by Justice Marshall. Scalia's opinion as narrative is on the surface an impoverished and abstract story.... Seeing judicial opinions as narratives and then linking that conception to ideology is, in one sense, a simple matter. A judge chooses to tell the reader one thing and not another. For example, in *Richmond*, Justice Marshall chooses to tell the reader the story of Richmond's resistance to school desegregation. Justice Scalia chooses not to speak of Richmond's school desegregation at all.... Telling, or not telling, the reader that this is a city with a 'disgraceful history' of race relations is a rhetorical move connected to ideology."

19. For a discussion of the "ordinary person" in the defence of provocation, see Grant, Chunn and Boyle (1994). See also *Lavallee* v. *R.*, [1990] 76 C.R. [3d] 329, [1990] 1 C.C.R. 852, [1990] 55 C.C.C. [3d] 97, [1990] 1 S.C.R. 888 [S.C.C.].

20. See also L'Heureux-Dubé J.'s opinion, *R.D.S.* v. *The Queen*, 1997, at para. 28, and Gonthier J.'s opinion, *R.D.S.* v. *The Queen,* 1997, at para. 26.

21. See also L'Heureux-Dubé J., *R.D.S.* v. *The Queen,* 1997, at para. 31.

22. Also see Hutchinson (1991: 241), where he notes that "insofar as we continue to turn to courts on issues of social justice, it is vital that more attention is paid to the ideological make-up of judges and that we explode the myths of judicial objectivity and neutrality.... The 'good judge' is someone who knows that there are no easy and objective answers.... [H]e or she attempts to listen to and empathise with the plight of litigants, retains a willingness to rethink their own views in light of that experience, and makes decisions that they are prepared to take personal responsibility for."

23. Interestingly, Justice Cory avoided the issue of judicial notice by making a rather curious reference to the fact that an intervener and not the appellant raised the issue and therefore it was not proper for the Court to consider the argument. This is curious since it completely ignores the fact that the respondent in the case argued that the case was in fact about judicial notice.

24. L'Heureux-Dubé J., *R.D.S.* v. *The Queen,* at para. 40, states "Further, notwithstanding that their own insights into human nature will properly play a role in making findings of credibility or factual determinations, judges must make those determinations only after being equally open to, and considering

the views of, all parties before them."

25. At least one commentator notes that the main difference between the position taken by Justices Cory and Iacobucci and Justices L'Heureux-Dubé, McLachlin, Gonthier and La Forest appears to be that "the former two judges would approve of the limited and perhaps even tacit use of the social context of racism in making the credibility judgement in question, while the latter four would encourage open acknowledgement of the social context of racism in making such determinations" (Archibald 1998: 62).

26. *R.D.S.* v. *The Queen,* Interveners' Factum, Women's Legal Education and Action Fund and National Organization of Immigrant and Visible Minority Women of Canada, at 13.

27. See, for example: *Juries Act,* R.S.N.S. 1989, c. 242; *Juries Act,* R.S.O., 1980, c. 226; *Jury Act,* R.S.P.E.I., 1988, c. J-3.1; and *Jury Act,* R.S.M., 1987, c. J30.

28. L'Heureux-Dubé, J. *R.* v. *Sherratt* (S.C.C.), at 204; see also *R.* v. *Bain* ([1992] 69 C.C.C. [3d] 481 [S.C.C.], [1991] 1 S.C.R. 91).

29. Criminal Code, s. 634, states that: "(1) A juror may be challenged peremptorily whether or not the juror has been challenged for cause pursuant to section 638; and (2) Subject to subsections (3) and (4), the prosecutor and the accused are each entitled to (a) twenty peremptory challenges, where the accused is charged with high treason or first degree murder; (b) twelve peremptory challenges, where the accused is charged with an offence, other than an offence mentioned in paragraph (a), for which the accused may be sentenced to imprisonment for a term exceeding five years; or (c) four peremptory challenges, where the accused is charged with an offence that is not referred to in paragraph (a) or (b)."

30. Criminal Code, s. 638, states that: "(1) A prosecutor or an accused is entitled to any number of challenges on the ground that (a) the name of a juror does not appear on the panel, but no misnomer or misdescription is a ground of challenge where it appears to the court that the description given on the panel sufficiently designates the person referred to; (b) a juror is not indifferent between the Queen and the accused; (c) a juror has been convicted of an offence for which he was sentenced to death or to a term of imprisonment exceeding twelve months; (d) a juror is an alien; (e) a juror is physically unable to perform properly the duties of a juror; (f) a juror does not speak the official language of Canada that is the language of the accused or the official language of Canada in which the accused can best give testimony or both official languages of Canada, where the accused is required by reason of an order under section 530 to be tried before a judge and jury who speak the official language of Canada that is the language of the accused or the official language of Canada in which the accused can best give testimony or who speak both official languages of Canada, as the case may be. And (2) No challenge for cause shall be allowed on a ground not mentioned in subsection (1)."

31. A "presumption" is a rule (in this case a judicial rule) which requires that certain facts simply be accepted (in this case the fact that duly sworn jurors will put aside their prejudices and decide the case on the evidence) until the contrary is shown to be true.

32. See also *R. v. Griffis (no. 2)* (December 1993, 20 C.R.R. [2d] 104), and Tanovich's well-researched article, "Rethinking Jury Selection: Challenges for Cause and Peremptory Challenges" (1994), where he notes that Justice Macdonald allowed a modified version of question 5 because it was necessary "for the purpose of exposing to view that which, on the evidence of Dr. Henry, I find becomes discrimination if given the opportunity in the jury box, namely, attitudinal prejudice or overt bigotry." Tanovich argues that, perhaps in cases other than racial prejudice, a simple question is all that is required.

33. Justice Doherty states at 360 that "Before turning to the principles controlling the challenge for cause process, the nature and ambit of the proposed question must be clearly understood. Counsel did not seek to challenge for cause based on race. He did not suggest that a person could be successfully challenged on the basis of his or her colour, or that only persons of a particular race would be challenged for cause. The question posed was race-neutral and did not assume that only non-blacks would be subject to the challenge. The question also did not seek to challenge prospective jurors based only on their opinions, beliefs or prejudices."

34. *R. v. Cole (D)*, (1996, 152 N.S.R. 2d 321 N.S.C.A.), Preliminary Inquiry Transcript, Vol. 1 at 339.

35. *Spencer Dixon* v. *The Queen*, C.A.C. No. 126136; *Guy Robart* v. *The Queen*, C.A.C. No. 126420; *Stacy Skinner* v. *The Queen*, C.A.C. No. 126474; *Herman McQuaid* v. *The Queen*, C.A.C. No. 126612; *Cyril J. Smith* v. *The Queen*, C.A.C. No. 126473. The judges sitting on the Court of Appeal for this decision were different than in the *Cole* case. The decision of the Nova Scotia Court of Appeal in these cases was heard on appeal at the Supreme Court of Canada. The appeals were denied in all but one case on February 19, 1998 (*R. v. McQuaid et al.*).

36. Royal Commission on the Donald Marshall Jr. Prosecution (1989), "Prosecuting Officers and the Administration of Justice in Nova Scotia, Vol. 1, Recommendation 39. A Directive of the Attorney General of Nova Scotia issued in 1994 pursuant to section 6(a) of the *Public Prosecutions Act* states that, "There is a duty on the Crown to make full and timely disclosure to the defence of all relevant information known to the investigator and the Crown Attorney in Criminal Code prosecutions conducted by agents of the Attorney General. The obligation applies to both inculpatory and exculpatory information.... One measure of the relevance of information is its usefulness to the defence. If it is of some use, it is relevant and should be disclosed. Accordingly, information is relevant if it can reasonably be used by the defence either in meeting the case for the Crown, advancing a defence or otherwise in making a decision which may affect the conduct of the defence such as, for example, whether to call evidence." This directive was in effect at the time of the trial of the six Black men accused of the aggravated assault of Darren Watts.

37. The Royal Commission on the Donald Marshall Jr. Prosecution states on page 162 of the commissioner's report (1989) that: "We have concluded that Donald Marshall Jr.'s status as a Native contributed to the miscarriage of justice that has plagued him since 1971. We believe that certain persons within the system would have been fore rigorous in their duties, more

careful, or more conscious of fairness if Marshall had been white." The Royal Commission (1989: 182) also concluded with respect to Black Nova Scotians that: "Based on the evidence and the information now before us, we can say definitely that many Nova Scotians—both Blacks and Whites—believe the criminal justice system discriminates against Black people at all levels."

Chapter 4

1. Cahn (1991), in the context of feminist analysis, argues that "Feminist litigation requires a feminist position in any issue—with the recognition that there are many 'feminist positions' ... feminist litigation certainly occurs when we work collectively on precedent-setting cases ... but it also occurs when we individually represent single mothers seeking public benefits. Feminist litigation is not defined solely by its focus on the goal of enhancing women's rights through substantive outcomes. It requires the integration of substantive goals with the actual process of representation." Critical Race Litigation differs from feminist litigation in significant ways; however, the developing goal of integrating theory and practice is similar.

2. Thornhill (1994) quotes from a working paper co-authored by herself and Monique Lortie: "To define Racism is at one and the same time both easy and difficult. Easy if one already has the conviction that this phenomenon exists, and one consequently acknowledges Racism's various components. Difficult if one expects and demands that any proposed definition be so complete as to encompass all of its possible manifestations. However, one irrefutable fact remains: A vast difference exists between the victim's perspective and that of the un-informed individual. Victims have an uninterrupted and continuous perspective of the dynamics or workings of Racism which permit them to put each 'isolated incident' into the proper perspective. Victims are already wearing the eyeglasses that allow them to see accurately. It is possible that the person who has not experienced Racism will merely see some 'isolated incidents' which are themselves reprehensible but this uninformed individual will not necessarily spontaneously perceive or grasp the cumulative and fluid nature of Racism which tends to generate its own energy. It becomes therefore imperative to valorize the victim's reality, by being particularly attentive to the victim's perspective and by hearing the victim's voice."

3. This trend is slowly being changed in Canada, where a new law school curriculum which deals with the issue of race is being developed and taught. For an example, see Aylward and Thornhill (1997).

4. Boyle (1994: 203) notes that "It is not uncommon for the Women's Legal Education and Action Fund [LEAF] to be asked to intervene in a case where the lawyer did not wish to make the equality arguments, as if they might somehow be embarrassing."

5. Brooks (1994: 88), in explaining the methodology of Critical Race Theory as applied to federal pleadings, calls what I refer to as *deconstruction* as the "subordination question," which he says entails a two-pronged inquiry that

asks whether a rule of law subordinates important interests and concerns of racial minorities and, if so, how is this problem best remedied? However, for reasons of clarity, I prefer to treat these questions as separate issues. *Deconstruction* asks the subordination question by placing people of colour at the centre of the analysis and also requires an in-depth analysis of the rule, while *reconstruction* requires a solution to the problem raised.

6. In June of 1990, as noted by Pomerant (1994: 6), the federal Minister of Justice directed a Reference to the Law Reform Commission of Canada in which the Minister stated that it was "desirable" in the public interest that special priority be given to a study of the Criminal Code and related statutes, and the extent to which they ensure that "(a) Aboriginal persons and (b) persons in Canada who are members of cultural or religious minorities have equal access to justice, and are treated equitably and with respect." In 1992 the Attorney General of Ontario announced that Ontario would review the jury selection process to ensure that jury panels include all members of society and to eliminate any possibility of excluding visible minorities from jury service in criminal trials. The Attorney General also called on the federal government to review the entire jury selection process in criminal cases, including the ability of jurors to be disqualified by counsel at trial for other than valid reasons. Letter of Reference from A. Kim Campbell, P.C., M.P., Minister of Justice and Attorney General of Canada, to Mr. Justice Allan M. Linden, President, Law Reform Commission of Canada, June 8, 1990; Justice Canada (1992b).

7. Section 629 of the Criminal Code states that: "(1) The accused or the prosecutor may challenge the jury panel only on the ground of partiality, fraud, or wilful misconduct on the part of the sheriff or other officer by whom the panel was returned and (2) A challenge under subsection (1) shall be in writing and shall state that the person who returned the panel was partial or fraudulent or that he wilfully misconducted himself, as the case may be." Section 630 of the Criminal Code states that: "Where a challenge is made under section 629, the judge shall determine whether the alleged ground of challenge is true or not, and where he is satisfied that the alleged ground of challenge is true, he shall direct a new panel to be returned."

8. *Juries Act*, R.S.N.S., 1989, c.242, s.5. The *Juries Act* also governs jury selection in civil trials. See NSLRC (1993): "Structurally, the procedure [for jury selection in civil trials] is similar to that for criminal trials.... A card with the name, number and address of each Panel member is put into a box, shaken up, then names are pulled randomly out of the box with each name being called and, subject to 3 challenges by each side or being excused by the Judge from service, the jury is formed once 7 people have been selected."

9. All references to the Nova Scotia jury selection process have been taken from this discussion paper (NSLRC 1993a).

10. Section 7(5) of the Nova Scotia *Juries Act* says: "The jury committee shall prepare the jury list from any or all of the latest available lists of electors prepared in accordance with the Municipal Elections Act, the Elections Act or the Canada Elections Act but, if it is not practical to do so, may use assessment rolls and other available information respecting persons qualified to serve as jurors." And under section 7(1) of the *Juries Act,* the jury

committee is to "select by random choice, in the case of the Halifax Jury District, the names of twelve hundred persons and, in the case of each other jury district, the names of three hundred persons, qualified and liable to serve as jurors."

11. For an excellent overview and analysis of Canadian case law in the area of challenges to the array, see Petersen (1993).
12. Discussion with Department of Justice official David Kiefle, 1998.
13. *R.* v. *Williams*, ACLC Factum, Supreme Court of Canada, File No. 25375, at para. 17–23. The African Canadian Legal Clinic is a non-profit organization funded by the Ontario Legal Aid Plan with a mandate to address systemic racism and racial discrimination in Ontario and Canada through test-case litigation and intervention strategies.
14. Ibid.
15. For a detailed discussion of human rights law in Canada and the reasons for its proliferation, see UNESCO (1945: 93), referred to by Mendes (1995: 1-18): "The great and terrible war which has now ended ... was a war made possible by the denial of democratic principles of the dignity, equality, and mutual respect for men, and by the propagation in their place, through ignorance and prejudice, of the doctrine of the inequality of men and races."
16. Jurisdiction of the federal commission includes but is not limited to federal government departments; Crown corporations, such as the CBC, the Royal Canadian Mounted Police and the Canadian Mint; federally regulated agencies, such as the National Transportation Agency; chartered banks; airlines, railroads, interprovincial communications and telephone companies; and other federally regulated industries. Jurisdiction of the provincial commissions includes but is not limited to provincial ministries, provincial Crown corporations, education, health care, housing, retail stores and other businesses not regulated by the federal government, such as manufacturing. See Baylis and Rudner (1995).
17. *Robichaud* v. *Brennan* ([1987] 2 S.C.R. 84 at 90–91), referred to by Mendes (1995: 3-32).
18. "Bill S-5, an Act to amend the Canada Evidence Act and the Criminal Code in respect of persons with disabilities, to amend the Canadian Human Rights Act in respect of persons with disabilities and other matters and to make consequential amendments to other Acts," reprinted as amended by the Standing Committee on Justice and Human Rights and as reported to the House on April 2, 1998, 46–47 Elizabeth II, 1997–98, by the Senate of Canada.
19. Section 32: "(1) This Charter applies (a) to the Parliament and government of Canada in respect of all matters within the authority of Parliament including all matters relating to the Yukon Territory and Northwest Territories; and (b) to the legislature and government of each province in respect of all matters within the authority of the legislature of each province."
20. Note the caveat that the views expressed in the study are solely those of the authors and do not necessarily represent the views of Justice Canada.

Chapter 5

1. See, for example, Alfieri (1995 and 1998: 1295). Alfieri (1995: 1653) states that "the record to date lacks any substantial evidence that CRT aspires to meet that challenge. The continued failure to come to the aid of the subordinated clients and communities it airily celebrates will undermine CRT, just as it does Critical Legal Studies. This type of failure condemns jurisprudential movements not to death, but to irrelevance or, worse, triviality." Also see Crenshaw et al. (1995).
2. *MacDonald Estate* v. *Martin*, [1990] 3 S.C.R (S.C.C.) 1235, and MacKenzie (1993: 25-4).
3. Chapter 21, Chapter 22 and Commentary 22.9.
4. See, for example, Law Society of Alberta, *Alberta Code of Professional Conduct* (1995); Law Society of British Columbia, *Professional Conduct Handbook* (1970); Law Society of Upper Canada, *Professional Conduct Handbook* (1987, as amended); and Canadian Bar Association, *Code of Professional Conduct* (1987, as amended).
5. Much of this section on class actions and public interest litigation is derived from Friedlander (1995: 82–83).
6. In *Hy and Zel's Inc.* v. *The Attorney General for Ontario* ([1993] 3 S.C.C. 675 at 660–61), Justice Major stated the Court's position: "Following this Court's earlier decisions, in order that the Court may exercise its discretion to grant standing in a civil case, where, as in the present case, the party does not claim a breach of its own rights under the Canadian Charter of Rights and Freedoms but those of others, (1) there must be a serious issue as to the Act's validity, (2) the appellants must be directly affected by the Act or have a genuine interest in its validity, and (3) there must be no other reasonable and effective way to bring the Act's validity before the Court." This case is discussed by Bowal and Cranwell (1994); see also Mosoff (1992).
7. *Law Society Amendment Act (Class Proceedings Fund)*, S.O. 1992, c.7; referred to by Friedlander (1995: 83).
8. For a discussion of the role of lay advocates in the courts and community activism, see Hoyte et al. (1996).
9. *R.D.S.* v. *The Queen*, 1997, Notice of Motion by the African Canadian Legal Clinic, the Afro-Canadian Caucus of Nova Scotia and the Congress of Black Women of Canada, at 12–13.
10. *R.D.S.* v. *The Queen,* 1997, Motion of the Intervener, Parent Student Association of Preston, Nova Scotia.
11. See Nova Scotia Barristers' Society, *Legal Ethics and Professional Conduct: A Handbook for Lawyers in Nova Scotia* (1990, consolidated May 1998), Chapter 21 and note 3. See also Nova Scotia *Gazette*, "Civil Disobedience and the Lawyer" (1967), and response (1968), 2:3 Gazette 44, referred to in Chapter 21, in the Nova Scotia code of professional conduct (NSBS 1990).
12. Abrams (1994) notes that not only is there very little literature on the topic, but there is also a paucity of discussion concerning the matter in American professional responsibility texts. This is also true of Canadian texts on professional responsibility; see, for example, MacKenzie (1993).

References

Canadian Legislation

Bill S-5, an Act to amend the Canada Evidence Act and the Criminal Code in respect of persons with disabilities, to amend the Canadian Human Rights Act in respect of persons with disabilities and other matters to make consequential amendments to other Acts. 46–47 Elizabeth II, 1997–98.

Canadian Bill of Rights, R.S.C. 1985.

Canadian Human Rights Act, R.S.C. 1985, c. H-6.

Canadian Multiculturalism Act, 1985, S.C. 1191, c. 8.

Class Proceedings Act, 1992, S.O., c. 6.

Criminal Code, R.S.C. 1985, c. C-46 as amended, ss. 634(1) and (2), and ss. 638(1) and (2).

Education Act. S.N.S. 1918.

Juries Act, R.S.N.S. 1989, c. 242.

Law Society Amendment Act, 1992, S.O., c. 7.

Narcotic Control Act, R.S.C. 1985, c. N-1 repealed 1996, c. 19, S. 94.

Supreme Court Act, R.S.C. 1985, c. S-26, s. 40.

Canadian Legal Cases

Alberta (A.G.) v. Gares (1976), 67 D.L.R. (3d) 635 (Alta. T.D.).

Andrews v. *Law Society of British Columbia*, [1989] 1 S.C.R. 143 (S.C.C.).

Bhadauria v. *Seneca College of Applied Arts and Technology (Board of Governors),* [1981] 2 S.C.R. 181 (S.C.C.).

Bradley and Martin (no. 1) (1973), 23 C.R.N.S. 33 (Ont. S.C.).

Canada Trust Co. v. *Ontario (Human Rights Commission)* (1990), 74 O.R. (2d) 481 (Ont. C.A.).

Christie v. *York,* [1940] S.C.R. 139 (S.C.C.).

Committee for Justice and Liberty v. *National Energy Board,* [1978] 1 S.C.R. 369 (S.C.C.).

Cyril J. Smith v. *The Queen.* C.A.C. No. 126473.

Franklin v. *Evans* (1924), 55 O.L.R. 349 (H.C.).

Hy and Zel's Inc. v. *The Attorney General for Ontario,* [1993] 3 S.C.C. 675.

Lavallee v. *R.*, [1990] 1 S.C.R. 852 (S.C.C.).

Loew's Montreal Theatres Ltd. v. *Reynolds* (1919), 30 Que. B.R. 459.

MacDonald Estate v. *Martin,* [1990] 3 S.C.R. 1235 (S.C.C.).

Narine-Singh v. *Attorney General of Canada*, [1955] S.C.R. 395.

Noble and Wolfe v. *Alley,* [1951] 92 S.C.R. 64 (S.C.C.).

Ontario (Human Rights Commission) v. *Simpson-Sears Ltd.,* [1985] 2 S.C.R. 536 (S.C.C.).

Quong Wing v. *The King* (1914), S.C.R. 440 (S.C.C.).
R. v. *Bain,* [1992] 1 S.C.R. 91 (S.C.C.), [1992] 69 C.C.C. (3d) 481 (S.C.C.).
R. v. *Biddle* (1993), 24 C.R. (4th) 65 (Ont. C.A.).
R. v. *Bird,* [1984] 1 C.N.L.R. 122 (Sask. C.A.).
R. v. *Cole (D)* (1996), 152 N.S.R. (2d) 321 (N.S.C.A.).
R. v. *Crosby* (1979), 49 C.C.C. (2d) 255 (Ont. H.C.).
R. v. *Drakes* (1998), 122 C.C.C. (3d) 498 (B.C.C.A.).
R. v. *Griffis (no. 1)* (1993), 16 C.R.R. (2d) 322 (Ont. Ct. Gen. Div.).
R. v. *Griffis (no. 2)* (1993), 20 C.R.R. (2d) 104 (Ont. Ct. Gen. Div.).
R. v. *Hill* (1985), 51 C.R. (3d) 97 (S.C.C.).
R. v. *Hubbert* (1975), 29 C.C.C. (2d) 279 (S.C.C.).
R. v. *Kent, Sinclair and Gode* (1986), 40 Man. R. (2d) 160 (Man. C.A.).
R. v. *McPartlin,* [1994] B.C.J. No. 3101 (B.C.S.C.).
R. v. *McQuaid et al.* (1998), 1 S.C.R. 298 (S.C.C.).
R. v. *Nepoose (no. 1)* (1991), 85 Alta. L. Rev. (2d) 8 (Alta. Q.B.).
R. v. *Parks* (1993), 84 C.C.C. (3d) 353 (Ont. C.A.).
R. v. *Sherratt* (1991), 63 C.C.C. (3d) 193 (S.C.C.).
R. v. *Siew Thiam Koh, Eng Chuan Lu, and Buan Haut Lim* (unreported).
R. v. *Williams,* [1998] 159 D.L.R. (4th) (S.C.C.), rev'g (1996) 106 C.C.C. (3d) 215.
R. v. *Wilson* (1996), 47 C.R. (4th) 61 (Ont. C.A.).
R.D.S. v. *The Queen,* [1997] 151 D.L.R. (4th) 193 (S.C.C.).
Robichaud v. *Brennan,* [1987] 2 S.C.R. 84 (S.C.C.).
Rogers v. *Clarence Hotel* (1940), 55 B.C.R. 214 (C.A.).
Spenser Dixon v. *The Queen,* C.A.C. No. 126136 (N.S.C.A.).
Stacy Skinner v. *The Queen,* C.A.C. No. 126474 (N.S.C.A.).
Streng v. *Winchester (Township)* (1986), 25 C.R.R. 357 (Ont. H.C.).

U.S. Legislation

Civil Rights Act, 1964, 1.78 Stat. 243, 42 U.S.C.
Civil Rights Act, 1968, 42 U.S.C.
Civil Rights Act, 1991, 105 Stat. 1071 (as amended in 2, 16, 29 and 42 U.S.C.A.).
Emancipation Proclamation, 1863, 12 Stat. 68.
Fair Housing Act, 1968, 42 U.S.C. 804.
Voting Rights Act, 1965, 79 Stat. 437.

U.S. Legal Cases

Batson v. *Kentucky* (1986), 476 U.S. 79.
Board of Education of Oklahoma City Public Schools v. *Dowell* (1991), 498 U.S. 237.
Brown v. *Board of Education of Topeka (Brown I)* (1954), 347 U.S. 483.
Brown v. *Board of Education of Topeka (Brown II)* (1955), 349 U.S. 294.
City of Richmond v. *J.A. Crosen Co.* (1998), 448 U.S. 469.
Dred Scott v. *Sandford* (1857), 60 U.S. (19 How.) 393.

Freeman v. *Pitts* (1992), 112 S.Ct. 1430.
Hopwood v. *State of Texas* (1996), 861 F. Supp. 551.
Koon v. *U.S.* (1996), 116 S.Ct. 2035.
Missouri v. *Jenkins* (1990), 495 U.S. 33.
People of the State of California v. *Orenthal James Simpson,* No. BA097211, (Cal. S.Ct.) 1994, 1995 WL 516132.
People v. *Powell et al.* (1991), 232 Cal. App. (3d).
Plessy v. *Ferguson* (1896), 163 U.S. 537.
Presley v. *Etowah County Commission* (1992), 502 U.S. 491.
Regents of the University of California v. *Bakke* (1978), 438 U.S. 265.
Screws v. *United States* (1945), 325 U.S. 91.
State v. *Russell* (1991), 477 N.W. (2d) 866 (Minn.).
United States v. *Classic* (1941), 313 U.S. 299.
United States v. *Fordice* (1992), 112 S.Ct. 2727.
United States v. *Koon* (1994), 34 F. (3d) 1416.
United States v. *Los Angeles Police Department* (1993), 883 F. Supp. 769.
Whren v. *United States* (1996), 116 S.Ct. 1769.

British Legal Cases

R. v. *Camplin,* [1978] 2 All E.R. 168 (H.L.).

Other References

Abrams, Kathryn. 1991. "Lawyers and Social Change Lawbreaking: Confronting A Plural Bar," commentary on "Breaking the Law: Lawyers and Clients in Struggles for Social Change" by Martha Minow, 52 U. Pitt. L. Rev. 753.
Aleinikoff, Alexander. 1991. "A Case for Race-Consciousness." 91 Columbia L. Rev. 1060.
Alfieri, Anthony V. 1998. "Race Trials." 76 Tex. L. Rev. 1293.
_____. 1995. "Black and White." Book review of Richard Delgado (ed.), *Critical Race Theory: The Cutting Edge,* Philadelphia: Temple University Press.
Allen, A., and F.L. Morton. 1997. "Feminists and the Courts: Measuring Success in Interest Group Litigation." Paper prepared for the Annual Meeting of the Canadian Political Science Association, St. John's, Newfoundland, June 8–10.
Alschuler, Albert W. 1995. "Racial Quotas and the Jury." 44 Duke L.J. 704.
Altman, Andrew. 1990. *Critical Legal Studies: A Liberal Critique.* Princeton, N.J.: Princeton University Press.
Altman, T.L. 1986. "Affirmative Selection: A New Response to Peremptory Challenge Abuse." 38 Stanford L. Rev. 781.
American Civil Liberties Union (ACLU). 1996. *Briefing Paper.* <www.aclu.com>
Appleby, Timothy. 1989. "Police weigh strategy on manslaughter charges." *Globe and Mail,* January 14, A10.
Archibald, Bruce P. 1998. "The Lessons of the Sphinx: Avoiding Apprehensions of

Judicial Bias in a Multi-racial, Multi-cultural Society." 10 C.R. (5th) 56.

Aylward, Carol A. 1999. "'Take the Long Way Home': *R.D.S.* and Critical Race Theory." 47 U.N.B.L.J. 249.

_____. 1995. "Adding Colour—A Critique of: 'An Essay on Institutional Responsibility: The Indigenous Blacks and Micmac Programme at Dalhousie Law School.'" 8 C.J.W.L. 470.

_____ and Esmeralda M.A. Thornhill. 1997. *Critical Race and Legal Theory: "Race," Racism and Law in Canada.* Upper year course materials. Halifax: Dalhousie Law School.

Backhouse, Constance. 1994. "Racial Segregation in Canadian Legal History: Viola Desmond's Challenge, Nova Scotia, 1946." 17 Dalhousie L.J. 299.

Barnes, Robin D. 1995. "Politics and Passion: Theoretically A Dangerous Liaison." In Richard Delgado (ed.), *Critical Race Theory: The Cutting Edge.* Philadelphia: Temple University Press.

Baylis, Paul, and Karen L. Rudner. 1995. *A Media Guide to Canadian Human Rights.* Ottawa: Human Rights Research and Education Centre, University of Ottawa.

Bell, Derrick. 1992a. *Race, Racism and American Law.* 3d ed. Toronto: Little, Brown and Company.

_____. 1992b. "Racial Realism." 24 Conn. L. Rev. 363.

_____. 1990. "Racial Realism—After We're Gone: Prudent Speculations on America in a Post-Racial Epoch." 34 St. Louis U. L.J. 393.

_____. 1985. "The Civil Rights Chronicles." 99 Harv. L. Rev. 4.

Berlin, Mark L. 1996. "Human Rights Law: A Legal Remedy." In Carl E. James (ed.), *Perspectives on Racism and the Human Services Sector: A Case for Change.* Toronto: University of Toronto Press.

Bowal, Peter, and Mark Cranwell. 1994. "Case Comment: *Persona Non Grata: The Supreme Court of Canada Further Constrains Public Interest Standing.*" 33 Alta. L. Rev. 192.

Boyle, Christine. 1994. "The Role of Equality in Criminal Law." 58 Sask. L. Rev. 203.

_____, Donna Martinson, Marilyn MacCrimmon and Isabel Grants. 1991. "A Forum on *Lavallee* v. *R.*: Women and Self-Defence." 25 U.B.C. L. Rev. 21.

Brooks, Roy L. 1994. "Critical Race Theory: A Proposed Structure and Application to Federal Pleading." 11 Harv. Black Letter L.J. 85.

_____ and Mary Jo Newborn. 1994. "Critical Race Theory and Classical-Liberal Civil Rights Scholarship: A Distinction without a Difference?" 82 Calif. L. Rev. 787.

Brown, Rosemary, and Cleta Brown. 1996. "Comments: Reflections on Racism." In Carl E. James (ed.), *Perspective on Racism and the Human Services Sector: A Case for Change.* Toronto: University of Toronto Press.

Butler, Paul. 1997. "Affirmative Action and the Criminal Law." 68 U. Colo. L. Rev. 841.

_____. 1995. "Racially Based Jury Nullification: Black Power in the Criminal Justice System." 105 Yale L.J. 677.

Cahill, Barry. 1994. "Slavery and the Judges of Loyalist Nova Scotia." 43 U.N.B.L.J. 73.

Cahn, Naomi R. 1991. "Defining Feminist Litigation." 14 Harv. Women's L.J. 1.

Calliste, Agnes. 1993. "'Women of Exceptional Merit': Immigration of Caribbean Nurses to Canada." 6 C.J.W.L. 85.

Calmore, John C. 1997. "Close Encounters of the Racial Kind: Pedagogical Reflections." 31 U.S.F. L. Rev. 903.

Canadian Bar Association (CBA). 1987. *Code of Professional Conduct.* As amended. Toronto: Canadian Bar Association.

Canadian Centre for Police-Race Relations. 1993. *Federal and Provincial Royal Commissions, Task Forces and Inquiries into Police/Aboriginal and Police/Visible Minority Relations: A Compilation.* Ottawa.

Canadian Journal of Women and the Law (C.J.W.L.). 1993. Editorial. "Racism ... Talking Out." 6 C.J.W.L. v.

Carasco, Emily. 1993. "A Case of Double Jeopardy: Race and Gender." 6 C.J.W.L. 142.

Carbo, C. 1993. *Task Force on the Relations Between the MUC Police and the Black Community of Montreal, Canada.* Ottawa: Canadian Centre for Police-Race Relations.

Cherif, M., and F. Niemi. 1984. *And Justice for All: A Report on the Relations Between Police and Visible Minorities in Montreal.* Montreal: Centre de recherche-action sur les relations raciales.

Christopher Commission. 1991. Report. Los Angeles: Los Angeles Police Department.

Claridge, Thomas. 1994. "Court Reporter." *Globe and Mail,* May 26.

Cleaver, Kathleen. 1997. "Racism, Civil Rights, and Feminism." In Adrien Katherine Wing (ed.), *Critical Race Feminism: A Reader.* New York: New York University Press.

Cochran, Johnnie L., Jr. and Tim Rutten. 1996. *Journey to Justice.* New York: Ballantine Books.

Commission on Systemic Racism in the Ontario Criminal Justice System. 1995. Report. Ontario: Queen's Printer.

Cook, Anthony E. 1990. *Beyond Critical Legal Studies: The Reconstructive Theology of Dr. Martin Luther King Jr.* 103 Harv. L. Rev. 986.

Cox, Kevin. 1991. "Halifax police under fire for probe of racial brawl—Reports of officers beating black not fully investigated, group says." *Globe and Mail,* December 20, A8.

Crenshaw, Kimberlé Williams. 1988. "Race, Reform, and Retrenchment: Transformation and Legitimation in Antidiscrimination Law." 101 Harv. L. Rev. 1331.

_____, Neil Gotands, Gary Peller and Kendell Thomas, eds. 1995. *Critical Race Theory: The Key Writings That Formed the Movement.* New York: New York Press.

Culp, Jerome McCristal, Jr. 1993. *Rodney King and the Race Question.* 70 Denver Univ. L. Rev., 200.

Currents: Readings in Race Relations. Urban Alliance on Race Relations (founded 1975).

Davis, Abraham L., and Barbara Luck Graham. 1995. *"The Supreme Court, Race, and Civil Rights."* Thousand Oaks, Calif.: Sage Publications.

Davis, Angela J. 1977. "Race, Cops, and Traffic Stops." 51 U. Miami L. Rev. 425.

Delgado, Richard. 1995. *Critical Race Theory: The Cutting Edge.* Philadelphia: Temple University Press.

_____. 1993. "The Inward Turn in Outsider Jurisprudence." 34 Wm. & Mary L. Rev. 741.

_____. 1990. "Recasting the American Race Problem." A review of Roy L. Brooks, "Rethinking the American Race Problem." 79 Calif. L. Rev. 1389.

_____. 1987. "The Ethereal Scholar: Does Critical Legal Studies Have What Minorities Want?" 22 Harv. C.R.-C.L. L. Rev. 301.

Dershowitz, Alan M. 1996. *Reasonable Doubts*. New York: Simon & Schuster.

Devlin, Richard F. 1995. "We Can't Go On Together with Suspicious Minds: Judicial Bias and Racialized Perspective in *R. v. R.D.S.*" 18 Dalhousie L.J. 408.

_____. 1991. *Canadian Perspectives on Legal Theory*. Toronto: Edmond Montgomery.

Downey, Donn. 1992. "Rowlands calls for healing, Chretien sees unrest as 'wake-up call,' blacks fear troubled summer." *Globe and Mail,* May 6, A1.

_____. 1991. "Teen held hands out, witness testifies; Officer seemed angry, trial told." *Globe and Mail,* October 19, A12.

Duclos, Nitya. 1993. "Disappearing Women: Racial Minority Women in Human Rights Cases." 6 C.J.W.L. 25.

Epstein, Lee. 1993. "Interest Group Litigation During the Rehnquist Court Era." 9 J.L. & Pol. 630.

Falardeau-Ramsay, Michelle, Chief Commissioner. 1997. *Annual Report*. Canadian Human Rights Commission. Ottawa.

Forte, David F. 1998. "Spiritual Equality: The Black Codes and the Americanization of the Freedmen." 43 Loy. L. Rev. 569.

Francis, Natalie. 1992. *Black Perspectives on Criminal Justice: The Individual and the State*. Indigenous Blacks and Mi'kmaq Programme Curriculum Review Project. Halifax: Dalhousie Law School.

Frashier, Pam. 1995. "Fulfilling Batson and Its Progeny: A Proposed Amendment to Rule 24 of the Federal Rules of Criminal Procedure to Attain a More Race-and-Gender-Neutral Jury Selection Process." [1995] Iowa L. Rev. 1327.

Freeman, Allen. 1988. "Racism, Rights and the Quest for Equal Opportunity: A Critical Legal Essay." 23 Harv. C.R.-C.L. L. Rev. 295.

Friedlander, Lara. 1995. "Costs and the Public Interest Litigant." 40 McGill L.J. 55.

Geller, W.A., and M.S. Scott. 1992. *Deadly Force: What We Know*. Washington, D.C.: Police Executive Research Forum.

Gibbs, Jewelle Taylor. 1996. *Race and Justice: Rodney King and O.J. Simpson, A House Divided*. San Francisco: Jossey-Bass.

Glasbeek, H.J. 1995. *A Report on Attorney-General's Files, Prosecutions and Coroners' Inquests Arising out of Police Shootings in Ontario*. Ontario: Queen's Printer, 8.

Globe and Mail. 1992a. "Blacks and the Police." Editorial. April 4, A14.

_____. 1992b. "L.A.'s Northern Echoes." Editorial. December 30, D6.

Gordon, Andrew G. 1993. "Beyond Batson v. Kentucky: A Proposed Ethical Rule Prohibiting Racial Discrimination in Jury Selection." 62 Fordham L. Rev. 685.

Grant, Isabel, Dorothy Chunn and Christine Boyle. 1994. *The Law of Homicide*. Toronto: Carswell.

Halifax Police Department, Incident Review Committee. 1991. Report. December 17. Halifax: Halifax Police Department. (Available from the author.)

Hampton, Howard. 1991. "Jury clears Metro constable." *Globe and Mail,* October 29, A12.

Harris, Angela P. 1997. "Race and Essentialism in Feminist Legal Theory." In Adrien Katherine Wind (ed.), *Critical Race Feminism: A Reader*. New York: New York University Press.

_____. 1994. Foreword to "The Jurisprudence of Reconstruction." 82 Cal. L. Rev. 743.

Harris, Paul. 1997. *Black Rage Confronts the Law*. New York: New York University Press.

Henry, M., and F. Henry. 1996. "A Challenge to Discriminatory Justice: The Parks Decision in Perspective." 38 Crim. L.Q. 345.

Herbert, Jacinth. 1989–90. "'Otherness' and the Black Woman." 3 C.J.W.L. 269.

Holman, H.T. 1982. "Slaves and Servants on Prince Edward Island: The Case of Jupiter Wise." *Acadiensis* 12: 100.

Hoyte, Shawna Paris, et al. 1996. *Ujima: Collective Work and Responsibility*. Nova Scotia Black Community Resource Manual. Halifax: Public Legal Education Society of Nova Scotia.

Hutchinson, Alan C. 1995. "Calgary and Everything After: A Postmodern Re-Vision of Lawyering." 33 Alta. L. Rev. 768.

_____. 1991. "The Politics of Law." In Garry D. Watson et al. (eds.), *Civil Litigation, Cases and Materials*. 4th ed. Edmond Montgomery.

Issac, Mr. Justice. 1997. Chief Justice of the Federal Court of Canada's address to the Dalhousie Black Law Students' Association, Dalhousie Law School, Halifax, February. Unpublished.

James, Carl E., ed. 1996. *Perspectives on Racism and the Human Services Sector: A Case for Change*. Toronto: University of Toronto Press.

Johnson, Alex M., Jr. 1994. "Defending the Use of Narrative and Giving Content to the Voice of Color: Rejecting the Imposition of Process Theory in Legal Scholarship." [1994] Iowa L. Rev. 803.

Judicial Council Advisory Committee on Racial and Ethnic Bias in the Courts. 1994. *Executive Summary*. <www.aba.com>

Justice Canada. 1992a. *Response of the Federal Government to the Recommendations of the Nova Scotia Advisory Group on Race Relations: Taking Action*. Ottawa.

Justice Canada. 1992b. "Visible Minority Representation on the Criminal Jury." Paper prepared for the Uniform Law Conference, August 1992. Ottawa: Justice Canada.

Kennedy, Duncan. 1990. "Legal Education as Training for Hierarchy." 38 *Politics of Law: A Progressive Critique*. Edited by David Kairys.

Kennedy, Kirk A. 1995. "Book Review: *Thurgood Marshall's Enduring Legacy: Thurgood Marshall and the Supreme Court, 1936–1961* (Oxford Univ. Press). 38 How. L.J. 383.

Kessler, Mark. 1990. "Legal Mobilization for Social Reform: Power and the Politics of Agenda Setting." 24 Law & Soc. Rev. 121.

Khan, Shahnaz. 1993. "Canadian Muslim Women and Shari'a Law: A Feminist Response to 'Oh! Canada!'" 6 C.J.W.L. 52.

Kimber, Steven. 1996. "Young, black, and shafted." *Halifax Daily News,* June 14, 18.

King, Martin Luther, Jr. 1963. "Letter from a Birmingham Jail." April 16.

Kivel, Paul. 1996. *Uprooting Racism: How White People Can Work for Racial Justice*. Gabriola Island, B.C.: New Society Publishers.

Kline, Marlee. 1989. "Race, Racism, and Feminist Legal Theory." 12 Harv. Women's L.J. 155.

Kushnick, Louis. 1998. *Race, Class & Struggle: Essays on Racism and Inequality in Britain, the US and Western Europe*. London and New York: Rivers Oram Press.

Law Reform Commission of Canada. 1980. *The Jury in Criminal Trials*. Working paper no. 27. Ottawa: Supply and Services Canada.

Law Reform Commission of Nova Scotia (NSLRC). 1993a. *A Discussion Paper on Ju-*

ries. Halifax: NSLRC.

———. 1993b. *Dissenting Opinions on Issues in the Report, Dissenting Opinion of Commissioner Dawna Ring and Commissioner Beverly Johnson on the Random [Jury] Selection process*. Halifax: NSLRC.

Lawrence, Charles R. 1987. *The Id, the Ego, and Equal Protection: Reckoning with Unconscious Racism*, 39 Stanford L. Rev. 317.

———. and Matsuda, Mari J. 1997. *We Won't Go Back: Making the Case for Affirmative Action*. New York: Houghton Mifflin Company.

Law Society of Alberta. 1995. *Alberta Code of Professional Conduct*. Calgary: Law Society of Alberta.

Law Society of British Columbia. 1970. *Professional Conduct Handbook*. Vancouver: Law Society of British Columbia.

Law Society of Upper Canada. 1987. *Professional Conduct Handbook*. As amended. Toronto: Law Society of Upper Canada.

Levenson, Laurie L. 1994. "The Future of State and Federal Civil Rights Prosecutions: The Lessons of the Rodney King Trial." 41 UCLA L. Rev. 509.

Lopez, Ian. F. Haney. 1996. *White by Law: The Legal Construction of Race*. New York: New York University Press.

MacKenzie, Gavin. 1993. *Lawyers and Ethics: Professional Responsibility and Discipline*. Toronto: Carswell.

Manitoba. Public Inquiry into the Administration of Justice and Aboriginal Peoples. 1991. Report. *The Justice System and Aboriginal People,* vol. 1. Winnipeg: Queen's Printers.

Matsuda, Mari. 1996. *Where is Your Body? And Other Essays on Race, Gender, and the Law.* Boston: Beacon Press.

———. 1987. *Looking to the Bottom: Critical Legal Studies and Reparations.* 22 Harv. C.R.-C.L. L. Rev. 323.

———, Charles R. Lawrence, Richard Delgado and Kimberlé Williams Crenshaw. 1993. "Words That Wound: Critical Race Theory, Assaultive Speech and the First Amendment." Boulder, Colo.: Westview Press.

McCone, John A. 1965. *McCone Commission Report.* December 2. Sacramento: State of California.

McKaque, Ormond. 1991. *Racism in Canada.* Saskatoon: Fifth House.

Mendes, Errol, ed. 1995. *"Racial Discrimination": Law and Practice.* Toronto: Carswell, in cooperation with Justice Canada and the Canada Communications Group, Supply and Services Canada.

———. 1994. *Complaint and Redress Mechanisms Relating to Racial Discrimination in Canada and Abroad.* TR1994-16e. Ottawa: Human Rights Research and Education Centre, funded by Research Section of Justice Canada.

Mollen Commission (Commission to Investigate Allegations of Police Corruption and Anti-Corruption Practices of the Police Department). 1994. Report. New York. July 7.

Monture-OKanee, Patricia A. 1993. "Ka-Nin-Geh-Heh-Gah-E-Sa-Nonh-Ya-Gah." 6 C.J.W.L. 119.

Mosoff, Judith. 1992. "Do the Orthodox Rules of Lawyering Permit the Public Interest Advocate to 'Do the Right Thing?' A Case Study of HIV-Infected Prisoners." 30 Alta. L. Rev. 1258.

NAACP Legal Defence and Education Fund. 1992. "The Color of Justice." 78 A.B.A.J. 62.

National Association of Criminal Defence Lawyers (NACDL). 1997. "Racism in the Criminal Justice System." NACDL newsletter. <www.criminaljustice.org.>

Neilson. *Study Team Report to the Task Force Program Review* (Neilson Report). 1985. Ottawa.

Nolan, Nicole. 1996. "Metro Cops More Likely to Shoot than LAPD." *Now Magazine*, July 11–17, 20.

Nova Scotia Advisory Group on Race Relations. 1991. Report. Halifax.

Nova Scotia Barristers' Society (NSBS). 1990, consolidated May 1998. *Legal Ethics and Professional Conduct: A Handbook for Lawyers in Nova Scotia.* Halifax: NSBS.

Nova Scotia *Gazette*. Editorial. 1967. "Civil Disobedience and the Lawyer." *Gazette* 1: 5.

O'Byrne, Shannon. 1991. "Legal Criticism as Storytelling." 23 Ottawa L. Rev. 487.

Oliver, W.P. 1949. "The Negro in Nova Scotia." *Journal of Education.* Halifax: N.S. Department of Education.

Ontario Human Rights Code Review Task Force (Cornish Report). 1992. *Achieving Equality: A Report On Human Rights Reform.* Toronto.

Petersen, Cynthia. 1993. "Institutionalized Racism: The Need for Reform of the Criminal Jury Selection Process." 38 McGill L.J. 147.

Pomerant, David. 1994. *Multiculturalism, Representation and the Jury Selection Process in Canadian Criminal Cases.* Working document. Ottawa: Justice Canada.

Quigley, William P. 1994. "Reflections of Community Organizers: Lawyering for Empowerment of Community Organizations." 21 Ohio N.U. L. Rev. 455.

Razack, Sherene. 1996. "Speaking for Ourselves: Feminist Jurisprudence and Minority Women." 4 C.J.W.L. 440.

———. 1991. *Canadian Feminism and the Law: The Women's Legal Education and Action Fund and the Pursuit of Equality.* Toronto: Second Story Press.

Roach, Kent. 1995. "Challenges for Cause and Racial Discrimination." 37 Crim. L.Q. 410.

Rosen, Jeffery. 1996. "The Bloods and the Crits." *New Republic*, December 9.

Rosenburg, Charles B. 1995. *Detective Fuhrman, the Tapes, and the Ruling (Part 2): Do We Need A New Evidentiary Paradigm for Evidence of Police Misconduct?* WL (Westlaw) 550008 (O.J. Comm.), 1.

Rosenthal, Peter. 1989–90. "The Criminality of Racial Harassment." 6 H.R. Y.B. 113.

Ross, Thomas. 1990. "Innocence and Affirmative Action." 43 Vand. L. Rev. 297. Reprinted in Richard Delgado (ed.), *Critical Race Theory: The Cutting Edge.* Philadelphia: Temple University Press.

———. 1989. "The Richmond Narratives: City of Richmond v. J.A. Croson Co." 68 Tex. L. Rev. 381.

Royal Commission on the Donald Marshall Jr. Prosecution (Marshall Commission). 1989. Report. Halifax: Nova Scotia.

Ruby, Clayton. 1992. "Clayton Ruby takes a look at the white face of policing and doesn't much like what he sees." *Globe and Mail*, May 5, A18.

Russell, Margaret M. 1997. "Beyond 'Sellouts' and 'Race Cards': Black Attorneys and the Straitjacket of Legal Practice." 95 Mich. L. Rev. 766.

Sarick, Lila. 1992. "Police officers acquitted in Lawson shooting." *Globe and Mail*, September 4, A1.

Saunders, Charles. 1995. "Speaking out can be hazardous." *Sunday Daily News*, May 7, A17.

Spann, Girardeau A. 1993. *Race Against the Court: The Supreme Court and Minorities in Contemporary America.* New York: New York University Press.

———. 1990. "Pure Politics." 88 Mich. L. Rev. 1971.

St. Lewis, Joanne. 1996. "Racism and the Judicial Decision-Making Process." In Carl E. James (ed.), *Perspectives on Racism and the Human Services Sector: A Case for Change.* Toronto: University of Toronto Press.

Tanovich, David M. 1993. "Rethinking Jury Selection: Challenges for Cause and Peremptory Challenges." 30 C.R. (4th) 310.

Target Magazine. 1975–. Toronto: Coalition Against Racist Police Violence.

Thornhill, Esmeralda M.A. 1994. "Focus on Racism: Legal Perspectives from a Black Experience." *Currents* 8.

———. 1993. "Regard sur le racisme: Perspectives juridiques à partir d'un vécu noir." 6 C.J.W.L. 1.

Trubeck, Louise G. 1996. "Embedded Practices: Lawyers, Clients, and Social Change." 31 Harv. C.R.-C.L. L. Rev. 415.

Turpel, Mary Ellen. 1991. "Patriarchy and Paternalism: The Legacy of the Canadian State for First Nations Women." 6 C.J.W.L. 174.

UNESCO. 1945. *Conference for the Establishment of the United Nations Educational, Scientific, and Cultural Organization.* ECO/CONF/29, November 16, 93.

Unger, Roberto Mangabeira. 1986. *The Critical Legal Studies Movement.* Cambridge, Mass.: Harvard University Press.

Urban Alliance on Race Relations. 1993. "The Impressions of Black Males of the Ontario Criminal Justice System." *Race and the Canadian Justice System* 8, no. 4, 41.

U.S. General Accounting Office (GAO). 1990. *Death Penalty Sentencing: Research Indicates Racial Disparities.* Washington, D.C.: U.S. Government Printing Office.

U.S. Senate Special Task Force on a New Los Angeles. 1992. *New Initiatives for a New Los Angeles: Final Report and Recommendations.* Washington, D.C.

Vijay, Agnew. 1993. *Resisting discrimination: Women from Asia, Africa, and the Caribbean and the Women's Movement in Canada.* Toronto: University of Toronto Press.

Walker, James. 1997. *"Race," Rights and the Law in the Supreme Court of Canada.* Ontario: The Osgoode Society.

Williams, Patricia J. 1987. "Alchemical Notes: Reconstructing Ideals from Deconstructed Rights." 22 Harv. C.R.-C.L. L. Rev. 401.

Wilson, Bertha. 1990. "Will Women Judges Really Make a Difference?" 28 Osgoode Hall L.J. 507.

Winks, Robin. 1971. *The Blacks in Canada: A History.* New Haven, Conn.: Yale University Press.

———. "Negro School Segregation in Ontario and Nova Scotia." *Historical Review* 50, no. 2, 169.

Wotherspoon, Terry, and Vic Stzeqick. 1991. *First Nations: Race, Class and Gender Relations.* Scarborough: Nelson Canada.

Yamamoto, Eric K. 1997. "Critical Race Praxis: Race Theory and Political Law–yering Practice in Post–Civil Rights America; Symposium: Representing Race." 95 Mich. L. Rev. 821.

Index

Indigenous Black and
Mi'kmaq (IB&M)
program (Dalhousie
University Law
School), 197
Individual rights, 19,
23–25
Inglis, Officer, 87, 88
Integration, 32
"Interdependent
community," 25
Islam, 46
Issue spotting. *See*
Race, identification
of, as an issue
Ito, Judge, 69–71, 202

Japanese, 80
Jews, 43, 77, 165
"Jim Crow," 31, 196;
Canadian version of,
40, 78; in the United
States, 40, 53, 61, 78
Johnson, Albert, 87–89
Johnson, Alex M., Jr.,
31
Johnston, James
Robinson, 44
Jones, Burnley, 93
Judicial accountability,
110
Judicial (racial) bias,
issue of, 84, 93, 95–
100, 103–11
Juries, 57, 124;
Aboriginal people on,
113, 142, 146, 149,
150, 152; all-White,
15, 50, 51, 60, 61,
68–89, 112, 150, 151,
154, 200; Blacks on,
16, 18, 71, 73, 81,
113, 114, 139–42,
144, 145, 148–53,
155, 157, 158, 200,
202; in Nova Scotia,
113, 143; in Ontario,
113; Whites on, 15,

18, 71, 73, 74, 114,
140; women on, 113,
146
Juries Act of Nova
Scotia, 143, 145, 149,
209
Juries Acts, provincial
and territorial, 112,
142, 144, 148
Jury nullification, 18,
71–73, 202
Jury selection, 59, 68,
111–25, 132, 137,
139–65, 209; federal,
153–58, 209;
provincial, 142–53,
209; racism and, 140
Justice Canada, 142,
145, 146

Kennedy, Duncan, 20,
26,
Kimber, Stephen, 126,
127
King, Martin Luther,
Jr., 14, 53, 54, 186
King, Rodney, 9, 50–
52, 60–67, 69, 73,
146, 197, 198. *Also
see* Rodney King
case
Kivel, Paul, 37, 38
Klare, Karl, 22,
Koon, Sergeant Stacey,
62, 64, 65, 197
Koon v. *U.S.*, 64
Ku Klux Klan, 52, 58,
59
Kushnick, Louis, 31,
36, 37

La Forest, Justice, 102,
105–8, 205, 206
Labour law, 174, 191
Lamer, Chief Justice,
102, 105, 205
Lambert, Justice, 120,
121

Lange, Detective, 71
Lavallee v. *R.* 46–48,
108
Law, duality of, 34, 82,
101; as a tool of
oppression, 82; as a
tool against racism,
13, 132, 191, 203.
Also see Racism in
the law and legal
system
Law Reform
Commission of
Canada, 144, 146,
154, 155
Law Reform
Commission of Nova
Scotia, 113, 142, 149,
150
Law schools, 136, 201;
Canadian, 44, 176,
208; in the United
States 26, 27, 38
Lawrence, Charles R.,
57–59
Lawrence, Raymond, 76
Lawson, Wade, 89, 91
LEAF. *See* Women's
Legal Education and
Action Fund
Le Jeune, Oliver, 41
Legal analysis,
noncontextualized
and ahistorical, 136.
Also see Abstraction;
"Contextualized
analysis"; Formalism
Legal ethics. *See* Codes
of professional
responsibility;
Ethical issues
Legal indeterminacy,
21, 28, 30
Legal Liberalism, 12,
19–26, 30, 31, 38
Legal Publishing, 46–
47
Legal Realism, 7, 21,
24

Washington, D.C., 91
Watts area of Los
 Angeles, 61, 62, 199
Watts case, 126–31,
 207. *Also see* Cole
 case
Watts, Darren, 126,
 127, 129, 207
White supremacy, 34,
 35, 52, 68
Whites, and
 discrimination, 155;
 legal treatment of,
 15, 67. *Also see*
 Juries
Whren v. *United States,*
 200
Wilson, Madam Justice
 Bertha, 98, 99
Wind, Officer Timothy,
 62, 197
Winnipeg, 91
Women, 100;
 Aboriginal, 46;
 Black, 36–38, 46, 48,
 49, 74, 87, 195;
 judges, 98, 99;
 White, 36–38, 74, 77.
 Also see Battered
 woman syndrome
Women's Action
 Against Racist Police
 (WAARP), 203
Women's Legal
 Education and Action
 Fund (LEAF), 101,
 110, 185, 208

Yale Law School, 26
Yale University, 196
York University, 117